# Searching for Hassan

# Searching for Hassan

## An American Family's
## Journey Home to Iran

TERENCE WARD

HOUGHTON MIFFLIN COMPANY

BOSTON · NEW YORK

2002

For information about permission to reproduce selections from
this book, write to Permissions, Houghton Mifflin Company,
215 Park Avenue South, New York, New York 10003.

Visit our Web site: www.houghtonmifflinbooks.com.

*Library of Congress Cataloging-in-Publication Data*
Ward, Terence.
Searching for Hassan / Terence Ward.
p.   cm.
ISBN 0-618-04844-8
1. Iran — Social life and customs. 2. Ward,
Terence — Journeys — Iran. I. Title.
DS266.W37 2002
955.05 — dc21     2001039526

Printed in the United States of America

Book design by Robert Overholtzer

QUM 10 9 8 7 6 5 4 3 2

The author is grateful for permission to quote from the following: *The Essential Rumi*, translated by Coleman Barks. Copyright 1995 by Coleman Barks. Reprinted by permission of Coleman Barks. *The Gift: Poems of Hafiz, the Great Sufi Master*, translated by Daniel Ladinsky. Copyright 1999 by Daniel Ladinsky. Reprinted by permission. *The Green Sea of Heaven: Fifty Ghazals from the Divan of Hafiz*, translated by Elizabeth T. Gray, Jr. Copyright 1995 by Elizabeth T. Gray, Jr. Reprinted with permission from White Cloud Press, Ashland, Oregon. Lines of Rumi, translated by Roy Mottahedeh, in *The Mantle of the Prophet* by Roy Mottahedeh. Copyright 1985 by Roy Mottahedeh. Reprinted by permission of the author.
The author wishes to thank Maryam Ghasemi for her kind permission to reprint her personal letters.

*To Donna, Patrick, and Idanna*

Neither fame nor fortune guided us to this gate;
We approach as refugees, here guided by fate.

— Hafez

# Contents

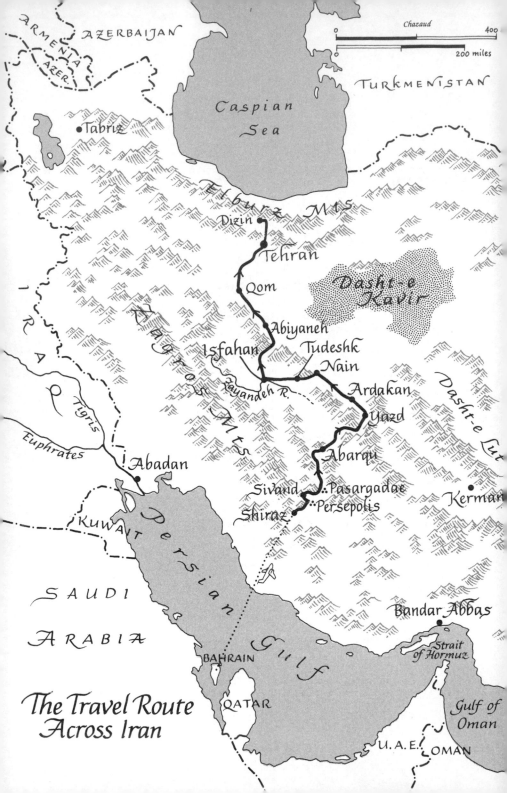

The Travel Route Across Iran

*Searching for Hassan*

 PROLOGUE

# Blood from Pomegranates

Where am I? That is the first question.

— Samuel Beckett, *The Unnamable*

I REMEMBER a brisk evening long ago. Fires glow red across the city's roofline. Explosions of firecrackers break the spring silence. It is March 1963, the last Tuesday night before *Nowruz*, the Iranian New Year. Snowmelt surges down alpine ravines. Hyacinths pierce through wet clay. Budding plane trees greet the warming season. For two thousand five hundred years Iranian astronomers have scanned the heavens for the sign. When the sun crosses the equator, a fresh year rises, heralding the first day of spring.

*Chaharshanbe Souri*, the Zoroastrian fire festival, echoes with all-night drumming and chanting. Piles of leaves, broken twigs and branches line the street. Moonlight washes over snowcapped mountains. A breeze blows through our Persian garden. Hassan prepares us for the ceremony. Brushing back our hair, he repeats Farsi phrases. Tonight, he says, we will leap over bonfires.

Older than Islam, this festival is interwoven with Zoroaster's sacred flame. Sins collected over the year are burned away under the night skies. Just leap. And you become clean.

Celebrations start at twilight. Hassan, our housekeeper, our cook, our young "Persian father," emerges from the shadows, swaying a glowing Coleman lantern and twitching his proud mustache. With the physique of a gymnast, he moves fluidly. His strong chin juts out with dramatic effect. He strides toward us, eyes flickering under the streetlamps. He bears the quiet nobility of an actor taking the stage.

My three brothers, Chris, Rich, Kev, and I watch mesmerized as he reaches down and sets each dormant pile alight. Before us, seven bonfires rage along our narrow street, grandly named the Alley of the Brave. An odd number for good luck. The flames crackle in the darkness, illuminating the mud-and-brick walls that line the alley. Neighborhood friends assemble, twittering nervously before the bright corridor of light.

Our runway is marked by the hypnotic dance of the fires. Hassan pats my head. "Be careful *pesar*, little boy. Don't slip like last year." Slowly, he starts chanting, "*Sorkhi-ye to az man o zardi-ye man be to.* Give me your healthy red glow and take away my sickly color." These will be our words for the fire. "*Sorkhi-ye to az man . . . ,*" we repeat. My oldest brother, Kevin, impulsively pushes forward. Curly-haired Chris stands ready, little bow-legged Richard holds his hand, eyes wide open.

One by one, children of the neighborhood, their grandparents and the young men gather up courage as they move toward the bonfires. Shouts and laughter erupt. Songs and dancing break out, sudden blasts of firecrackers thrown by mischievous kids send mothers into squeals of fright. The jumping is about to begin.

Hassan, curling his eyebrow, gives me a quick wink with boyish delight. This is his sign! Loud yelps fill the air as we all scamper toward the blazing pyres with our adrenaline surging. Fatimeh, Hassan's wife, and the neighborhood women swarm like moths around the flames, clapping. I chase Hassan toward the burning bonfires. My three brothers trail close behind. My heart is pounding, my ears ringing. Then, in a startling moment, I see Hassan soar and vanish in the blinding light. "*Sorkhi-ye to az man . . .*" I inhale and jump too.

Sizzling branches, scorched leaves, wafts of smoke. Heat sears my bony knees. I smell singed hair. My feet hit the earth again, still churning. I open my eyes. In the darkness I see Hassan's silhouette. Again he disappears into a blazing wall. I jump. Flames lick at my legs. I mustn't lose him. Another fire, another breath. Again.

In the dream, somewhere on Tehran's high plateau, under the rugged Elburz peaks and a dizzying canopy of stars, I chase after Hassan's vanishing heels. Across chessboard squares of darkness and light, I run with my brothers in hot pursuit long into the night as the sacred flame washes over me.

Leaping over fire always marked the first act of this magical eve. As the flames die down, we all scurry back inside our gate and Fatimeh quickly dresses us in black shroud costumes. Hassan hands me a copper soup ladle. Out on the verandah, my father casts an approving glance at our commotion, lifting his eyes from his book, puffing on a pipe. He beckons to me. Jazz tunes float around us in the evening air, mixing with classical Persian *santur* and *tar* music drifting over the vine-covered wall from a garden party next door. Out into the night pours Louis Armstrong's silky gravel voice in "When It's Sleepy Time Down South," followed by Leonard Bernstein's hit musical of gritty rhythms from Manhattan's West Side.

Back in the kitchen, Hassan counsels my brothers and gives Chris a spoon. "Now you must pray to God. It is time for spoon-hitting. Go to the houses around the neighborhood and bang on your bowl. If somebody gives you something, it means that God will also give. But if nobody gives you anything, then God will give you nothing."

He tells me to put a key in my shoe. Stumbling out in the dark, we head for the alley again. Our red gate swings open and we creep under the lamplight up to a neighbor's wrought-iron door. Chris nervously presses the bell. We bang on my empty bowl with our spoons. Copper on iron rings loudly. When the door opens, we quickly cover our faces and thrust our bowls forward. My face is hidden, yet through the black veil I watch an elegant long hand with gold rings reach out in a clenched fist.

In that hand lies the prophecy. If empty, all wishes are lost. Then it opens, and with God's blessing, *ajeel* — assorted nuts, seeds and dried fruits — drop into my bowl like promises for the New Year. We run home thrilled, but I remember there is one more thing to do.

Stopping before the gate, I hang back in the shadows of the alley, feeling the sharp teeth of Hassan's key in my shoe. The night air is still. Now I must listen to those who pass by, as Hassan said. An older couple shuffles home and I overhear their words: "Praise God. She and Ahmad will be well together." With that cryptic message, I slip through the gate and rush up the drive to Hassan for its decoding. Interpretation is always left to elders.

"Well, Terry *ghermez*" — he calls me "Red" for my hair — "these parents were speaking about their daughter and her beloved. This is a good sign. You've been a good boy, God is telling you."

Hassan asks me what I have wished for. Shyly, I stumble and speak of Sara and my hope that she'll be in my class next year.

"Your wish for Sara will be granted."

On each day of the two-week New Year's festival, Hassan initiates us with equal passion. On the actual day of *Nowruz*, he invites us to his red-brick home, which faces the cherry orchard, for *chai o shirini*, tea and cookies. We exchange small gifts, and he explains the meaning of *haft sin*, the seven offerings — green sprouts, apple, garlic, vinegar, sumac, wild olive, and a dish called *samanoo* — that adorn his table. The sprouting wheat grass wrapped with red ribbon symbolizes new growth, while the garlic is meant to keep away bad omens. A candle burns brightly next to his holy Koran, and a mirror reflects its light. A sour orange floating in a bowl of water, he tells us, is our Earth floating in the cosmos.

During that festive fortnight, as my father sits on the porch with his nightly glass of Shiraz wine, Hassan counsels him: "If you're drinking wine, Mr. Ward, you might as well throw some in the garden for the spirits. Then they see you're not selfish, that you're willing to share. It purifies your act. You know, it's good to do that."

After he leaves, I watch my dad look twice over his shoulder, then splash some red wine into the bed of roses below, before filling his glass again.

On the morning of *Sizdeh Bidar*, the thirteenth day of *Nowruz*, Hassan says to my mother, "Your family can't stay here today. Impossible." My mother asks him to explain. "To stay indoors is a bad omen," he insists. "We must go to the countryside and throw all bad things of the past away. Nature will take care of them. They'll become wind, trees, rivers and blossoms."

So together we join the entire city in the search for a spot of green where we can lay down our picnic blanket, samovar and rice, and spend the day with nature. Walking to the nearby stream, Hassan carefully places the green sprouts in the rushing water. With that final ritual, the days of *Nowruz* come to a close, and life returns to normal.

Spring gives way to summer. When the sun's suffocating heat falls over Tehran like a thick wool blanket and melts the asphalt into soft pools of black gelatin, the people abandon their brick homes.

"From tonight, we will sleep under the stars," Hassan announces. We drag our beds out onto the verandah, into the sweet breath of night, and a whole new cycle begins. During these months it never rains. All the bedding goes outdoors — mattresses, blankets, pillows and sheets — and when the light fades in the west and trembling stars begin spinning across the heavens, Hassan arrives with his lamp and his treasure chest of stories: King Solomon's ring; Moses and the shepherd; parables of holy Ali, Jesus and the donkey; passages from the Koran; poems by Hafez; and tales from *Hazar Afsane*, composed for Humai, the daughter of Bahram, the legendary ancient king of Persia. Each evening, we boys gather under the cool night skies with unbridled excitement, never knowing where we will set sail. Each night is hopeful, even in defeat.

A princess can fall in love with a common boy. God will open the heavens and speak. A hidden hand shall direct our path. Lovers take the stage: Leili and Majnoon, Shirin and Farhad. Each new night reveals a secret, a truth. The mythical bird Simorgh awaits us. As we listen, Chris, Rich and I watch Hassan's impish eyes glisten. Struck with surprise as his saga unfolds, we are also hypnotized by his enthusiasm. With a talent for mimicry, he imitates expressions, gestures and gaits of people, deftly slipping into the skins of colorful characters in his pageant of morality tales. Thieves, grand viziers, prophets, street urchins, princesses, fishermen, barbers, con artists, vagabonds, warriors and fortunetellers, all come alive.

Lying on his back, Kevin, the dreamer, gazes up at the moon's pale white mountains and shaded Sea of Tranquillity. Some nights he uses our telescope. As each story unfolds, we imagine the geography: castles in the clouds, ruby-filled tombs, windswept monasteries, night caravans, alchemists' studios. When the tale-weaving stretches too late and little Richard nods off to sleep, Hassan pauses. In that time of silence, as slumber sets in, he slowly draws away, leaving us with the burping frogs, buzzing crickets and blowing wind. Like Scheherazade, he keeps us waiting until the next night to complete the tale. Somewhere out there, we know, a princess is falling in love with a brave farmer, another will run off with a young mariner. Hope, Hassan tells us, there is always hope.

Our household staff grew to embrace not only Hassan and Fatimeh but also her mother, Khorshid, who took care of Fatimeh's two children, Ali and Mahdi. And then there was Hassan's brother, Mohammad. Just discharged from the army for overturning a jeep, he was out of work. So he became our driver. Although we generally rode in the back seat while he negotiated traffic, we had to hold on tightly to avoid being vaulted into the windshield by his sudden braking. Once Hassan asked my mother to go to the police station in his brother's place when an infraction was traced to our car. Hassan rightly feared his brother's license might be in jeopardy if Mohammad appeared before the police. In his gentle and humorous way, Hassan ruled our lives.

Although officially he managed our household, Hassan was for us much more than that. Like Virgil, he guided us through the labyrinths of dimly lit bazaars and lovingly taught us all the customs needed to ease our way into his culture. He became an important part of our family, feeding our imaginations, enlarging our world. Stocky and strong, with his splendid black mustache, he offered his folk wisdom with a deft wit. In the absence of television, he gave us the comic antics of the confounding "Mullah Nasruddin," presenting life's dilemmas and wise solutions in a hilarious way. In his eye, a spark was always lit.

We longed for the moment when Hassan would call us to see the musicians and Haji Firouz black-faced clowns who appeared dancing at our gate just before New Year, amid feasting and gifts. My brothers and I chattered away in our broken street-Farsi and danced to Iranian pop music. As the seasons changed, so did our frantic occupations: buying silkworms in mulberry groves, riding the grumpy mules of passing nomads, trekking up poplar-lined river gorges, playing hide-and-seek in hollowed-out caves outside our back wall, skiing in the high snows of Shemshak, wandering deep into treasure-filled bazaars, licking saffron-flavored ice cream under thick shade trees, and dressing up for the U.N. festival at our polyglot Community School.

On the Fourth of July, we would lie outstretched on our blankets and gaze at the booming fireworks exploding above the great lawn of the U.S. embassy. We had heard only faint rumors about a giant called Willie Mays and the mythical Central Park. We were oblivious of distant America. For us children, Iran, not the United States, was home.

Describing her passage back to Ireland in *A Book of Migrations*, Rebecca Solnit writes poignantly about the meaning of home in one's memory. "Home, the site of all childhood's revelations and sufferings, changes irrevocably, so that we are all in some sense refugees from a lost world. But," she goes on to say, "you can't ever leave home either; it takes root inside you and the very idea of self as an entity bounded by the borders of the skin is a fiction disguising the vast geographies contained under the skin that will never let you go."

For my family, after ten years it all came to an abrupt end. Our decision to leave Iran and return to the States was reluctantly agreed upon after Kevin, separated from the family for the first time, found only misery at Deerfield Academy, a prep school in New England. He described it as being like *Lord of the Flies*. I was scheduled to leave for the same boarding school the following September. My parents couldn't bear the idea of casting their four boys to the winds. Our family would remain united, they decided. And so we left Iran.

Sadness and confusion clouded our last days in Tehran as we packed up our lives into boxes, walked under pergolas and mulberry trees in a haze, bit into Hassan's last supper of *chello kebab*, fighting back the tears. My mother had found someone to take over our rented villa. He vowed to treat Hassan Ghasemi and his family with respect, and pay them well.

We stood somberly outside our gate to say our goodbyes. Strangely, it was July 4. Hassan and Fatimeh hugged us all while we made solemn promises to stay in touch. He pulled my ear one last time, telling me to "respect mother and father." Choked up, I nodded my promise. He countered with a contented wink. Young Fatimeh reached out and took my mother's hand in hers. The two women held each other closely. Time slowed for that long farewell. Then we heard the beeping horn.

As the taxi pulled away, our last sight out of the rear window was of Hassan, Fatimeh, baby Maryam, little Ali and Mahdi, grandmother Khorshid, and Mohammad, clustered together, waving sadly at the red gate.

Once in America, my mother wrote to Hassan and Fatimeh. She waited. Finally, an air-mail letter arrived, with its red stamps with the Shah's portrait on them.

Dear Donna,

Hectic always seems to be the way in Tehran and this fall is no exception. I know that news about your family is what's most important for all of you. I spoke to them before the new tenants moved in and at the time Hassan and Fatimeh said they did not think they could work for anyone but Mrs. Ward.

I urged them to give the new people a chance. About three weeks later, Mrs. G. was at home in the villa, with workmen all about. Hassan had stayed on for a month to get her started and was marvelous, and she said she cannot find anyone else like him and so on. But, she understood that they wanted to leave, and Fatimeh apparently said she never did like Tehran, etc. I said nothing.

From what I can put together they have bought a truck with Mohammad, and left Tehran. Hassan and M will be truckers? So it goes. But don't be upset. You did so much for the family and they no doubt learned the Ward esprit and that, after all, is all anyone can do . . .

That letter seared like a hot iron. Written by my mother's dear friend Elie Dugan, who helped her pack in our final days, these words announced the unimaginable. My mother was distraught. "How will we ever find them?"

Hassan had told her that he would stay at the house for years to come. She hadn't expected the Ghasemis to leave. At least not so soon. And despite the letter's warm spirit, her friend never thought to ask Hassan for his new address. Or to send it to us.

My mother faintly remembered his village's name: "Toodesht," she thought it was. Soon, telephoning and writing letters, she enlisted Tehrani friends in the search. Al Gross, the director of the Bank of America in the capital, told her that no one on his staff had ever heard of any village by that name. Our friends the Farmanfarmaians wrote diplomatically of the daunting task of locating Hassan with such sketchy information. Other responses came back. The village Toodesht? It didn't exist.

So what began as a small break in contact grew into a chasm. The Ghasemis had vanished. Gone. Without a trace.

\*    \*    \*

Meanwhile, we had become nomads as well. Back in America, we moved four times before settling in Berkeley's redwood-studded hills above the University of California campus, where both my mom and I enrolled, she in the School of Nutrition, I in the Near Eastern Studies Department. Kevin headed off to Harvard. Chris packed his bags for Cornell, and Rich chose Stanford. Later, seeking to be closer to Iran, I traveled to Egypt to study.

On my dust-coated balcony that overlooked the palm trees of the American University in Cairo, in 1978, I first heard the ominous news: BBC reports of riots and massacres crackled in from the provincial Iranian city of Tabriz. Students were demonstrating, government troops opening fire. Many lay dead, scores wounded. On Cairo's hazy horizon, the red afternoon sun was setting behind the pyramids.

These warnings, like Cassandra's, would fall on deaf ears. Diplomats ignored the signs. Martyrs would now be buried. The Shia forty-day mourning period passed, and then new protests ignited in Mashhad, Tehran, Isfahan. Bullets were said to have been fired into unarmed crowds. Mothers wept offstage. Iranians had finally lost their fear. A tidal wave no army could control rose up from this storm-blown ocean of resentment against the ancien régime. Soon this revolution would blow the Shah off his peacock throne along with his dazzling court of posers and sycophants. All would be swept away, stunning the world.

My brothers back in the States couldn't believe or accept that the Iranian people had so drastically changed. The Islamic Republic was proclaimed and Ayatollah Ruhollah Khomeini hailed as the Supreme Leader. Arrests filled the prisons. Revolutionary courts ordered the execution of "traitors" by firing squad. Factories, homes, land and private wealth were confiscated, sending thousands fleeing into exile.

Then, on November 4, 1979, hostage fever gripped America in a drama that would last 444 days. Foreign Minister Sadegh Ghotbzadeh's nightly rhetorical games and Ted Koppel's arching hairstyle became bizarre sources of fascination.

Refugees kept flooding out of Iran by air, sea, on horseback and on foot. A diaspora of a million Iranians was born. The Islamic Republic closed its borders. Ayatollah Khomeini proclaimed America the "Great Satan" and Americans *personae non gratae*. Then a terrible war broke out. Saddam Hussein, without warning, invaded the southwest province. Iranian soldiers battled Iraqis in trenches and nerve-gas horror. Hundreds of thousands would die.

All our attempts to contact Hassan over the years had failed. A wall of silence had risen. He and his family had disappeared. Their fate was unknown. His young sons, Ali and Mahdi, had surely joined the war.

At night, I dreamt of pomegranate groves with blood-red fruit so ripe it burst its skin. Time passed. One decade, then another.

# 1

## Fellow Travelers

> The start of a journey in Persia resembles an algebraical
> equation: it may or it may not come out.
>
> — Robert Byron, *The Road to Oxiana*

IN EARLY April 1998, my family began our long-awaited journey back home. Not to our ancestral Ireland, but to Iran.
While most Americans still recoiled with images of ranting
hostage takers and wild-eyed terrorists, we put our fears aside.
My three brothers and I, with our elderly parents, would cross the
vast Iranian plateau on a blind search for Hassan, our lost friend
and mentor who had taken care of us in Tehran so many years
ago. Our seven-hundred-mile overland trek, from the ancient
southern city of Shiraz, once called the Paris of Persia, all the way
north to Tehran, the metropolis of modern Iran, would be a
cross-cultural odyssey to rediscover a country, its people and our
much-loved adopted Iranian family.

Journeys are often conceived in a miraculous split-second flash
that illuminates the purpose and route of passage. Once the em-
bryo forms, everything else falls into place in scattered pieces —
visas and plane tickets, weathered maps, oblique itineraries — a
jigsaw puzzle of fact and fantasy.

In early December 1997, my youngest brother, Richard,
phoned me with surprising news from his home in Saudi Arabia.
In the Gulf island state of Bahrain, he said, visas for Iran could be

found. His voice, broken up by a poor connection, barked and echoed.

"Just heard that ladies from Arabia-bia flew into Iran on a shopping binge. They landed in Isfahan, bought their carpets-pets and got out safely . . . a rug under each arm."

"No!"

"Got their vi-sas . . . in Bahrain."

"For how long?"

"Less than a week."

"Any Americans?"

"Don't know. Tomorrow I'll find out. So, *baba*, are you ready-eady to go back-ack?"

"Mamma mia," I stammered.

"Goo-ood. Great id-ea! Ask Mom and Dad . . . What about the whole family-mily?"

His question fell through the receiver with the weight of heavy granite. The entire family?

"A tough sell," I remarked.

"No tougher-er than the Karakoram-ram."

After living in the Persian Gulf for eight years with his wife and two young boys, Richard had developed a thick skin. His baptism in Middle Eastern turbulence began in 1991. Overnight, Saddam Hussein's army poured across the Saudi border into Kuwait, only to be stopped by an accidental and chaotic firefight in a small village called Khafji, a few hundred miles from Rich's green suburban lawn in Dhahran. While his kids played in their treehouse, Scud missiles rained down.

For his latest vacation — Rich was an environmental geologist — he had climbed in Pakistan's rugged Himalayas, the infamous Karakoram Range. His hiking trip swiftly turned into a feat of endurance. Halfway into the trek, his companion fell twenty feet onto a rock ledge, fracturing his leg. Single-handedly, Rich fashioned a leg splint, lifted him onto his shoulders and hauled him down to the Hunza Valley to be airlifted out. Rich had long before earned my admiration as a fearless, no-nonsense scientist. He was in love with nature's geological wonders and was determined to witness each one in person. But Iran seemed daunting, as remote and impassable as his snowbound Karakoram peaks.

When I asked my brother Chris whether he would be coming along, he replied, "Are you nuts?"

For years, only the odd foreign journalist had dared venture into the somber Islamic Republic. News reports were dismal. Boys used as human minesweepers on the Iraqi front. Women trapped under black chadors. Clenched-fisted zealots led by mullahs in the ritual chant *"Marg bar Amrika,* Death to America." Cast as a pariah, Iran had been cut off from the world. All travelers except the foolhardy few kept a safe distance. And rightly so. This fundamentalist state had flogged offenders, covered women and defiantly thumbed its nose at the West. Yet there was reason to be upbeat: a moderate cleric had just been elected president.

Mohammad Khatami's surprise landslide victory in August 1997 ushered in a new era. Many hailed this heady period as "Tehran Spring." In a CNN interview with Christiane Amanpour on January 7, 1998, President Khatami welcomed cultural exchange. He offered an olive branch to Washington for the first time since the Shah's fall in 1979 and spoke of "people-to-people" contacts with Americans. His fluency in German and English surprised world leaders, as did his penchant for quoting Kant and Tocqueville. The smiling, soft-spoken leader dared to suggest reform, democratic rights and change. Responding characteristically to his critics, he spoke of the need for a "kinder, gentler Islam." Women and young voters had responded with overwhelming support. In Tehran's bazaars, this refreshing moderate who promised to restore a "civil society with rule of law" was jokingly being called "Ayatollah Gorbachev."

If Ping-Pong diplomacy helped normalize relations with China, could soccer and wrestling do the same for Iran? Iranian hard-liners were concerned, and for good reason. Thunderous applause and chants of "USA! USA!" echoed when American and Iranian wrestlers hugged each other after a friendly match in Tehran a month later, in February. The recently announced

World Cup draw was nothing less than miraculous. Iran was scheduled to play Team USA in Lyon, France, on June 2 1.

A black-and-white photograph had haunted my family for years. It was a weathered picture sitting on my mother's desk in Berkeley in which Hassan, the proud father, stood with his young wife and his mother-in-law. Both women wore scarves. Fatimeh peered sheepishly with large brown eyes through her horn-rimmed glasses. Khorshid held baby Ali, who grinned under his pointed elfish cap with drooping earflaps. Hassan beamed handsomely, and his smile bore a half-moon of white teeth under his mustache, aquiline nose and glistening eyes. Four faces shining in the living room as silent reminders.

Late at night, during spirited reunions, when our talk circled back to earlier days in Iran, my mother would always raise the same ghostly question left hanging in suspended conversation: "I wonder what happened to Hassan. I just pray he's all right, that his family is safe." My mother, especially, was tortured by a lingering guilt about not having done enough for the Ghasemis. Frustration and worry would swell in her eyes.

"But what more could we have done?" my father would ask.

My father's Irishness weighed in heavily whenever my family spoke of those halcyon days. In the wee hours of the morning, after we had conversed our way back through Persian time with bittersweet memories of cherry orchards, the snow-crested Elburz and Hassan's magical fables, my father would repeat Daniel Patrick Moynihan's Celtic adage to remind us, "It's no use being Irish unless you know the world is eventually going to break your heart."

"Nostalgia" comes from the Greek word *nostos*, to return home, and *algos*, pain. The ancients used the term to describe the state of mind of Hellenic soldiers of Alexander the Great garrisoned in far-off Asia. There was only one effective cure: the journey back. André Aciman, the New York–based writer, haunted by his native Alexandria, described his sense of separation in *Shadow Cities:* "An exile reads change the way he reads time, memory, self, love, fear, beauty: in the key of loss."

My parents' exuberant voices were firm and fearless when I first asked them about the journey back. Playing the seer, my father chose the departure date that he felt symbolically mirrored our quest: April Fool's Day, 1998. I was elated, but also troubled.

I wondered how our search would alter our cherished memories and our nostalgia for Hassan's "Mullah Nasruddin" tales, mint tea, buttered steamed rice and glistening eyes. Any journey of return runs that risk. Odysseus's crew paid dearly for their homing instinct: only the captain survived. Peering through smoked glass blurs memories. Aging mirrors may reveal strangers. And what if the past were to be erased, finally and completely, no longer there? What then? Were we doomed to Chekhovian dreams of lost cherry orchards?

After the Islamic Revolution, questions haunted my family for years. Did Hassan pay a terrible price before a judge? Had he become embittered, betraying our memory, denouncing my family as crude imperialists? They were unresolved questions, a haunting abandonment, unfinished business. My mother's worries about Hassan surfaced whenever the word "Iran" was mentioned, while in my brothers' homes, Hassan's storytelling antics were carefully being passed on from one generation of wide-eyed children to the next.

But what of Hassan himself? Had he survived? After two decades, the Islamic Republic's impassable gate, long padlocked, was finally creaking open. The answer lay inside.

Yes, the time for our journey back had finally come. To arrive at his doorstep we would need Irish luck and Allah's blessing. In the cold light of day and on close study, our search for Hassan seemed improbable. Only two clues existed. The first one was that faded black-and-white photograph taken in the spring of 1963. The second lay embedded in my mother's memory: the name of his ancestral village, "Toodesht." Our only hope was that he had settled there. But the multiple pronunciations of the town were daunting. Over the years, her uncertainty bred extraordinary mutations.

At dusk, as the thick San Francisco fog crept up the Berkeley hills to engulf my parents' redwood observation deck on Grizzly Peak, my mother ran up and down her scales of names, hoping to catch the true melody of Hassan's mysterious village, wedged somewhere in the mountains between Isfahan and Nain. It was a recurring theme, a broken record that always ended with gasps and laughs, exasperation and hopelessness.

"Think back, Mom. Now, what do you remember Hassan telling you before we left Tehran?"

"That one day he'd return to his village."

"And it was?"

"Toodesht."

"You're certain?"

"Absolutely. Well, just a minute . . ."

"Yes?"

"Maybe it was . . . Tadoosht. Or . . . Qashtood."

"Sure?"

"Toosquash!"

My father summed it up: "No Ithaca this, I assure you."

No matter how upbeat we all tried to be, we were certain that Hassan hid behind clouded mists, never to be seen again.

U.S. State Department officials mouthed predictable doom. My brother Chris voiced his fears repeatedly. No visas could be obtained in America. Kevin remained skeptical. Only my parents and Richard were defiantly thrilled. When a Foreign Service officer told me, "Americans are strongly advised not to visit the country," I countered by saying, "A moderate mullah has been elected president." Unfazed, he snapped, "And public floggings have tapered off."

Chris skittishly pleaded with my father over the phone, "You know, I've got two sons to worry about."

Dad cut him short. "So what? I've got four and I'm going."

The Ward clan's view about the journey remained divided. It was decided that the wives would not join us, which suited them just fine. Terror and dire omens underlined our phone conversations. Friends kindly offered unsolicited advice, showering us with warnings. "It'll be hot, dry, dangerous, dirty and scary. There's no embassy to protect you, you'll be taken hostage, your books will be confiscated. *You'll* be confiscated. And your parents, how can you put them at such risk?" One dapper bicoastal socialite reminded me darkly, "There'll be no fashion."

I asked my father, "What's the dress code?"

"Dress for a funeral," he advised.

So, like fashionable New Yorkers, we packed black.

Riffling through my files, I found a faded piece of paper. At the top was written: *Useful Arabic Translations.* During the height of Lebanon's civil war, in the early 1980s, it was slipped to me before I boarded a flight for Beirut. I realized only later that this sorry attempt at Arabic was gibberish mixed with a few Farsi words. I faxed it to Chris and Kevin:

*Meternier ghermez ahliah, Gharban.*
  The red blindfold would be lovely, Excellency.
*Balli, balli, balli.*
  Whatever you say.
*Shomah fuhr tommeh geh gofteh bande.*
  I agree with everything you have ever said or thought of in your life.
*Akbar kheli kili hfir lotfan.*
  Thank you very much for showing me your marvelous gun.
*Khrei, japahah mansh va fayeti amrikany.*
  I will tell you the names of many American spies travelling as reporters.
*Suro arraigh davatsaman mano sepahen-hasi.*
  It is exceptionally kind of you to allow me to travel in the trunk of your car.

My brothers faxed back terse responses. They were not amused.

*        *        *

For advice, I browsed through Lonely Planet's *Iran: A Travel Survival Kit*, the only serious guidebook published since the Revolution. The author, David St.Vincent, a tenacious English chap, was not one to flinch. All his tips came from firsthand experience. During one of his four trips, he was dragged before a revolutionary court on the charge of "plotting to import Salman Rushdie's *The Satanic Verses.*" Wedged between the exhaustive lists of hotels and monuments lay a few unorthodox words of counsel: "Never underestimate the ruthlessness or strength of the *Komiteh* and its network of informers . . . Don't be the first to discuss politics with a stranger." He described the Revolutionary Guards as "a combination of Spanish Inquisition and the Gestapo." About photography and cameras he offered further advice: "There's still a certain amount of paranoia about foreign spies, and Iranians can get very suspicious of Westerners with cameras." He suggested getting OKs before shooting, "if you don't want to risk having your camera smashed or stones thrown at you — don't think it doesn't happen." I especially appreciated his culturally sensitive how-to advice in dealing with authorities: "Answer your interrogators in such a way that their curiosity is satisfied, their suspicion allayed and their self-importance flattered." And, most of all, his upbeat succinct reminder: "You have been warned."

Another young writer, William Dalrymple, had also passed through Iran recently. In his book *In Xanadu: A Quest*, he delivered a witty and learned trans-Asia travel account, tracing Marco Polo's thirteenth-century footsteps to the East, from Jerusalem's Church of the Holy Sepulcher to Kublai Khan's mythical palace in Mongolia. He was stunned by contemporary Iran: "Mullahs speeding past in their sporty Renault 5s. Iran was proving far more complex than we had expected. A religious revolution in the twentieth century was a unique occurrence, resulting in the first theocracy since the fall of the Dalai Lama in Tibet."

It was so true. Some historians suggest that the Iranian Revolution stands as the most original of this century. Only Iran's Revolution defied Marxist ideology. Dalrymple explained: "Yet this revolution took place not in a poor banana republic, but in the richest and most sophisticated country in Asia. A group of clerics was trying to graft a mediaeval system of government and a pre-mediaeval way of thinking upon a country with a prosperous modern economy and a large and highly educated middle class."

My Florentine wife, Idanna, told me of her ancestral city and a fiery Dominican priest named Savonarola. When Lorenzo the Magnificent ruled Florence during the Renaissance, a brilliant and charismatic friar spoke audaciously from the pulpit of San Marco, railing against the city's decadence. With Lorenzo's death in 1493, Florence's *popolo* sent the entire Medici clan fleeing for their lives. The new Repubblica Fiorentina was born. Its guide was a visionary monk.

Quickly, the world's wealthiest and most cultivated city re-invented itself. Florence found renewed faith. Humility was in order. Dark shrouds and capes became de rigueur. Church attendance overflowed. In the Piazza della Signoria, the political heart of the city, a symbolic public repentance of sins took place. All frivolous, beautiful things — makeup, pendants, embroidery, mirrors — were gathered in a monstrous pile and set to the torch. It all went up in smoke. Savonarola, with his "bonfire of the vanities," openly challenged the moral authority of and even dared to reject the infamous Borgia pope Alexander VI.

Unfortunately for Savonarola, his prophetic vision could not replenish the gold in Florence's dwindling coffers. Popular support eventually waned. His fate and that of the republic were tied to a promise of new prosperity that never came to pass. Artisans in Lyon and Amsterdam made lovely silks and textiles, sapping sales of Florence's traditional money spinners. Trade routes east to the Indies and west to New Spain opened new markets in Lisbon and Seville that bypassed Italy altogether. It all ended abruptly when the pope struck back, excommunicating the charismatic priest and his noble city. Enemies rallied, and Savonarola was burned at the stake.

Yet today his theocratic guidance and inspiration is greatly admired by many Florentines. Idanna reminded me that, after all, it was *the* republic. This was the epic moment when Michelangelo and Leonardo faced off in the Palazzo Vecchio's Hall of the Five Hundred, composing frescoes of war battles. Florentines called their city the New Athens. There was no Machiavellian prince. Elected councils served. The Medicis, she said, had been cast out like the Shah.

Was theocratic Iran in the same position? I wondered. Some historians and journalists had drawn parallels, even comparing Khomeini's rule with that of Savonarola. But where were the elected councils these days? And where were Iran's Michelangelos and Leonardos?

It was late when the phone rang in my apartment in Manhattan. I recognized the singular voice of Amir, my Iranian friend, who wailed loudly.

"Listen to your friend, *baba*. You're crazy to go to Iran."

"You think so?"

"I know so! Your sweet *madar*, Donna, and dear *pedar*, Patrick, what if something happens and they never get out?"

"There won't be any —"

"Police! I know they will catch you at Tehran airport."

"But we fly to Shiraz."

"Even worse."

"Then we drive north."

"Followed by secret police."

"Come on, Amir."

"You come on, *baba*. First American family to go back, and you think you only will hear big *salaams*, drinking tea, with big welcome?"

"We're also Irish, remember?"

"Haaah! Think again."

"Chris is very afraid," I said.

"He's smart, your brother. Not like rest of Ward family, who won't listen. *Baba*, promise me one thing. Don't ask anyone about Hassan."

"I promise."

"Tell no one. *Khub*, I go now."
"Goodbye, Amir."
"*Khoda Hafez*. May God protect you."
"*Khoda Hafez*, my friend."

Few friends viewed our family journey as anything less than raving mad. Amir was no different. Since the Revolution, he had not set foot on the soil of his homeland.

After hearing my parents' irreversible decision to make the trip, fence-sitting Kevin was finally pressured into saying yes. A week later, ever-wary Chris also reluctantly agreed. The entire family planned to converge on the humid island sheikdom of Bahrain, just fifty miles east of Richard's home in Saudi Arabia. There we would secure our all-important visas.

Two days before leaving New York, I found a detailed atlas of Iran, printed in the Persian script that resembles Arabic. At a friend's apartment on 44th Street, near Times Square, I leafed through the pages, searching the index for phonetic sounds, beginning with *t*, then *oo*, then *d*, and suddenly my eyes rested on a village: T-u-d-e-sh-k. Was this it?

I double-checked the lettering and stared at the map in disbelief. There it was, our needle in a haystack, a tiny speck hidden in a central mountain range bordering the Dasht-e Kavir Desert! Perhaps my mother had been right all these years. Tudeshk.

To be scrambling after this forgotten village in a distant Asian desert in hopes of finding our long-lost friend seemed unconventional, to say the least. Then again, we had never followed a predictable life, one cast in the classic American mold. In fact, at times it seemed as if our life in Iran had been scripted by an unseen hand.

My father, Patrick, first saw the writing on the wall in Manhattan in 1950. Young GIs were bleeding in deep Korean snow. The question of "Who lost China?" raged in the Potomac's corridors of power. President Harry Truman promised a new hydrogen bomb. A blacklist was brewing. Bizarre new expressions were creeping into the political lexicon: "premature antifascist," "radical New Dealer," "social activist." And, of course, there was "fellow traveler."

The words always had an allure for me when I was a child. A fellow traveler was clearly someone to confide in, swap stories with, a partner in adventure. It sounded endearing, something I would have liked to be called, until my father explained its cold-war meaning. "Fellow travelers," he said, "were once thought to be special. They didn't carry Communist Party cards because they were the true subversives, and worked under cover. Aiding and abetting. Puppet masters behind the scenes. Always seen in curious places, much more dangerous."

In 1950, Senator Joe McCarthy and his House Committee on Un-American Activities had already launched their conspiracy crusade. Fires of inquisition burned; their hearing room had become a celebrity circus. Their tactic: naming names. Anyone who had questioned the system in the thirties and forties was at risk. Intellectuals, writers, actors, activists, labor organizers, all became targets.

My father would be one of them. As a natural rebel with a flame of red hair, he embodied an exotic mix: a Yeatsian romantic son of Irish parents, a passionate socialist and a natural ham with dreams of acting on Broadway.

Born of Donegal immigrants, Pat had served as an altar boy, and by the sixth grade he had read every book in the Bayonne, New Jersey, library. Even though he was the top student in St. Henry School, he was denied the annual scholarship award. It went instead to the son of the rich man who had secretly pledged to donate a new wing to the school. Thank God for this injustice: the scholarship that broke his heart would have whisked my father off to Ireland to follow the path of a priest. And nothing of what I am about to tell would have come to pass.

At sixteen Patrick walked away and began organizing apprentice welders in the taverns and wooden warehouses along the Hudson River, where he cut his eyeteeth as a union activist on

New York's waterfront. His politics and wavy ginger hair earned him the nickname Paddy the Red. It was the Depression. Everyone's world had collapsed, few had jobs, pay was meager, the future looked grim. Strikes led to battles with police. When my father was arrested, my grandfather came to bail him out of jail, with the simple question "Patrick, but why?" Young Pat looked up with conviction and pain: "Because we have to." His father never truly understood. He was a quiet man who worked the night shift at "the Hook," Bayonne's refinery. His real voice was in his fiddle, which came alive for feasts and weddings.

The world then plunged into savage war, and a generation was sent overseas. In December 1941, with his welding torch in hand, Pat headed west for Hawaii to patch up the crippled Pacific fleet still floating in Pearl Harbor. Like Yossarian in *Catch-22*, he signed up with the U.S. Air Corps and became a bombardier. By 1944, he was in a creaking B-17 Flying Fortress, searching for German targets. He watched raiding Focke Wolves circle their prey, sending planes spiraling earthward in flames with his friends trapped inside. On the ground, he drank heavily with his crew, while fresh faces arrived like clockwork after each mission to step into dead men's shoes.

But, like Yossarian, he survived. His brother Sean was badly wounded and frostbitten in the Battle of the Bulge, and his brother Jimmy faced down *banzai* charges on the bloody beaches of Guadalcanal. Never a great believer in the system, Patrick was certain their Irish luck had something to do with it. At the final hour, as he was released from active duty, Berlin lay in smoldering ruins. On a misty night in June, standing outside an aerodrome in Kettering, England, ticketed and bound for America, an airman begged him for his seat.

"Hey buddy, I'm tryin' to get back to my doll. Our wedding's planned! Come on Red, be a pal, let me take your place." Sympathy overcame my father. The teary-eyed airman grabbed his gear and rushed to board the plane. Pat walked back to the pub to wait for his name to be called for the next available flight. A few hours later, news circled with a hush. The B-17 had crashed into the Irish Sea. No survivors.

Once the war was over, Pat ran to the farthest place he knew on the American continent, the majestic Rocky Mountains. He found the granite flatirons of Boulder that shielded the green lawns of the University of Colorado, and there he met Donna Jean Ball.

My mother's earliest awareness of the world and her place in it came from a huge map of the United States in her elementary school classroom. Hutchinson, Kansas, she learned, was the geographic center of the nation and, for her, the center of the world. As a young girl growing up in a small town near her grandparents' farm, she dreamed of emerald-green jungle outposts and a dark, slow-moving river called Congo, where her Uncle Otto and Aunt Gladys served as missionaries. Each year, she waited in vain for her promised gifts: a scarlet-colored sassy parrot and a swinging silver-haired gibbon. When her father picked up and moved the family west to Colorado, everything would change for Donna. Lured onto the university stage by a sorority girlfriend, she was cast in a forgettable production of Josefina Niggli's *Red Velvet Goat*. When she confidently strode out as a señorita during an evening rehearsal of a south-of-the-border crowd scene, she came face to face with Patrick Ward, playing the part of a mustachioed boisterous Mexican señor, sporting a broad New York Irish accent. He was, in her words, "unintentionally hilarious."

Apart from being a unique character on campus — a side-splitting actor in theater and an honors student in economics — he was the most impoverished human being she had ever met. Almost immediately, she decided to desert her secure life and join him in a true adventure. Pat was a veteran, nine years older than she. He was irresistible. Suddenly her orderly life evaporated, and she became an avid interloper and a political activist in his world, a heady mix of idealistic dreamers unlike any she had known before. She was captivated. Donna chose their companionship even though she was never sure they really trusted her. By day, she and Patrick drove food supplies to striking miners in the mountain village of Louisville, and by night he acted in and directed plays, while she designed sets. Pat was drama critic for the college paper, she became society editor. The world was fresh and new. They were in love.

Penniless, Pat borrowed a hundred dollars for the wedding. With only his air force uniform to his name, a much ridiculed wedding present — an Irish Sweepstakes ticket from his sister Sue — proved to be the next miracle. It was a winner. Not the big money, but with $500 in fresh loot, the newly married couple bought a thirdhand '39 Oldsmobile and blazed east, to New York's 98th Street. One end of the street led to Madison and Fifth Avenues, and the other end was blocked by emerging subway trains. At night, bonfires blazed in vacant lots across the street, and the sounds of Latin music and drumming on car hoods filled the air.

Patrick enrolled at Columbia University, landed a job and even found time to coach the neighborhood Puerto Rican baseball team to their first league championship. When Donna strolled past men lounging under the yellow-splashed bodega awnings, they greeted her with smiles, proud of their victory. Pat was earning his master's degree and Donna studied at Hunter College. On weekends, friends from Greenwich Village gathered to sing, discuss theater or play charades; every now and then a young writer named Norman Mailer joined them.

The mood in Washington, D.C., however, was less jovial. The witch-hunt had begun. Senator Joe McCarthy's hearings on "un-American activities" raised anti-Communist hysteria to fever pitch as the country followed the fate of the "Hollywood Ten." At the University of California at Berkeley, loyalty oaths were demanded. Dozens of professors resigned in protest. And there was the blacklist. On it were Zero Mostel, Dashiell Hammett, Lillian Hellman, Paul Robeson and many others. Old friends at the University of Colorado were caught in the net of suspicion and careers were destroyed.

Freshly graduated, my father landed a job at the staid Bureau of

Labor Statistics in Manhattan. Soon gruff, chain-smoking FBI agents began to appear at his office. J. Edgar Hoover's G-men were relentless, full of distrust and, above all, humorless. They peppered him with questions.

"At Colorado, were you a member of the Social Science Reds?"

"I played third base and batted lead-off. Almost won the championship."

"Were you in San Francisco with Harry Bridges in '39?"

"Along with about ten thousand other union men."

"As drama critic at Colorado, you wrote about street scenes with tenements?"

"Our theater had a motto: Art should be real."

"Are you sure you didn't use it for social activism? Weren't some of your friends members of the Communist Party?"

"I had lots of friends."

In truth, Pat and Donna had stopped seeing those colleagues whose fanaticism denied the reality of the Korean War. The faithful were adamant: the North did not invade the South. Dogma bred denial. Pat felt there was no point in contesting their beliefs. Instead, he continued to organize relief for striking miners trapped in the frigid mountains above Boulder's bucolic campus.

In those heady days, my mother said to Patrick, "There's only one way for us to fit in. We have to move to someplace like Afghanistan." Betrayal, suspicion, treason, blackmail and espionage were shrill new buzzwords of the advancing cold war. Pamphlets like *Red Channels* had surfaced listing Communist Party members. Fingers were pointed. Rumors were started. Doors slammed shut on anyone with a past.

His old socialist friend at the Bureau of Labor Statistics, Harry Lawson, had warned him to say — if ever questioned — that they never met. The next morning, two agents escorted Harry down the bureau's long hall. Pat watched silently from his office as Harry was whisked out the door. Inside Pat's desk drawer lay a fat wallet forgotten by the young FBI agent during his previous visit. Pat tossed it into the hall. The relieved agent reappeared an hour later, sweat on his brow, thanking everyone. "Oh, thank God. If I'd lost that badge, I'd've lost my job. How can I ever pay you guys back?" Pat didn't ask him for the obvious favor. After the visits by FBI agents and the resignation of Lawson from the bureau, Pat knew it was time to move on. The decision became more urgent because Donna was pregnant, and as another icy winter gripped Manhattan, she knew the city was no place for their new baby.

Reading the *New York Times* one dreary afternoon, she came across a job listing that would change their lives. She tore it out and rang the number from a pay phone across the street. A telegram arrived soon after. The next morning, Pat and Donna entered the Park Avenue office of Aramco — the Arabian American Oil Company — and were quickly questioned by a bespectacled interviewer. He asked Pat if he knew anything about Saudi Arabia. Pat bluffed. Donna studied the posters on the walls: lovely white bungalows, blue skies and grinning expatriates in the sun. The site lay half a world away striding the Persian Gulf, in a province called Al-Hasa, where temperatures soared above 100 degrees in the summer. My mother's allergy to the sun was never raised. They left the office, contract in hand and a list of necessary tropical gear that resembled a summer camp directive. They imagined balmy desert breezes as they shopped in cruisewear departments for summer outfits, including a white dinner jacket that spent many years in splendid isolation.

One week later, Pat slipped into exile. It was 1952. That same year Charlie Chaplin sailed from New York and was informed at sea that, as a politically unacceptable foreigner, he could never return to America. Pat, a voluntary expatriate, boarded an Aramco plane headed for Lebanon, where he studied Arabic for a month in Sidon before finally landing on the barren sands of Saudi Arabia. My mother followed later with her new baby, Kevin.

In the sandy wastes along the Gulf, their footsteps would mark the beginning of a twenty-year journey. At Aramco, Pat sent the first Saudi employees to American universities and pushed for workers' rights — unheard-of in the oil companies operated by British colonials in neighboring Kuwait, Bahrain and Iran. There, English bureaucrats fresh from liberated India still clung jealously to their imperial practices of social apartheid and exclusion. In the Gulf and Iran, Victoria's raj was very much alive.

In the American compound, raucous theater and homemade hooch were de rigueur. Pat's performance in *South Pacific* and his production of *Night Must Fall* riveted the culture-hungry crowds, while the fierce *shamal* sandstorms pounded the frontier town of Dhahran. Most of the Yanks were in their twenties and thirties, Ivy League and Stanford graduates, a thin slice of the best and the brightest. Pat shone onstage and off, co-writing *Blue Flame*, a do-it-yourself company-issued guide for brewing alcohol in your kitchen.

Then one day a young doctor from Huntington, New York, warned Pat that the company's chief of security had boasted that he had a file on Pat Ward from the FBI. Envious of Pat's friendship with the camp doctor, this security man, in an absurd pique of jealousy, proclaimed that my father was a "security risk to American interests."

Furious, Pat pleaded with his manager to strike back. His boss quietly advised, "Let it pass. There's no need to concern yourself. It will only create a tempest, and I may not be able to protect you. After all, he is head of security." So the matter rested, but with a certain smoldering resentment. Years later, Pat requested his government files under the Freedom of Information Act. The search revealed a completely blank record.

After John F. Kennedy won the 1960 presidential election, Pat again decided to move on. He accepted a post as economic adviser to the National Iranian Oil Company. When we all stumbled out into the crisp mile-high air of Tehran's Mehrabad Airport, Kevin was only seven years old, I was five, Chris was four and little Richard had just turned two. The Shah on his peacock throne had adopted a brassy new title, *Aryamehr*, Light of the Aryans. Across the Caspian Sea, Stalin's fresh corpse lay in state in Moscow's Red Square.

2

# A Second Coming

Flee, then, to the essential East.

— Goethe, *Hegira*

**B**AHRAIN'S AIRPORT, April Fool's Day, 1998, was an unlikely site for a reunion of the four Ward brothers. Richard had dutifully driven over from his home in Saudi Arabia to pick us up after a grueling New York–London–Bahrain flight. But we had to find him first amid the chaos.

Without warning, we were engulfed by oncoming waves from Pakistan International and Air India 747s that disgorged a sea of guest workers, maids, nannies, laborers, clerks, accountants, grandmothers and boy Fridays, whose massive influx from South Asia kept the Gulf economies afloat. At the mention of Iran our request for seventy-two-hour transit visas was met with suspicious looks. The inquisitive eye of Colonel Abdullah, in his smart khaki uniform, signaled to Kevin that he wanted to know more.

"Why, sir, are you wanting to go to Iran? Business?" he asked through the transit visa window.

"No, for pleasure."

He laughed. His stamp crashed down.

Swept up again in the boisterous human tide, we passed a rose-colored Mercedes with shining gold hubcaps raised on a revolving platform in the spanking-clean marble arrival hall, the prize in this month's airport raffle. Overhead, flashy advertisements winked seductively about Silk Cut cigarettes, Rolex watches, and Chanel perfume.

It was Kevin's and Chris's first time in the Middle East since we all gathered in Egypt fifteen years before, when I was studying Pharaonic history and singing in a jazz band led by Leonidis, my Greek classmate from Alexandria. Back then, we all scaled Cheops's pyramid at dawn to watch the sun rise over the timeless Nile Valley, clambered down into the dusty Old Kingdom tombs of Saqqara and lost ourselves in medieval Cairo's labyrinthine Khan al-Khalili souk.

The flashy Gulf, Kevin and Chris soon discovered, was wildly modern, cut from those achingly poor and antiquated Arab neighbors to the north: Jordan, Egypt and Iraq. As Kevin drank in the strange cocktail of quick wealth, glossy construction and raffle prizes, he announced that Bahrain felt more like Las Vegas. Chris agreed. Then a black-masked woman passed by, silencing them both. Jet-lagged and exhausted, we waited until Rich finally strode in through the sliding glass doors. His loud whoops of joy drew the immediate scrutiny of airport security as Rich bear-hugged us in his massive arms. Giddy, tense and a bit shaken, we climbed into his waiting van, parked illegally outside the arrival hall.

The teardrop shaped island of Bahrain illustrates the demographic rift that divides Islam's two major sects, Sunni and Shia. Bahrain's population, I knew, was overwhelmingly Shia, as are more than 98 percent of Iranians. Yet all political power rests with Bahrain's ruling family, and the security apparatus remains in the hands of the Sunni minority. Democracy had not come to this part of the world. Sheikdoms and hereditary kingdoms were the rule.

Bloodied and bowed, the Gulf's Shia Arabs have forever been persecuted as heretics by their Sunni hereditary rulers in Saudi Arabia, Kuwait, Bahrain and the United Arab Emirates. Ancient fears and mistrust fueled the hatred of these Arab rulers. In Riyadh, the Saudi capital, a senior oil company executive calmly assured me once that the Shia "had tails."

Clustered around the Gulf in settlements, these Arab Shia had a natural affinity for Iranian believers across the Gulf through their common faith. Many see them as a fifth column with hidden Iranian allegiances. During the explosive days of the 1979 Islamic Revolution, the Saudi princes feared they would suffer the same fate as Iran's Shah. In nearby Bahrain, explosive student protests periodically signaled discontent.

I had grown fond of these Shia Arabs, having conducted many management training seminars in Gulf countries for eight years. Like most persecuted minorities, they held a quiet dignity and a yearning for justice. There was no sense of entitlement among them. In the Gulf, American diplomats took great pains never to criticize any petrokingdoms over human rights abuses. Silence kept the oil flowing.

In the back of Rich's minivan, surrounded by my brothers, I felt liberated from the impending gloom of another round of consulting projects in Disneyesque desert sheikdoms. During a decade of self-imposed exile from Ronald Reagan's America, I had lived in Athens and traveled down to the Gulf as a consultant to companies with a multicultural work force. The awkward mix included Japanese, French, Saudis, Egyptians, Bengalis, Filipinos, Yanks, and Greeks, reluctantly thrown together in golden-cocoon Arabian city-states, sprinkled on shifting sands and pounded by blazing sun.

In the Gulf, strangely enough, no one was exposed to the natural elements anymore. Everything was indoors. The sound of wind on a tent flap had been replaced by the perpetual hum of air conditioning. Cases of pneumonia brought on by the artificial chill reached epidemic levels in summer.

Social life and entertainment had been reduced to marathon video viewing and, of course, drinking liters of the banned but ever-flowing alcohol. Meanwhile, women in purdah — otherwise known as "bimos," or black independent moving objects — scurried through enclosed marble shopping malls, keeping their exposed ankles one step ahead of the dreaded *Mutawas*, the religious police. The ancient Bedouin culture of Arabia had traded in its camels for Cadillacs, gained a huge waistline and an obsession for Louis XV furniture, and, somewhere along that superhighway to the modern age, lost its charm and mortgaged its soul.

In contrast, the thought of returning to Iran was profoundly appealing. Something there had snapped. Globalization had received a swift and unexpected kick in the teeth. America's cultural icons of McDonald's, Nike, MTV, pierced eyebrows and Planet Hollywood had been mercifully kept at bay.

Careening in Rich's van along the palm-lined corniche, we circled the Gulf waters that shimmered silver in blinding sunlight. Blasts of thick humidity poured through our windows. Strolling Bahrainis flowed by in white gowns with soft cotton headscarves and black camel-hair double coils that held their headgear in place.

Rich told us he planned to spirit us across the bridge to his home in Saudi Arabia, where our eager parents had arrived. Apparently, Mother was limping from a recent fall and a sprained ankle that would have kept any of us bedridden. Dad was in marvelous shape for seventy-three.

Observing my brothers one by one, I realized how much had changed since our Tehrani childhood days. Chris's blond curls had straightened, Kevin's black mane of hair had disappeared, as had Richard's.

Chris stood taller than all of us, athletically slender at six feet. His artistic hands — which once gathered talismans, stones, and shells into an aquamarine jar he called his "magic box" — now shaped elaborate sculptures, pouring molten bronze into life-size white plaster casts. In his Philadelphia studio, he endowed his figures with a viridian patina similar to that of the ancient Luristan bronzes of Iran. His creative gift mystified my parents. "He walks lightly," Dad once told me. "He touches the earth every fourth step."

Kevin, on the other hand, enjoyed playing two roles: "brother number one" and Ivy League literary aesthete, quoting T. S. Eliot at the drop of a hat. After graduating from law school he turned his back on the profession, confessing to my father that he found all lawyers to be insufferable masochists. He wrote a satirical work called *Not the Official Lawyers' Handbook* while navigating the currents of New York's nightlife, sporting black tie, tennis sneakers and a faded Hudson Riverkeeper baseball cap. A non-conformist and self-styled futurist, he now crafted speeches for high-tech CEOs and created gargantuan productions for corporate powwows. He did his best work while seated in a boat off Shelter Island, where J. M. Barrie wrote *Peter Pan*. Once a week, Kevin enthusiastically commuted to Cambridge to teach a course in American literature at Harvard.

Chris and Kevin had carved out their own worlds in America. But at nightfall, when they herded their little children off to sleep, the echo of a familiar Persian voice rose in their bedtime stories. In this way, verbal heirlooms — like Hassan's tale of Solomon's ring — were gently passed on to a new generation.

The Bahrain causeway, a seven-mile bridge constructed over salt flats and the Gulf's choppy waves, presented a cultural shock. Saudi Arabia's Islamic restrictions were more severe than anywhere else in the world, except perhaps in Taliban-ruled Afghanistan. Women, always covered, were not allowed to drive, work or vote. But there was folly. Saudis still joked about the original design plans for the causeway that included an arrow-straight bridge crossing to the "pleasure island" of Bahrain, where wet bars served cocktails and draft beer while Gulf Air stewardesses tanned their pale English skin by luxurious hotel swimming pools. Coming back, the joke went, the engineers' design had the road weaving left and right to compensate for all the drunk Saudi drivers returning to teetotal Arabia.

At the wheel, Richard, with his close-cropped hair and round spectacles, radiated an unruffled, Indiana Jones air. He was an explorer at heart. Since childhood, nature's wild grandeur had pulled him by the collar. When he was in a geology program at Stanford, he once trekked for months in Nevada's remote Snake Range to map unknown lands. From there, a package arrived at my door. In it I found the skin of a five-foot rattlesnake on which Rich had scrawled: "They say these mountains are just outside of God's country — California. But if you only knew what my eyes have seen. Whispering crocus, alpine poppies, hidden springs, beguiling ravines, screeching F-16s overhead, deadly rattlers underfoot. This one is special. It almost got me."

Richard's job in Saudi Arabia seemed to be a twist of destiny. Aquifers trapped underground in geologic folds had become his obsession. His environmental mission with Aramco centered on preserving the Saudis' most precious patrimony: water.

With his wife, Ellen, and their two young boys — both born in Saudi Arabian hospitals like their daddy — he lived in Dhahran, an American-designed town that had a golf course, a bowling alley, baseball fields, a library, a movie theater, a snack bar, a gymnasium, an elementary school, and ranch-style homes. It was a strange oasis. To enter and exit, one had to cross military-style security checkpoints.

As we pulled into Richard's driveway, I saw my brother's eccentric imprint on Dhahran's Levittown monotony: on his garage door was painted a giant replica of Mondrian's *Broadway Boogie*. Inside, among hand-carved Rajput columns, brass doors and inlaid tables, we all sat down for our last supper.

Intrepid Ellen laid out our lavish feast while their two young boys hovered close to their father. Little Brendan and Ames knew they would not be coming on the trip. Over the meal, we caught up on old family news and retold stories that brought gales of laughter and tears to our eyes. Then we turned to the business at hand.

Tomorrow at dawn we would leave. We discussed our itinerary, which Richard had researched and painstakingly arranged. Instead of flying to Tehran, we would go in through the back door, landing in the southern city of Shiraz. From there, we would strike north, past Persepolis and the Zoroastrian city of Yazd to the edge of the Dasht-e Kavir Desert. According to my map, a village spelled "Tudeshk" — we hoped Hassan's birthplace — lay in the mountains east of Isfahan.

Over dinner, our old friend Tom Owen, whose month-long Land Rover treks into the lifeless Rub al-Khali Desert were legendary, rose with a toast. "To the Ward clan." He raised his glass of homemade red wine. "To your audacious leap into the familiar and the unknown."

"This," Chris said, sliding our itinerary across the table to Tom, "is so you'll know where to begin your search in case we don't return." Then he asked about survival tips.

"Each person keep a separate stash of money," Tom counseled, "in case you need to bargain yourself out of tight situations."

Over dessert, Chris read slowly from the Lonely Planet guide. "Before entering Iran, memorize the address and phone number of your diplomatic mission in Tehran." He paused. "The right of a foreigner to telephone his consul is not always observed, so insist before being whisked away."

Tom rose to leave with a time-honored Arabic farewell: "*Allah maakum*. God be with you."

Chris circled the telephone number of the Irish embassy. "Now, everybody listen carefully to this number . . ." Three of us carried Irish as well as American passports.

At one-thirty in the morning, the warmth of our reunion gave way to the cool desert breeze. We had four hours left to sleep. Unearthly howls of cats fighting outside my window fueled my insomnia. Fresh doubts surfaced about the sanity of this whole affair. Were we placing ourselves in jeopardy for a dream that no longer existed? Where could Hassan be? Could he sense our homecoming, I wondered. Richard had told us the reward bounty of $1,000 that he had offered to several travel agencies was still uncollected.

Lights of a yellow gas flare at a nearby refinery danced on the bedroom's white lace curtains above my pillow. Crickets' chatter pulsed in the shadows. As I drifted off to sleep, images of the flare sparked in my mind. I saw Hassan's face lit by a long row of crackling bonfires. He started to run. Taking a deep breath, I followed his footsteps. My brothers cried out behind me. Over the first flame I leapt. Sweating and panting, blinded by the light, I ran through the night chasing his vanishing heels.

Early the next morning, I awoke to Chris's loud complaints about the books I had packed for the trip. He was emphatic, his voice trembling from frayed nerves.

"Are you trying to get us arrested?" He held up Sandra Mackey's *The Iranians* as evidence.

"Not at all."

"Good, then you're leaving it here."

"But when I travel to Italy, I bring Barzini's *The Italians.*"

"We're not going to Italy."

He tossed it on the table. I showed him the cover.

"Look, women in chadors," I said.

"But there's the Shah with his crown."

"You can barely see him."

"Go ahead, put all our lives at risk." Opening my suitcase, he peered at the rest of my movable library. "What else do you have in there?"

One by one he inspected: Calvino's *Invisible Cities*, Borges's *Labyrinths*, Marco Polo's *Travels*, Robert Byron's *Road to Oxiana*, Freya Stark's *Valleys of the Assassins*.

"And this?" Chris held it aloft. "When was it written?"

"Are you bothered by the word 'assassins'?"

"Before or after the Revolution?"

"It's a classic."

"Answer my question."

"In the thirties. I told you, it's a classic. Calm down, Chris."

"Look, you don't have kids, but I do. And you're trying to smuggle in these hand grenades." His pleading eyes radiated only grim fear. "Why don't you bring the whole damn Salman Rushdie collection while you're at it!"

The Iranian embassy in Bahrain is tucked away in Fashaneya, a shabby suburb strewn with rundown villas, blinding white sand, paved roads that abruptly end and street signs that have nothing to do with the official government map that Richard was using to navigate. We arrived late. A lonely guardhouse was abandoned. As we entered the embassy, the sound of overworked air conditioners drowned out conversation. We handed over our passports and sat down to wait. A coffee table offered promising travel brochures of Isfahan, the turquoise city of Shah Abbas, and of jungle-lush Mazandaran, a province on the Caspian Sea.

A book lay in full view: *The Imposed War*, an official pictorial record of the Iran-Iraq War. Imposed? Yes, it was the Iraqis who had started the war. Saddam Hussein attacked across the Shatt al-Arab, annihilating the oil cities of Khorramshahr and Abadan, crippling Iran's economy and launching a killing rage. The photos told the gruesome story. Unspeakable slaughter in Mesopotamian marches matched the horror in the fields of Flanders eighty years before — blinded men, severed torsos, trenches full of contorted dead. I closed the book quickly, thinking about Hassan and his two sons.

The Iranian consul general's office was businesslike and roomy. The consul greeted us graciously, in the no-nonsense revolutionary attire of a white shirt without a tie and a three-day beard that partially hid his dimpled chin. We chatted, his voice deep and formal. Ayatollah Khomeini's stern face stared down at us with eyes like black olives. After our ceremonial cup of tea, an ink-coated stamp pressed down on our passport pages. He signed all six visas with a flourish, smiled and offered us good wishes in Farsi. It was done.

We drove off in disbelief. A Saudi Shia friend, Abdullah, seeing us off at the airport, dismissed the antipathy between Arabs and Iranians. "We are all Shia here in eastern Saudi Arabia and Bahrain. We need ten more years to catch up. We can learn from the Iranians. They have a civilized ancient culture like Egypt."

Few Westerners know that all the great oilfields of Saudi Arabia lie beneath historically Shia land. A dream for any Saudi Shia is to reach the Iranian holy cities of Mashhad and Qom, the Vatican of the faithful.

"They'll like you because you have respect," Abdullah said.

"*Insha'allah*, God willing," I replied.

Armed with hollow bravado, residual fears and my mother's wheelchair, we joined other pilgrims, mostly Arabian Shia traveling to the holy sites. Judging from our half-empty Iran Air 727, we seemed to be the only Westerners on board. The plane cruised above the Persian Gulf, home of the U.S. Navy's Fifth Fleet, and flew over a phalanx of American warships, plying the iron-gray waters like a sleek school of sharks.

To my left, Richard began chanting his special "get out of jail" mantra quietly to himself: "*Bebakhsheed, nemedonam, man kami divaneh hastam.* I'm sorry, I don't know, I'm a little crazy."

Recent reports in the Gulf press were ominous. The sudden jailing of the popular mayor of Tehran, Mohammad Karbaschi, on trumped-up corruption charges signaled another sinister offensive from hard-liners. Moderate technocrats were "on the run." My mother quizzed a stylish Iranian businessman from Hamburg, Germany, who was returning for a visit. Recent political events were the subject. Karbaschi, accused of embezzlement, was a rising star in the reform coalition and one of the brains behind President Khatami's surprise 1997 election victory, which upset the conservatives no end. Always probing for controversy, my mother asked her usual incendiary questions.

"He's such a wonderful man, Karbaschi."

"Yes, madam, he's done many good things."

"So why in heaven's name is he in jail?"

"Only Allah knows."

"But Mr. Karbaschi is such a vital leader for the country."

"But things change."

"So why won't the mullahs leave him alone?"

"Well, maybe he's guilty," he answered, looking over his shoulder.

"Oh, come on now."

"Some people know much more about this than we do, madam."

I noticed Chris's flurry of elbow pokes had failed to stop her. Ignoring him, Mom kept chattering away about the mayor, the mullahs, Khatami, and the ruling right wing. Sliding into the seat directly behind the businessman was a suspicious-looking fellow with the same three-day beard as the Iranian consul in Bahrain. He leaned forward to listen.

"No more politics, please," Mom's conversation partner pleaded, waving her off. He slithered over to the far window.

"We're surrounded," said my father.

"Now, will you please shut up, Mom, and put on your head-scarf," muttered Chris.

"But dear, it's too hot."

"I don't care," said Chris.

"You really mustn't worry so much, boys."

My father groaned. "Can't we change the subject?"

Kevin closed his eyes and began reciting Yeats's prophetic poem "The Second Coming" as the airplane's wings dipped one last time over the bleak Zagros Range on its descent toward the greening Fars Plateau and the Persian heartland.

"'Turning and turning in the widening gyre the falcon cannot hear the falconer.'"

We sipped our warm mint tea.

"'Things fall apart; the center cannot hold; mere anarchy is loosed upon the world . . . and everywhere the ceremony of innocence is drowned.'"

The onboard snacks had included pistachio nuts, a yellow apple, peach halves and a violet box in which two Persian winged lions held a chocolate wafer. Curious, I thought, that these pre-Islamic images survived. Even Darius the Great's "heathen" winged griffin still reigned as the Iran Air mascot, not the newer calligraphy of *Allah al-Akbar*, God is great. A grape juice container had a label that read, "Don't stare at me, drink me." I obeyed.

When the wheels touched ground with a violent skid, Kevin was voicing the last stanza: "'And what rough beast, its hour come round at last, slouches towards . . .'"

The engines roared, drowning him out. We had landed in Shiraz.

Looking over at me, Chris sighed. "Getting through customs will be a highlight of our trip."

I took stock of our contraband: my books, Richard's vitamin pills, my forty rolls of film and telephoto lens, a tape recorder with ten cassettes, *New York Times* articles, *Herald Tribune* editorials, and my mother's ever-questioning curiosity. Her wheelchair was stuffed with dollar bills. I hoped for mercy.

Taxiing to the terminal, we were all visibly nervous, but clearly not alone. Every passenger on the plane looked equally skittish, filled with his own private trepidation. Soon we would be confronted by our first Revolutionary Guards and customs officials. What reception awaited us? Would books and papers be confiscated? Would we be followed?

The battered airport terminal spoke silently of past Iraqi bombing raids; the chipped concrete and faded paint were signs of neglect and an impoverished economy.

All those anxious feelings melted with our first steps off the plane. My mother gazed up at the sky and filled her lungs with a gasp of crisp air. Passing clouds seemed so close. Familiar smells, distinct and faint, dislodged childhood memories. An immediate feeling of home washed over us. A warm and ancient welcome was in the air.

At passport control I solemnly pushed my mother's wheelchair. She smiled at the bearded military guards. They showed pity. At customs, no search took place. We walked straight through.

Chris, expecting the worst, stood frozen in disbelief until I pulled his arm. Then, grinning splendidly, he grabbed my bag of contraband and we wheeled past the armed soldiers.

At the doorway, we were greeted gravely by Avo, a middle-aged Armenian who bore all the attributes of Inspector Clouseau or a low-level spy. Avo had been assigned to join us by our travel agency. There was no room for protest: it was regulation, he told us in English; all Americans had to be accompanied twenty-four hours a day.

Stepping outside, I stood overwhelmed. Luminous sunlight reflected off the surrounding Zagros peaks under the immense sky. I could taste the altitude. It colored every sense. Floating a mile above sea level, I felt featherweight. There was a lightness of being, as if gravity's hold had just slipped.

Rich, always the scientist, described to us the geological havoc that created the plateau. He spoke of the late Cambrian continental dance when the supercontinent Gondwanaland split up into smaller pieces. By the late Miocene period, he explained, east of Madagascar the Indian tectonic plate had broken free from the African continent. Racing out to sea, it surged northward, aiming directly at the underbelly of Asia. The final impact was cataclysmic. Wrenching and buckling collisions of these continental plates threw coastal beaches and sea shells high into the clouds, forming the Himalayas. The Middle East was also sculpted this way. North of the sweltering Persian Gulf, two plates had slammed together over the sea floor and lifted a vast plateau more than a mile high.

I scanned the sculpted mountains that rose like hunched copper bones out of the green-streaked plain. With my heart pounding, I read the landscape like an excited boy.

Our eyes searched the expansive sky, which pulled our gaze from east to west. Against this spectacular Asian topography, Montana's mind-stretching horizons would look mundane, even parochial. Iran's strength spoke through her mountain ranges, through her forbidding ramparts, brown and purple, framed in silent, rugged wonder. Familiar sensations gripped us in this sanctuary of Fars, home of the ancient Persians.

The lofty Iranian plateau is shaped like a trapezoidal tabletop and ringed by snowy shark-tooth peaks. Hemmed in by two formidable ranges, the Elburz and the Zagros, the plateau is bone dry.

The only water seeps down from melting mountain snows; it rarely rains. Sweeping west to east along the Caspian Sea's lapping shore, the colossal Elburz Range — topped at nineteen thousand feet by Iran's Fujiyama, the volcano Demavand — links Eurasia's rugged Caucasus with central Asia's Hindu Kush and the soaring Pamirs of the Himalayas. The Zagros chain slashes north-south like a crescent-shaped scimitar down the long Iraqi border and along the Persian Gulf coastline, demarcating the eastern limit of the Arabic-speaking world. On this plateau, sensations are vivid. High altitude sharpens pathos. Senses open wide.

God's hand chose to be minimalist here. No humid sun-beaten river basins like the bilharzia-ridden Nile, no aching silt-washed Mesopotamia, no teeming eternal Ganges can be found. Instead, wild, dizzying peaks lift out of a rough moonscape with forceful enterprise. Copper-tinted flanks fold and buckle like accordion frames, leaving snowmelt-carved gorges and steep unnerving ravines. Yet when and wherever water runs, there is life. Erect steeples of poplar trees line up in sleek columns alongside riverbeds or bravely stand alone. Reaching to the sky, they remind passersby: look up. Look to the heavens.

3

# The Past Is a Foreign Country

The past is a country from which we all have emigrated.
— Salman Rushdie, *Imaginary Homelands*

A pearl beyond the shell of existence and time
was searched for by those lost on the seashore.
— Hafez

I N THE NORTH of Iran, buttressed by the flanks of the slate-gray Elburz Mountains, sits Tehran. Our old house, above the neighborhood of Tajrish, clung to the first wave of steeply rising sheets of stone. And for ten years it was home. "For those who have left it," Mircea Eliade wrote in *No Souvenirs*, "the city of their childhood and adolescence always becomes a mythical city."

I remember a warm spring evening. If memories of Tehran define my family's fabled cosmology, then a garden-encircled villa is our touchstone. Like the alchemist in his laboratory, Hassan in the kitchen swirls like a dervish. Mixing fire with water, he transmutes elements. Outside, coals burn white hot. Inside, steam rises from the cauldron. The table groans with vegetables and spices: turmeric and cumin, red peppers and eggplant, sweet garlic and tomatoes, all laced with herbs; mint, tarragon and dill are potions in his hands. Plums, quince, lemons and apricots add the sweet-sour flavors he seeks. With special care he creates mouth-watering feasts: seared lamb *kebab*, delicately softened with his secret marinade; crushed walnuts in pomegranate nectar flooded over braised duck called *fesanjan; jujeh kebab*, a grilled, saffron-yellow lemon-garlic chicken; all spread over a bed of *pollo* — hot basmati rice with melted butter and sumac.

Smoke and heat animate Hassan's storytelling. In his bag of tales, he picks from a wide range, comic buffoonery to operatic tragedy. Rich's favorite tragedy is from the *Shahnameh*, the Persian *Iliad*. The story begins: heroic Rustam, the Hercules of Iran, holds off the marauding Turan Turks from the east. While the battle unfolds, Hassan twirls his apron, grabs his chopping knife and flares his eyes for dramatic effect.

Rustam's mythic battle with his enemy, Sohrab, lasts three days. The country's destiny is at stake. The fight rages on, and even God pauses to watch. Rustam and Sohrab clash under thunderclouds. Finally Rustam fatally slashes Sohrab, who falls. When the mighty Rustam bends down over the bleeding warrior, he sees a magical armband that once was his own. In a flash he remembers: this was a gift to the only woman he ever loved. After one night of passionate love twenty years before, she vanished and he never saw her again. Now Rustam knows that his dying enemy can only be his long-lost son! Brave Sohrab, finally reunited with his father, dies slowly in his arms. *Noooo!* We gasp on cue as Hassan deftly pulls a hissing, puffed-up baked Alaska out of the oven.

In our living room and on the candlelit verandah, a lavish black-tie affair bubbles away. A Louis Armstrong record croons Fats Waller's "Ain't Misbehavin'" to a gathering of Iranian aristocrats and pipe-smoking professors, Western diplomats, covetous businessmen with their trophy wives, and thinly disguised spies as they gossip and guzzle Russian vodka. Dad recounts his "Dancing Master" story to uproarious laughter while my brother Kevin loiters around the caviar bowl like the thief of Baghdad, acting nonchalant as he scoops up large dollops of the black gold onto his waiting toast. Waiters and bartenders serve the crowd. Upstairs, brother Chris, inside his cardboard-box spaceship, soars past Mars.

Meanwhile, in the kitchen, Hassan continues to describe

Rustam's pain as he holds his son's head in his arms. Tears fill his eyes and ours. Outside, the jazz tempo changes. Billie Holiday languidly flies on "God Bless the Child."

As the summer months settle in, Hassan introduces us to a Tehran custom — when heat blisters the city's flatlands, families head into the hills for respite. We trek above Tajrish Square to Darband's roaring mountain river, where teahouses hang from cliffs, cooled by breezes cast off by the tumbling water. We climb along the winding path, and *kebab* smoke wafts from braziers, stoked by waving fans. From tiny stalls, vendors call out their temptations: tangy pressed sour-cherry rolls or young shelled walnuts, tender and white.

But in Tajrish there is another attraction: the bazaar. I remember it vividly as a world of deep shadows. Holding Hassan's hand, I step cautiously. Shafts of light shoot through the overhead mesh, slowly streaked by blue smoke and dust. Shops and stalls, bustling teahouses, even a post office lie hidden in this hooded cavern. Swirling through its arteries are ladies in chic dresses, students carrying their books home, laborers and hawkers, turbaned mullahs clutching Korans, women draped in long black cloaks, straggling children being dragged in tow.

Inside this labyrinth, people come to dip into exotica: shiny porcelain tea sets, copperbright trays, intoxicating perfumes, stacked rolls of textiles, plastic toys and telephones, shrill gold jewelry, burlap bags filled with rice, flowery carpets, nuts and dried fruits — Persian figs, mulberries, apricots, persimmons. And then there are the spices, standing upright in a row, waiting for you in their woven hemp sacks: fiery reds, simmering yellows, burnt tans and fading greens. Spilling from one pigment to another, they are the colors of blood, sunflower, amber, grass.

Parviz's quick hand swoops out of the darkness and tugs at the air. Hassan shakes his friend's hand warmly. I find my wooden stool and sit beside Parviz while Hassan goes off to buy vegetables. Shoppers scurry, streaming by. Parviz's dusty fingers rustle my red hair, leaving saffron dust behind. I smile. His fragrant

offerings fend off the ripe stench of lamb meat hanging at a
nearby butcher's. As usual, he offers me one of his treasures, a
strip of cinnamon bark or a mint leaf, and we sit silently to watch
the world go by. Like seasoned fishermen, we patiently wait for
the nibble, the bite; we wait for someone to stop and stare at his
rainbow of goods.

A searching hand caresses a root. Another rubs some seeds
or flicks through the dried leaves. Pepper, cardamom, nutmeg,
Parviz explains. Curious heads turn to listen. His soft voice re-
traces the spices' long journey across land and sea before their
auspicious arrival in Tajrish, to meet the welcoming touch of such
honorable customers.

Mostly, I remember, he begins the travels east along India's
Malabar coast; for the dried Omani lemon he sets out from the
southern Arabian deserts. I listen, pleased to join his verbal caravan. But no spice I know is more astonishing than his offering on
that spring day.

His weathered, cracked fingers place a dried dark flower stem
in my palm. He winks, says *"Beyah, bokhor,"* and shows me how he
tucks it under his tongue. His eyes roll with a smile. I do the same.
It slips quickly under my teeth and I bite into the thick petal,
breaking it into smaller pieces. My mouth explodes like a bomb.
Tongue ablaze, cheeks flush, blood races. My gums quickly go
numb. I break out in a sweat. A quick breath sends the rich, fiery
scent into my lungs. It is clean and heavy. My God, what is this? I
look up dazed at Parviz. I feel moist droplets on my forehead.

Still smiling, he gives me another. "Powerful, no?" he says.

I nod weakly.

"Feel that strength?"

"What is it?" I stammer, my mouth still in flames.

"Queen of the spices. Clove."

"From where, *baba?*" I ask.

"Farther east than all the others."

"How far?"

"The end of the world. *Maluku.* Islands of Kings."

"Where?"

"Where Asia ends and the oceans begin."

"*Ma-lu-ku.*" I repeat under my breath.

"Yes. Farther east than China, islands floating like gardens. One day, little brother, you will go there."

"*Insha'allah,*" says Hassan, just then returning to Parviz's stall.

Their eyes turn upward. Mine follow. "If God wills." Always the last words. The radio from the teahouse buries their words with a song by the great diva Parisa, about moonlight, narcissus eyes, the maiden in the white chador.

Each summer, my brothers and I swim like tadpoles for hours, escaping the sizzling heat in a turquoise-tinted pool. Overhead, a steel cable stretches from a treetop to the verandah across the water. A brainstorm of my mother's, this cable holds a pulley and a wooden swing. Climbing the steep ladder, we take turns jumping onto the swing, flying over the pool and leaping in midair, ending with wild splashes below. Exhausted by the afternoon, with chlorine-reddened eyes, we tiptoe across burning gravel to Hassan's home.

Under shady trees on a large wooden bench covered with maroon carpets, we find Hassan sipping tea with his wife and, occasionally, a friend. This is the seat of tradition. Jasmine, planted by his wall, floats its scent into the air. Chatting away, we drink glass after glass of tea. Between soft talk and naps, young Fatimeh and her friend giggle at Hassan's humor. A small brass samovar simmers. Smiles cross over tiny rims of tea glasses.

Often, Chris, Rich and I doze off. Fatimeh unrolls her mattresses and calls us inside. One by one we collapse by the pink cylindrical pillows that line her room. Slowly sunlight fades. When I wake to voices outside, gold streaks of the setting sun fall across the garden like jewels. Beyond our wall, purple and indigo shadows cover the mountain ridges. Onion, garlic and pungent simmering herbs drift from Fatimeh's kitchen. I nudge Chris and Rich, who wake up groggy and pleased. It's time to leave. We scamper back to the big house.

Often, after dinner, I wander again down the dark path to Hassan's warmly lit room. Before his nightly storytelling, Hassan always washes and Fatimeh sits before her loom. I play with baby Ali and watch Fatimeh weave. After his ritual ablution, Hassan wipes dry his damp hands. His face is refreshed. He lifts up his baby and kisses him. Then, without speaking, he lays out his prayer rug. In silence, he kneels. He raises his head, eyes half shut. His lips move. I cannot hear his words.

W. B. Yeats once suggested that the Irish, in times of great joy, know that tragedy lurks around the corner. The same holds true for Iranians.

Each year, the nation relives its collective suffering. Across Iran, the murders of Hussein, his sons and followers in A.D. 680 on the plains of Kerbela are reenacted in processions and plays. Though frowned on by the Shah's father as backward folk art, these centuries-old performances called *taziyeh* are the Islamic world's only indigenous drama. Because the Muslim lunar calendar contains twenty-nine fewer days than our Gregorian year, the holy month of Moharram — an emotional time of remembrance that plunges everyone into ritual grief — changes seasons with the years.

Dressed in mourning, Hassan tells us that this year too he will carry the green flag of Hussein in the Ashura procession. Somber music plays over the radio. The big day arrives. Jostled by the crowd, my brothers and I peer through the legs and arms of adults. Stern and dignified, Hassan marches past, followed by scores of black-clothed boys and men beating their chests with open palms or lashing their backs with chains before the watching crowds. Women trail behind them. Tears flow freely for their saintly martyrs. *"Yaaaah Hussein!"* they cry. The sounds of drums and chains echo down the street.

In the late afternoons of autumn, on our way home from school, we buy tart green almonds sprinkled with salt from stacked roadside carts. We dodge rocks tossed by rival kids, outpace growling street dogs or pluck bark off the towering plane trees before turning the corner near our house.

Once inside the red iron gate, we pad down our garden foot-path over well-worn stones by the cherry orchard and enter a doorway that opens onto a room with carpets from wall to wall. Fatimeh greets us with her round cherubic face and pomegranate cheeks. Inside, we find sips of hot tea, little Ali, baby Mahdi and the mystery of Fatimeh's loom. Her tiny pearl-white hands are ideal for carpet making. In her remote native desert village, Fatimeh tells us, she wove her first knot when she was only six years old.

Her father used to work in Tehran. My brothers and I knew about his tragic death — crushed while digging a water tunnel with his crew in north Tehran. Fatimeh did not remember him; she was far too young when the tunnel collapsed. The family was left in desperate straits. By the time her sixth birthday arrived, she was one of many girls weaving from dawn to dusk for the pay of just one rial. Seven days a week. No school, no breaks, no food. Only a piece of dry bread in her pocket. The loom's strings made her fingers bleed. Whenever child Fatimeh nodded off, the money-hungry matron, a Dickensian villain, would hit her on the back with a stick. The girl's heads were shaved to prevent them from wasting time fussing over their looks.

A month before he died, her father had announced in a boom-ing voice: "Young Hassan Ghasemi must marry my daughter." Fatimeh lay swaddled in the corner, barely two years old. A brown hat was placed on Hassan's ten-year-old head in front of both families, symbolizing their engagement.

Hassan lost the hat, but never forgot his obligation. Nor did the two plotting mothers. With the death of Fatimeh's father, Hassan's fate was sealed. When he finally agreed to marry, at the age of twenty-two, his bride was still a child. "She was a baby," Hassan later told us, laughing. "She just wanted to play with dolls."

Hassan's father was a scoundrel, a ne'er-do-well, a camel driver who set out across the desert trade routes, leaving his wife and children to fend for themselves, stranded and penniless in their desolate village. For months, even years, he would disappear.

During one inauspicious homecoming, young Hassan, then only five, did not recognize his father and attacked him with a stick, defending the family shack from the "Afghani" intruder. For his insolence, his father beat him with the same stick, long and hard. When food was scarce, his mother ordered the kids to scavenge trees for bugs and locusts. That was all the protein they ate. When she suggested killing a camel for meat, her husband said he'd rather kill one of his children. At seven, Hassan was taken away from his mother, dragged off to the capital by his father. In Tajrish Square, he was cast off and told to get a job. For the next year, he roamed the nearby hills as a shepherd, guarding a rich man's flock. He never saw his father until the winter snows fell again in Tehran and it was time to go home for the one-month vacation. Only then would his father reappear to collect his son's wages.

Hassan was a mature twenty-three when he first walked through our red gate with his young bride.

One day, a group of entertainers entered our garden, a strange tribe we had never seen before. On a whim and with his usual flair for hospitality, my father had invited for lunch the entire troupe from a sizzling downtown hot spot, Club Shokufeh-no.

In the kitchen, Hassan cursed, smashing pots and pans around. "God bless your father, but he should have told me all these *divaneh*, crazies, were coming," he complained.

Jugglers, bird trainers, a clarinet player, belly dancers and a white poodle were introduced to us. Out on the verandah, magicians traded tricks, pulling coins out of one another's ears and returning watches to one and all. French, Russian and Arab chorus girls sat next to the grotto in a cluster as prim and proper as young ladies at Sunday school.

Concerning important things, I was sure that my father consulted Hassan first. As a child, I suffered from warts. For more than a year, doctors with knives and red-hot cauterizers had left nothing but scars on my elbows and knees when trying to remove them.

After each operation, a new batch appeared, turning every fall and scrape into a painful ordeal. Frustration hung in my parents' voices.

One winter day, Dad arrived home from work and pulled out a ram's horn from his leather attaché case. Dusty with flecks of leaves and dirt, it curled like a nautilus shell. He carefully rested the horn on the walnut table by the fireplace in the chilly living room, where we rarely played. Hassan made a fire and lit a candle. My father had a mystical look in his eye and set his strong, gentle hand on my shoulder, drawing me near.

"I'm going to cure you, Terry," he said with conviction and then lifted my small arm and slowly waved the horn over my wounds, whispering a mantra: "Witch away, witch away, witch away . . ." My three brothers watched spellbound. Every night the sessions continued. After dinner, we would walk into the ice-cold room at the appointed hour, and Dad would make a fire and light a candle. Hassan stood by his side.

After two weeks, my brothers lost interest in this ritual. But we persisted, my father, Hassan, and I. Slowly, my wounds healed and the warts disappeared, never to return. The twisted horn and my father's chanting baritone had apparently worked. *Credo quia absurdum* — I believe it because it is absurd — became the family's unspoken motto.

A plethora of private clubs catered to foreigners and upper-class Iranians. Each protected oasis opened its gate onto leafy old estates with lovely gardens, swimming pools and clay tennis courts. Shaded watering holes served cocktails on verandahs to privileged members. It was a life, a friend mused dreamily to my mother, of "tropical nobility."

Downtown, there was the elegant French Club, where my father preferred to lunch, far from the brash Yanks. To accommodate the huge U.S. military population that kept mushrooming each year, there was the Officers' Club, the NCO Club and the Castle Club, which kept soldiers off the streets and in the bars.

There was also the British Club, the American Club and the German Club.

Meanwhile, the Shah's reliance on Western experts and U.S. military personnel to help create his "New Civilization" led to deep resentment and caused cultural clashes. I knew something was wrong when one afternoon I overheard some drunk marines boasting about beating up "ragheads."

In the northern suburbs, the new consumerism and American influence sprouted new curiosities. In Vanak, an elaborate miniature-golf course with a fast-food drive-in broke new cultural ground, as did an American-style diner called the Hot Shoppe. A crystal-white indoor skating rink, the Ice Palace, opened its doors, with Muzak and frigid air that blasted even in August. Downstairs a heated swimming pool with steamed-up windows hid bathers inside. All these places catered to wealthy Westernized Iranians, who often displayed more sophistication than their European or American counterparts.

Off Shemran Road, the sleek CRC — a glistening bowling alley of cream-streaked marble — reached an even loftier level. Overnight, a beer-swigging working-class sport was elevated in Tehran to refined high fashion. Upstairs at the elegant club, an intimate theater played the latest films. There, in the enveloping darkness, I first heard Sinatra's velvet voice singing *Strangers in the Night* and Mancini's hooting sax theme in Peter Sellers's *Pink Panther.* A movie poster for James Bond's *Goldfinger* splashed a nude gold-coated torso on the door. It seemed so risqué, so foreign.

In 1963, when civil rights protests culminated in the March on Washington, on August 28, where Martin Luther King gave his "I have a dream" speech, Duke Ellington's orchestra flew out of New York for its first tour of the Middle East. The orchestra would perform in Syria, Lebanon, Jordan, Iraq, Iran, and Pakistan, as well as in India. On September 9 in Damascus, the opening night of the Ellingtonians drew seventeen thousand Arabs and Westerners to "Syria's first big band jazz concert." "The applause," reported *Variety*, "was mixed with Arabic yells of *Ash al Duke*, Long live Duke!"

My father was thrilled about the visit. Our house rang with Duke's arrangements of "Satin Doll," "Mood Indigo," "Take the A Train." But then came the awful news from Dallas: JFK was dead. In Tehran, the shops closed. My parents were devastated. "The bastards," my father said. "They don't know when to stop." The State Department canceled the rest of Duke's tour. My mother that week took us to a theater in Tajrish to see *To Kill a Mockingbird*, and we were transported to a sinister, racially divided Alabama town where Gregory Peck, as Atticus Finch, fought his lonely battle for human dignity. What, we wondered, was the story all about? America, my father said. That night, I heard him playing Billie Holiday's wounded alto over and over again. It was the song "Strange Fruit," about lynching.

Far from America's painful divisive politics, my father and mother enthusiastically embraced the cosmopolitan life in Tehran. Their friends were a diverse set of Western-educated Iranians and diplomats, both foreign and American, who doubled as amateur performers in the Little Theater of Tehran. On summer evenings, as we boys scampered in our garden, they staged readings in the gazebo of *A Midsummer Night's Dream* and *Who's Afraid of Virginia Woolf?*

Unlike my parents, Tehran's American community kept to itself in privileged enclaves behind high walls. The residents lived, worked and played in a world apart, mixing little with Iranians. Among Western expatriates, only the Yankees seemed to dream of returning home.

That year, the Tehran bazaar shut down for another reason. An ayatollah had spoken out in Qom and been arrested. His daring words had reverberated throughout the city: "The Shah is the puppet of America. The Shah must go!" Hassan listened to the radio. From the closed bazaar, crowds streamed out in protest. Thousands filled the streets. Troops were mobilized. Clashes erupted. Gunfire ripped through the air. In Tajrish, chaos broke out. For three days, school was canceled. "Problems downtown," my father said. "Stay at home. Don't go out," advised Hassan. The city froze. Fatimeh stopped weaving. Mass arrests filled the jails, and the crackdown broke the protests. The ayatollah was placed under house arrest for nine months before being exiled to Turkey and then Iraq. That week in 1963 marked an ominous portent. It was the beginning of the Shah's fateful countdown with the clergy.

Every September, a rickety school bus appeared at our red gate, and my three brothers and I dutifully rode off to the Community School, in the heart of the city near the Majlis (parliament). Mr. Boghardi, the driver, raced with impunity through red and yellow traffic lights like a bull chasing a matador's cape. "We have to catch the green," he would shout, while over his radio, Petula Clark sang about going "Downtown" and the Supremes warned him to "Stop! In the Name of Love." On the tree-shaded red-brick campus, we found ourselves thrown together in a fruit salad of twenty nations spanning God's wide earth. Although founded at the turn of the century by American Protestant missionaries as a hospital, our school with its mix of students mirrored the United Nations. Instruction was in English, Farsi and French. In every sport except soccer, we predictably lost to our crosstown rival: the overcoached, overtestosteroned, overserious American School.

Our most celebrated school event obviously had to be the only date everyone could agree on: United Nations Day. Highlighting the event was a noisily merry and endearing kaleidoscope of national dress and flags. Clattering wooden clogs marched beside drooping sombreros; flowing saris and brassy pink turbans glided in front of cocky cowboy hats; soft cotton dishdashes chased silk kimonos; mahogany leather sandals shuffled under earth-colored batik sarongs; dashikis, tartan kilts and astrakhan hats trailed behind pearl lace-curled bonnets. A week before this "procession of nations," secret lots were drawn for the flag carriers. No one wanted to bear his own country's banner. Exotic beauty was the goal. Brazil, I always prayed for. Who wouldn't? Emerald Amazonian green, a helio-splash of tropical yellow and a cobalt-blue night sky lit with flickering constellations — surely this was the prize. I remember being crushed one year when my flag was announced: Canada, the plain red maple leaf.

The last vestige of the Community School's missionary past could be seen on Tuesday and Thursday mornings at eleven. Into the chapel we would reluctantly stream: Kanwarbir, my Sikh friend, to my right; Sara, my Jewish friend, to my left; Ahmad, my Bahai buddy, and Vali, the young aristocrat, right behind. Reverend Lockhart, a midwesterner, poured such emotion into his sermons that when he was "on" he could transport us to the royal court of Belshazzar and Nebuchadnezzar in ancient Babylon, or to ancient Egypt. Into those colossal cedar walls he bellowed, flames burning the words: *"Let my people go!"* I looked upon those walls and was shocked to see the same fiery words etched under our vaulted ceiling. Below them stood the unbending trio of Shadrack, Meshak and Abednego.

Impassioned and red-faced, after each spirited performance, Reverend Lockhart ordered us to stand and sing from the hymnal. One morning he called out, "Page thirty-five, 'Onward Christian Soldiers.'" We jumped up to launch into the song. The piano sounded and, in unison, we all belted out the first word, "On-waaaard," quickly followed by an incoherent jumble. Instead of "Christian," a cacophony of "Muslim-Sikh-Jewish-Armenian-Bahai-Buddhist-Catholic-Zoroastrian" ricocheted off the walls. Unfazed, we boomed on, "so-oool-dieeers, march-ing as to waaaar." The beamed ceiling reverberated and our voices held steady until "with the cross of Je-sus going on before" erupted with more confusion as the names of "Buddha-Mohammad-Singh-Moses" filled the air.

While Reverend Lockhart waved his arms, trying to synchronize our voices, his embarrassed face reddened deeper with the painful awareness that his young flock were already spoken for and defiantly holding on to their parents' faith. We were living proof of the Babel of tongues and the scattering of nations. But what the good reverend could not see was the glowing beauty in the chapel on that day. Standing next to Jew, Sikh, Muslim, Zoroastrian, I somehow knew we were united in purpose. Each voice that proclaimed his or her prophet and faith spoke the truth. Each, if you listened closely, echoed the ninety-nine names of God. "There is only one religion," George Bernard Shaw wrote, "though there are a hundred versions of it." In honor of my classmates, I could never choose one faith. I could never betray the lesson they taught me that day.

Seven hundred years ago, the Persian poet Rumi wrote of his God:

> Not Christian or Jew or Muslim not Hindu,
> Buddhist, sufi, or zen. Not any religion
> or cultural system. I am not from the East
> or the West, not out of the ocean or up
> from the ground, not natural or ethereal, not
> composed of elements at all. I do not exist,
> am not an entity in this world or the next,
> did not descend from Adam and Eve or any
> origin story. My place is placeless, a trace
> of the traceless. Neither body or soul.
> I belong to the beloved, have seen the two
> worlds as one and that one call to and know,
> first, last, outer, inner, only that
> breath breathing human being.

The eyes of Sara Haim were large, shimmering golden brown pools. Magnified by her Coke-bottle glasses, her doe's look of innocence gave off an endearing gleam that I hoped she saved only for me. An Iranian Jew, wafer thin in her Scotch plaid skirts and white frilled shirts, Sara was my secret girlfriend in fourth grade. Framed by her short-cropped bangs, her pale skin and dimpled chin glowed. But it was her eyes, radiating with quiet intelligence, that warmed me with a glance. Once, when we sat quietly in her synagogue, she wrote out a poem in Hebrew script, the words of

Queen Esther to her king, Xerxes (Ahasuerus). I asked her the meaning, she smiled behind her thick glasses, then turned away in silence. I hid this cherished poem in my small library at home.

While very smart, she was also terribly shy. An unspoken understanding kept our affection to cautious flirting. When I proposed marriage in the fifth grade, she said she would think it over. Her slender body was so frail that I feared a strong gust of wind would blow her away. When a sudden storm blew across the playground, I would race over to hold her hand until it died down. Although I knew she could fly, I wanted to keep her on earth one more day.

Whenever Hassan told us stories at night of Leili and Majnoon, the crazy young lovers of Nizami, my imagination turned to Sara. Years later, a rabbi in New York translated Sara's poem for me. "Love has no age," he read. By then, her family must have fled Tehran. Where is she now? I wonder. Tel Aviv? Paris? Los Angeles? An aching high wind more violent than we children could ever imagine surely lifted her away.

Unlike the rest of my friends, Kanwarbir arrived each morning at school with three fine rows of braids tucked neatly behind at the nape of his neck. He couldn't see them, but we could. With his small mousy face, large spectacles and skinny knock knees, Kanwarbir seemed far too fragile to be a Sikh warrior. I always ran to his defense when our class bully picked on him.

Eating green sour plums one day, he told me in confidence that soon he would wear a turban. His parents had scheduled the ceremony when he would become a man, and his hair would be wrapped for the first time. While we spoke about the color of the cloth — tangerine, salmon or burgundy — I felt a tinge of jealousy welling up inside me. How grand to enter the classroom of Miss Jose decked out in a flashy lemon turban! Sara Haim would surely be smitten by the sight of me in a turban and finally confess her love. Why had my mother and father never given me one? Lucky Kanwarbir, I thought.

The first time I was invited to his house, it was for afternoon tea. With a broad grin, Kanwarbir greeted me and led me inside. Pungent scents of coriander, curry, cloves and incense mingled in the living room. Before sitting down to chat, he showed me a small altar perched on a corner shelf. On it were silver-framed photographs of turbaned family members, uncles and grandfathers, all handsomely bearded and mustachioed.

Dressed in a flowing rose sari, his mother served us steaming cups of dark tea while my friend pulled out his collection of Tintin books, and we began reading together. When his mother called him, I paid no mind. Hers was a language I couldn't understand. The cartoons in front of me had swept me away. I was following Tintin, Hergé's red-headed Belgian reporter, into the Himalayan ice fields of Tibet to hunt for the footprints of Yeti, the abominable snowman.

Time passed. The setting sun cast a faded light into the room. When I looked up, I was alone. I wondered where my friend was. I began to look for him, but had no luck. The house was completely silent. I slowly began to climb the staircase. Nearing the top, I could hear a woman's soft whisper. I glanced into a bedroom to my left and saw two silhouettes seated on the carpet.

The sun's dying rays of gold streamed over them. Kanwarbir faced the light. His pigtails were undone and a stream of long black silky hair spilled down his back like a waterfall to the floor. With her long delicate fingers, his mother lifted his hair and stroked a brush through it, ever so slowly.

I felt nervous, I felt ecstatic. Was it wrong to witness this moment of privacy? I couldn't pull myself away. This silent image, intimate and tender, held me frozen in place. Her left hand moved with eyes of its own through her son's mane. Her right hand brushed his silky hair, pure and unviolated.

I watched my fragile little warrior, Kanwarbir, the lion cub, being groomed at day's end. His entire life was in front of him. A turban would soon crown his head. Each stroke of his mother's hand ran through his hair and down his naked bronze back. Gracefully, she dipped her brush under the nape of his neck and lifted strands out toward her until, in slow motion, they fell in an arc like an unfolding Japanese fan. The gold dying sun glinted through his hair. How long I stood transfixed, I'll never know. When dusk's light finally gave way to darkness, I tiptoed back downstairs. In the incense-filled room with its altar, I waited quietly for my friend to descend from his lair.

Twenty years later, I learned that just after we left Tehran, Kanwarbir had a dreadful accident. Hanging from the monkey bars at recess, surely trying to prove himself, his grip slipped and he fell. When he woke, he heard the doctor whisper that his spine was broken. Tragically, the rest of the lion's days would be spent in a wheelchair.

My buck-toothed classmate Vali hailed from the Farmanfarmaian "Givers of Orders" clan: an aristocratic, wealthy family descended from the deposed and defanged Qajar dynasty. His uncles were known for their cosmopolitan flair and their aggressive business practices, which led to vast fortunes. At his house, Vali showed me his collection of gold coins, which were thrown freely by the hundreds at family weddings. Under the Islamic regime, this wealth would make his family a target for persecution. Before that happened, Vali emigrated with most of his family. Unfortunately, his uncles Khoddadad and Rashid, who remained behind, were imprisoned during the Revolution. Although sentenced to be executed, Khoddadad was freed, thanks to a former tea boy who remembered him for his kindness. A Revolutionary Guard allowed him the chance to flee across the border into Turkey. Rashid was freed four years later.

Living next door to us was Ali, the angry, brooding son of our part-time gardener, a future Robespierre destined to finger those to be put up against the wall for *Komiteh* firing squads. Both Ali's and Vali's families, in the revolutionary turbulence, were fated to struggle over power and money. Feudal allegiances and religious obedience divided the classes, and many sought revenge.

The best metaphor for the divide between rich and poor could be seen in the journey of water. In our gully passed the pristine mountain-fed water that flowed into the street channels, called *jubes*, of north Tehran's wealthy, wending its way mile after mile through the city that washed, cleaned, drank and dumped garbage in it, until the water finally arrived, turbid and brown, in south Tehran, carrying cholera and infection. Begging was a way of life there, and eye disease was rampant. On Fridays, my mother joined a young woman from the Pasteur Institute to deliver rice and medicine to the shantytowns gripped by poverty. Their visits, while admirable, were a drop in the ocean.

The Shah's portrait followed us everywhere. His titles — King of Kings, Shadow of the Almighty, Center of the Universe, Light of the Aryans — framed his harvest of military ribbons, drooping off his chest like trophy animals hanging from sportsmen's walls. In 1968, the country braced itself for his coronation, and he crowned himself and his empress, the Shahbanou, in a ceremony of bejeweled narcissism. Strangely, I never heard his name spoken in public. Like a land mine, if touched, it could explode.

At a party, one of my father's Iranian friends, after drinking several glasses of wine, popped off with a joke about the Shah. The next morning, he disappeared. When my dad asked about him, fingers were raised to lips. "SAVAK," they whispered. It was the name of the Shah's secret police. His friend was held for a week. When he returned, my father said, he was a broken man.

In Iran's vast countryside, the poverty could only be described as inhumane. The vaunted land-reform program, called the White Revolution (hailed by Washington), failed to deliver on its promises. Forlorn villages — stripped of their feudal owners, who once injected capital to maintain complex irrigation systems — saw their all-important water networks collapse. Unprepared farmers cashed out, sold their "new" land and headed for the cities. Agribusiness and mechanized farming rushed in to fill the gap, pushing even more people off their lands. Imported machinery broke down in the fields, and there were no spare parts. By the 1970s, Iran could no longer feed itself. Prices skyrocketed, and food from abroad and inflation became facts of life. Abandoned in the Shah's ambitious plans, thousands of villagers began to pour into Tehran like sharecroppers from the Dust Bowl.

And in south Tehran, they stayed. It was a disaster waiting to happen. Anger was deep and simmering. Corruption within the royal family was common knowledge. Western-educated patriots felt betrayed by the reckless profiteers surrounding the imperial court. Expensive technology came with foreign experts, who got paid high salaries, drove up rents and lived in Tehran's best neighborhoods. The 1973 OPEC windfall hadn't reached the man in the street. Fortunes were rumored to be stashed in Switzerland. University students abroad staged protests against the Shah in European capitals. Cultivated democrats argued for a pluralistic society. The lit fuse would soon explode.

When the Islamic Revolution thundered through the streets, trampling the peacock throne, everyone was shocked by its massive, almost unanimous support. From the slums, shantytowns and even the wealthy northern suburbs, millions marched in the capital and across the country. Kleptocrats in the Pahlavi court packed their bags and scurried off to Europe. The Shah's "Great Civilization" fell apart like a flimsy Hollywood set.

On its tattered remains the Shia clergy began erecting the first purely theocratic state since the prophet Mohammad's rule in Medina. Uncompromising in tone, Khomeini's inspiration, *veleyat-e faqih*, "rule by Islamic jurists," soon became enshrined in the Islamic Republic's new constitution. Bitter disenchantment set in as middle-class technocrats and Western-educated intellectuals — once so intoxicated by and hopeful for the Revolution — felt betrayed by the clerics. They fled by the thousands. Many arrived in Europe and the United States, having lost everything. Tenaciously, they pieced their lives together, physically cut off from the country they loved, knowing they could not return.

Iran's portal to the world slammed shut.

As the years passed, occasionally I reminisced with Iranian friends, and in those moments a forgotten scent of roses would usher back a memory, like the rose water in Fatimeh's room.

One taste and, like a river, other memories would flow: crisp *sangak* bread pulled hissing from a baker's oven; tart bursts of a pomegranate *sharbat*, ruby red syrup poured over crushed ice during hot summer days; a bowl of rice at dusk by Fatimeh's loom; the soft breathing of a reed flute; rust-colored mountain passes lost in clouds; teahouses lit with yellow lanterns; little Ali and I watching a mustard dawn; the sounds of Colonel Shaki's stallions galloping to a dying dynasty; Hassan's eyebrows as black as crow wings; the bitter smell of *taryak*, opium smoked by a grinning white-haired grandfather; burgundy tribal carpets drying on river stones; long black cloaks brushing over knee-deep winter snows; rose petals crushed under departing feet.

All would come back to me.

Even the sight of Hassan's heels disappearing through walls of fire.

4

# Pasargadae's Stones, Zoroaster's Flame

> The Iranian plateau is a "soft centre" that panders to
> megalomaniac ambitions in its rulers without providing
> the genius to sustain them.
>
> — Bruce Chatwin, introduction to
> Robert Byron's *Road to Oxiana*

TUCKED INSIDE a craggy mountain gorge in northern Fars,
along the Shiraz–Isfahan trunk road, lies Sivand, a sleepy
village that still speaks a Persian dialect predating the
Arab invasions. For millennia, this road has connected the Persian heartland with the ancient seat of power in Pasargadae, the
original home of the Aryans. A rushing river carved a natural fortress for the people of Sivand within these bleak canyon walls.
Slender poplar trees guarded their stone-and-mud homes that lay
across a footbridge. Lining the main auto route, dozens of tin-
roofed, plywood-walled stalls leaned against one another like a
shaky house of cards, beckoning passing drivers with their wares.

It was midmorning. Truckers pulled over for a brief respite
from their cross-country marathons, hauling cargo north from
the Gulf to Tehran. For them, Sivand offered forbidden treasures: a bounty of banned tapes recorded by exiled Iranian singers
in southern California. The roadside stalls were full. Tables overflowed with boxes of cassettes. I listened to the cadence and sylla-
bles of the vendors. The guttural sounds of Arabic's throat-grab-
bing vowels had disappeared. No trace. Words sounded crisp
and clipped.

"History, like a badly constructed concert hall, has occasional dead spots where the music can't be heard," the American poet Archibald MacLeish once wrote. In our search for Hassan, we had resolved to seek out the nation's dead spots. For twenty years, the Islamic Republic had offered its version of truth, yet other truths existed. Only by listening to the past could we hope to reach beneath the surface. And where better to begin than at the dawn of civilization, when first stirrings sprang into myth. Not far from Sivand, two thousand five hundred years ago, a young and vigorous Persian Empire, shaped by Cyrus the Great, entered history's concert hall. We had resolved to drive first to his tomb. Our pilgrimage in the south was long overdue. During all our years in Tehran, we had never ventured south to the sacred site of Cyrus. Now it was time to pay our respects.

Passing a booth plastered with pro-Khatami election posters, I asked the young shopkeeper to speak into my tape recorder in his tongue, called Pahlavi or Middle Persian, not the usual Farsi of modern Iran. He did so with gusto and laughter. I understood nothing. "I'm sure he called you some funny names," said Avo, our official companion, who was standing next to me. Which beasts in the animal kingdom did he compare me to? "I don't know," Avo said. "Actually, he seemed very respectful." Sipping cherry juice, I returned the favor and browsed through his collection of bootleg cassettes.

"They've always been anarchists here in Sivand," Akbar, our guide, explained in his fluent English. "They've always done whatever they want. Everyone knows that, but no one does anything to stop it."

"And the music?"

"It comes from Tehrangeles," he said. "You know, L.A."

"And what about that?" Two raspy speakers pounded away with a noxious Abba sound, pop synthesizers, bass, a disco beat.

"Especially that."

On sunny California shores, an entire music industry flourished around the half-million expatriate Iranians in Los Angeles. This Iranian-American culture had produced a few legitimate stars. The downside was a host of flashy pseudoromantic MTV trendies. Their politics, taste and love of glitter seemed to mirror those of another American tribe in exile, Miami's Cubans. To be fair, however, the commercial tunes spun out of L.A. studios offered these shoppers a fresh alternative to the cleric-scrutinized music of contemporary Iran.

A few minutes of listening were more than enough. Rich and I preferred the shopkeeper's brogue with its deep Persian roots, free of any Arabic words. There was ancient defiance in this stubborn mountain village.

Akbar hailed from Shiraz. His handlebar mustache pointed grandly to the sky, and his eyeglasses and windblown hair gave him a bohemian look. A ruggedly handsome fellow resembling Omar Sharif, Akbar had spent his university years in southern California. After the Revolution, he returned to Iran to start a family, whom he proudly showed us in a wallet photo. Working at the local refinery, Akbar moonlighted as a guide, bringing foreign visitors to ancient Persian sites while explaining his country's curious proto-religion, which he pronounced "Zorro-astarian." Thankfully, Akbar's breadth of knowledge easily balanced Avo's deficiencies, which were glaring.

Our travel agency, Caravan Tours, had assigned us Avo, a slim, bespectacled, nervous thirty-five-year-old bachelor with expressive eyes and a puzzled air about him. Continually vacillating between disbelief and shock, bold smugness and conspiratorial intrigue, Avo knew nothing of history and didn't seem to care. Although his father ran a construction company in Tehran, Avo said he had decided to go out on his own. In Toronto, he had worked as a night manager in a convenience store. But after a few years he returned home and moved back in with his parents. His English was impeccable. We were his second assignment, he said. Six months had passed since his last job, when he led a group of Japanese through Tehran's bazaar. "They didn't understand a thing," he explained matter-of-factly. "Of course, it would have helped if I spoke some Japanese." A master of irony, Avo delivered most of his lines with a deadpan look.

At Sivand's roadside stalls, I gravitated over to Akbar to speak about the roots of Iran's so-called Aryans, which cannot be traced in bloodlines or genetics, as Nazi ideologues falsely claimed. In fact, the only place to search is in language — linguistic paleo-anthropology, to be exact. In the study of vanished peoples and their voices, fossils emerge of a massive trunk, a proto-language called Indo-European, spoken eight thousand years ago, from which sprouted branches of Farsi, English, Sanskrit, Swedish, Latin, Greek, Italian, Spanish, French, Russian and German. One linguistic historian, Cavalli-Sforza, has reached even further back, claiming to have identified the earliest mother tongue of all. He calls it Nostraic.

Since the source of all these related Indo-European languages has been agreed upon, more or less, scholars have been arguing over another mystery: its place of origin. Most scholars opt for the Russian steppes. Cold northern climates help explain the common words for snow, wolf and bee. The Mediterranean and Black Sea regions are rejected out of hand. It seems that no pre-historic word for sea ever existed. Colin Renfrew, the British ar-chaeologist, has lobbied for central Anatolia as the home of the proto-language. Others have pointed to the Danube Valley. We will never know precisely, but the source is surely embedded in chilly Eurasian soil.

More than two centuries ago, on the evening of February 2, 1786, a shocking revelation ruffled a buttoned-up, sweaty gather-ing of the Asiatick Society in Calcutta. Sir William Jones, an Eng-lish judge and amateur linguist, had stumbled upon evidence in his studies of Sanskrit that he could no longer deny. To every-one's surprise, he noted striking similarities among ancient San-skrit, Latin and Greek. The word for father in Sanskrit, *pitor*, he said, differed little from the Greek and Latin *pater*. The word for mother, *matar*, was no doubt a sister to the Latin *mater*. And his list of cognates grew. Before the audience — all functionaries of the East India Company and the British raj — he concluded, "No philologer could examine all three without believing them to have sprung from some common source which, perhaps, no longer exists."

When Hassan first uttered the Farsi word *baradar*, meaning brother, I recalled being pleasantly surprised by the resemblance. I had no trouble learning the words for father, *pedar*, and mother, *madar*. A quick scan of the Indo-European family for similar words for *baradar* reveals: *phrater* in Greek, *brathair* in Irish, and *bhratar* in Sanskrit. From the tip of J. M. Synge's Western world, the Wards' ancestral Donegal lashed by Atlantic storms, to Rabindranath Tagore's humid, cyclone-prone Bengal on the Indian Ocean, I realized that Irish, Iranians and Indians sang, cursed and told stories from ancient dreams that once shared a mother tongue.

Before Cyrus the Great's Persian epoch, there were wonderful creations forged by a people called the Elamites. Bronze figurines of cows, deer, griffins and sphinxes, earth goddesses and chariots colored by the turquoise patina of time have been found in the province of Luristan, on the western side of the Zagros Range. Each evokes "a world of mystery, magic symbols, savagely conflicting powers," wrote Roman Ghirshman, the noted archaeologist. He compared the first Iranian art that blossomed on the plateau with Greek art of the eighth century B.C. The influence of this art form may have spread wider than we imagine. So formidable were these Luristan bronzes that Ghirshman asked, "Have we here the *ultimate* source of Etruscan art, whose iconography was destined in the course of time to enrich Celtic art, then the art of the *Völkerwanderung*, and finally Romanesque sculpture, which has been described as 'steeped in the glamour of Eurasia'?"

The Aryan migration into Iran is pervaded by myth. Legend has it that Aryan tribes first arrived from the north after the fabled King Jamshid ordered his people to seek the sun. From the scrub and thistle steppes of Russia they moved to warmer places, to India, onto the Iranian plateau and westward into Greece and Italy. For three millennia the people of the plateau have called their land Iran. It is thought to be derived from the ancient name *Aryanam*, meaning Land of the Aryans. Persia, or *Persis*, was the Hellenized mispronunciation of Pars, the original name of the southwestern province, homeland of the rulers of the Persian Empire. The absence of the *p* sound in the Arabic alphabet led the Arab conquerors to call it "Fars."

I reflected on the linguistic archaeology that Hitler abused to create his biogenetic "Aryan" nation. By hijacking the concept of a communal Indo-European tongue to feed his pathology of "blood purity," he pushed social Darwinism to horrific limits.

Akbar, in our minivan, tried to clarify the muddle. In 1932, he told us, Reza Shah Pahlavi, the father of the last Shah, dismissed the internationally accepted name of Persia and officially replaced it with the centuries-old name of Iran, in tribute to the country's Aryan ancestry. Foreign ambassadors objected. Reza Shah announced that it was the ancient Greeks, and not Iranians, who first called his country Persia. In similar fashion, the Chinese more recently rejected British-named Peking for Beijing. This is now, and that was then. Bulldog Churchill characteristically resisted. "The Shah may call it whatever he likes," he growled, "it will always be Persia."

Today, perhaps the only people still using "Persian" are scholars and expatriate Iranians who resurrected the term during their long days in exile. Desperately hoping to renounce any connection to the Islamic Republic of Iran and its actions, the expats proclaim "I am Persian" as their collective refrain. At cocktail parties from Manhattan to London, Paris to Santa Monica, self-styled "Persian princes" speak only of the past. All the same, an upcoming soccer match scheduled in France, pitting archenemy America against Iran in the World Cup final, would put all their rejection to the test. At kickoff, I sensed, heart flurries would spark a renewed patriotism that few could disown.

\*     \*     \*

As we drove away from Sivand's Iranian-American musical road-side bazaar, Nasrollah, our driver, slipped my newly purchased cassette into his tape deck. Mournful wailing: an old favorite. Crackling through worn-out speakers, a heady woman's alto pierced its way into soprano range. Nasrollah signaled with a thumbs-up. His stubble-faced grin greeted my approval. A veteran warrior of Iranian highways, Nasrollah gripped the steering wheel with large strong hands and supreme confidence. He had two families, he told me — his wife and two children, and now us.

Instead of looking ahead like a proper navigator, Avo began talking loudly with Nasrollah, distracting him from the winding road. An argument was heating up. The driver's face reddened. In their tense exchange, Nasrollah glowered at Avo, who by now was clearly upsetting him.

"Avo, let him drive," Rich said from the back.

"Richard, it's OK," Avo said. "I am your guide. Driver must take *my* orders."

"We hate accidents."

"Don't worry, I'm in charge."

"That's what we're afraid of."

"We're safe, *baba*, don't worry."

"Not if you keep jabbering to Nasrollah on these mountain roads."

"He's only driver. I am the boss."

Suddenly, to our left, a fierce engine growl poured through our open windows. A bus full of terrified faces passed our battered minivan. Along its flanks, red calligraphy trumpeted the company name: *Rasool*, or Prophet. Avo began yelling at Nasrollah, who turned his head and flashed a violent look of rage at him. Then, around a blind curve, an oncoming car appeared, blowing its horn. The bus swerved into our lane, narrowly missing our front fender. Nasrollah screamed, braking. As he jerked on the steering wheel, we all howled. Over the road curb, I peered at the river raging in the gorge forty feet below. The bus roared past. On its tailgate, in bright green lettering, we all read: *One Way to Paradise*.

My God, I thought, some things hadn't changed. Driving in Iran was still a religious experience.

We soon passed a cluster of white flowering almond trees clinging to a narrow ridge above greening rows of grapevines. Arid land folded and buckled uplifts creating sudden rock-slab cliffs striped in amber, apricot and rust. Towering on either side of the Murghab River stood sculpted walls of rock sheared off by time's hand. Our winding passage climbed along the canyon floor. Black-winged crows dive-bombed our windshield, jauntily riding invisible updrafts. Sandstone hung above in petrified waves, defying gravity. Avo was tight-lipped now, with Rich seated just behind his shoulder, ensuring his silence. My mother slept, and Kevin chatted with Akbar about Zoroaster in the back. Chris and my father stared at the passing cliffs. It was a geography eerily similar to that in a western. "John Ford country," said Dad.

Nasrollah's track followed the river's course north through the gorge for over an hour until we burst out of the cliffs' shadows and onto a vast plain. Big sky country again. The high, treeless expanse seemed harsh and infertile. Then fields of greening alfalfa sprigs flashed by. Riding across the Dasht Murghab Plain, we broke from the main road and turned left for the village of Pasargadae. Herodotus, the Greek historian, informs us that when the Persians first entered these lands, they were still nomads on the march. The royal tribe, he says, was the Pasargadae, and this name was given to the capital of the Persians. Only a handful of trees sprouted behind the protective brick walls of the smallish settlement. We drove past the town and back onto the green plain, slowly approaching the tomb of Cyrus the Great, which shone like a white beacon.

Akbar told us that it was still intact only because of the quick-witted Pasargadae villagers. In the seventh century, invading Arabs bent on destroying all things ancient and pagan rode up to the tomb and asked who was buried there. "Solomon's mother," the villagers replied. The holy name from the Koran sent the coarse, illiterate Bedouins galloping on. The bluff worked. Now the resting place of Cyrus II, founder of the Persian Empire, sat starkly alone. His Achaemenian dynasty would not carry his name but that of his family, Hakhamanish, known to Greeks as Achaemenes.

As we walked to the tomb, Nasrollah joined us, leaving Avo in the minivan. He appeared genuinely interested in the monument. Then he pulled me aside and whispered, loud enough for others to hear, "We must get rid of him."

"Who?" I asked.

"Avo," Nasrollah said. "He's dangerous, and crazy."

"You think?"

"I'm sure. *Kheli divaneh*, very crazy."

"Let me speak to the others."

"*Kheli mamnoun*, many thanks."

"You're welcome."

"Perhaps we can leave him here."

Nasrollah's suggestion did not surprise me.

I spoke to Mom, who took pity. Her work with learning-disabled children gave her insights. Avo, she insisted, showed the telltale signs.

"Extreme dyslexia," she asserted.

"A clueless contrarian" was Kevin's assessment.

"A bozo spy," said Dad.

"And what if he's too spaced out to be working for the government?" I asked.

"You may have a point."

Akbar was diplomatic. "Avo is not intellectual. I worry for you."

We stopped short of the six tiers of stone, topped with a gabled chamber and its single sealed entrance. Iran's founding father had lain undisturbed for two and a half thousand years. As we gazed at his tomb, I was struck by its simplicity, unlike the grandiose ruins of Persepolis, which I had seen only in pictures. In the limitless vista that spread in all directions to the horizon, the humble monument stood solitary. The ancient capital, with its palaces, gardens and temples, had been dusted away from view. The only structure that had defied the ages belonged to Cyrus. Powdery white, without ornate carving or embellishment, it offered a philosophical perspective on power in the face of eternity. Shaped deliberately to human scale, it drew the eye to an inscription, weathered away by time. This was Cyrus's message to posterity. Akbar recited it from memory.

> WELCOME, PILGRIM,
> I HAVE BEEN EXPECTING YOU.
> BEFORE YOU LIES CYRUS,
> KING OF ASIA, KING OF THE WORLD.
> ALL THAT IS LEFT OF HIM IS DUST.
> DO NOT ENVY ME.

Robert Byron, in *The Road to Oxiana*, considered by many to be the finest travel book ever written, described Cyrus's tomb as "a sarcophagus of white marble on a high stepped plinth, standing by itself in the ploughed fields. It looks its age: every stone has been separately kissed, and every joint stroked hollow, as though by the actions of the sea. No ornament or cry for notice disturbs its lonely serenity."

I stared up at the white-worn tomb, silhouetted against the landscape, raised high to the azure sky. I touched the stone — the texture felt soft, hand rubbed over centuries, the object of veneration. Chris pulled out his sketchpad and began to draw.

Antiquity's ruins strewn throughout the Near East — whether it be Petra, the Great Pyramids, Hatshepsut's temple or Ephesus — have spawned generations of dubious dragomans, hucksters and hustlers. Like fishermen, they wait for the daily catch. In Iran, however, their absence has thankfully left Achaemenian sites pristine. Only two aged bearded farmers hovered nearby, as curious about us as we were about Cyrus's tomb. They waved their spades. I waved back. White puffy clouds passed overhead. A cool wind blew from the west where, on the horizon, circling snow-crested summits sealed off any western approach to the vast plain.

When Robert Byron wrote that "Alexander was the first tourist" to visit Cyrus's tomb, he was, of course, exercising poetic license. Generations of pilgrims had flocked to the site long before the Macedonian prince knelt in devotion here. Byron, in his subtle style, was signaling Alexander's worship of Cyrus, his classical hero. On his conquests, we know that Alexander carried Xenophon's book *Cyropaedia* (The Education of Cyrus) along with Homer's *Iliad*, which lay under his pillow with a dagger. Cyrus embodied the attributes of the ingenious general and compassionate conqueror, both powerful and merciful. Xenophon, the famed literary general, described the Achaemenian king: "Cyrus was the most handsome in person, most generous in his soul, most fond of learning, most in love with honorable fame, so that he would bear all suffering and all the dangers for the sake of praise."

Xenophon's portrait of the "ideal ruler" is inescapable. His *Cyropaedia* reads like a leadership guide for the ancient world, decidedly more humane than Machiavelli's guide for Renaissance rulers. We are given a full account of strategies and cunning. A lightning campaign across Anatolia. The swift defeat of the wealthy Lydian king Croesus of Sardis. Then his electrifying welcome at the gates of Babylon, the ancient world's metropolis. Cyrus possessed an uncanny psychological hold over his soldiers.

His management style was the dream of every general. Long night vigils at the bedside of his wounded men built fierce loyalty and love. "When the rest went to dinner at the usual time, Cyrus stayed [among the wounded] with his aides and doctors, for he would not leave anyone uncared for." Diplomatic touches and lightning assaults were not enough. "On the campaign the general must show he can bear better than his men the heat of the sun in summer, the cold in winter and hardship on a difficult march," Xenophon advised. In conclusion, he wrote, "All these things go to make [Cyrus] loved by those he leads."

Uniting the tribes of the Medes and the Persians into a formidable army in 547 B.C., Cyrus rode over the Zagros ramparts, off the Iranian plateau and onto the world stage. His empire was described by Xenophon as "the greatest and most glorious of all the kingdoms of Asia . . . bounded on the east by the Indian Ocean, on the north by the Black Sea, on the west by Cyprus and Egypt and on the south by Ethiopia. And although it was of such magnitude, it was governed by the single will of Cyrus; and he honored his subjects and cared for them as if they were his own children; and they, on their part, revered Cyrus as a father." Quite simply, he broke all the rules.

Akbar stood in quiet meditation. A graduate of the University of California at Santa Barbara, he lived in nearby Shiraz with his wife and two daughters. His black hair spun in the breeze. The curious farmers drew closer; rain clouds covered the snowy peaks. His head straightened, then he spoke. "You see, Cyrus is not just the father of Iranians, but also father to the free peoples of the world. He brought human thinking to a higher level. Talking about human rights is easy now, but it is he who began it."

"And before Cyrus?" Richard asked.

Akbar said, "The Assyrian ruler Sennacherib, who bragged that he killed all the men, all the women, even the cats and dogs."

"Even cats?"

"Of course. Then he demolished everything and ordered the harvest to be destroyed. He poured salt on the crops. Because God had told him to do it. That's what he said. And I haven't even told you about Nebuchadnezzar."

Rich cursed under his breath.

"Instead, when Cyrus goes to Babylon he orders his people to respect the temples of Jews and of Marduk, the god of the Babylonians. 'Respect civilians,' he says. 'Defend all those who are not fighting. Protect all women.'"

"How refreshing," said my mother.

As if awakened by a divine vision, Cyrus had marched from this plain at Pasargadae leading his loyal Mede and Persian armies through the Zagros mountain passes and down into the steaming flatlands of Mesopotamia, all the way to the gates of King Nebuchadnezzar's fabled Babylon. Ingeniously, he diverted the Euphrates in an epic engineering feat that later inspired Leonardo da Vinci to alter the course of the Arno so that Pisa could be subjugated by his Florentine paymasters. "The river should be diminished by leading off many streams as Cyrus, King of the Persians, did at the taking of Babylon," Leonardo wrote excitedly in his notebook. Heavy rains and bitter acrimony among Florence's elders dampened the initial enthusiasm for his bold project. It was abandoned. Where Cyrus succeeded, Leonardo didn't.

Herodotus describes that when Cyrus rode into Babylon, it was not as a feared conquering general but as a liberating hero. Nebuchadnezzar's son Nabonidus, a thoroughly inept and scandalous ruler, had earned the full scorn of his people. During his short reign, Nabonidus had defied the gods, enraged the priests of Marduk, instigated uprisings and provoked a virtual civil war. Cyrus appeared as a savior, and he played his role brilliantly. Welcomed by the priests at the city gates, he promised to honor and restore the temple of Marduk. He had arrived as a protector of their faith.

A stone cylinder, fashioned by Cyrus in 539 B.C., marks the event. The inscription reads: "I am Cyrus, King of Babylon, King of Sumer, King of Akkad, King of four countries . . . My great army entered Babylon peacefully and I did not allow any harm to come to the land of Babylonia and its people. Babylonians' respectful manner taught me . . . and I ordered that all should be free to worship their god with no harm. I ordered that no one's home be destroyed and no one's property be taken . . ."

Gusts of wind blew around us.

"The first declaration of human rights," Akbar proclaimed.

"A copy is on display in New York on the East River," I told my mother.

"Really, where?"

"At the General Assembly of the United Nations."

"You see," Akbar said, "Persepolis and Cyrus's tomb in Pasargadae were destined to remain for the people of the world, not
only for us Iranians. Because history is for every person. We are
the manifestation of past times, and we give what we are to our
children and to the future of the world. So the events of life, you
see, are all related. That's why I love history."

We all nodded, quite moved, not expecting his paean to history. He wiped his brow and looked up again at the tomb. I wondered if he had gone too far, whether he was about to reveal personal political beliefs. Avo had now joined us, and seemed to be
listening intently. Akbar kept up his impassioned delivery.

"For Iranian people, at least for the Muslims, there are two
Meccas. One is the Mecca of Saudi Arabia and the other is the
Mecca of Pasargadae and Persepolis. If Mecca represents Islamic
heritage, the other two speak of the true heritage of being Iranian. But some ignorant people don't know this. They want to
destroy the past. Here is the place where the Aryans chose to settle and live. The state of Fars is the heart of Iran. Geographically,
where we stand now, is unique to Iran. It links middle Asia with
Mesopotamia."

In silence, we stared out at the great expanse and at the passing
clouds overhead. Chris had finished his charcoal sketch of the
tomb. My mother looked on approvingly. I scanned the encircling mountains to the west, free of rain clouds again. I imagined
the euphoria greeting the Persian liberator in the Mesopotamian
capital where the tribe of Israel had been enslaved for two generations.

From "philosopher-king" of the Greeks, Cyrus was elevated
even higher by the Old Testament prophets, who described the
Persian as a savior-king touched by the hand of Yahweh. Ezra and
Isaiah proclaimed him "the Lord's anointed." Jeremiah declared,
"Yahweh stirs up the soul of the King of the Medes to smite the
wicked harlot, Babylon."

Antiquity's rogues, the Assyrians and Babylonians had perfected the wicked arts of sadism, deportation and genocide over

three centuries. Massacring innocents far and wide was one spe-
cialty, relocating entire populations another. Brazenly, they had
appointed themselves God's punishing hand. And no one was
safe. In 586 B.C., when Jerusalem collapsed after the second siege
that finally ended the dynasty of David, Nebuchadnezzar ordered
the great temple stripped of its riches and then marched the re-
maining survivors off to exile in sultry Mesopotamia, weighted
down with looted gold.

Almost fifty years later, when Cyrus stood before the gates
of Babylon, he appeared as a miracle. Not only did the Persian
king liberate the Hebrew people from captivity, but with states-
manlike kindness he did the unthinkable: he restored all the gold
seized by Nebuchadnezzar in Jerusalem and sent the exiles back
home, with orders to reconstruct the destroyed temple of Solomon.

Second Isaiah hails Cyrus as a "messiah." The Persian king is
the living sign of God's redemption — a loving God who has
finally forgiven his people, ended their exile and freed them to
leave the rivers of Babylon and begin their long trek home to
Zion. But that's not all. Yahweh's servant Cyrus has been sent
to "bring forth justice to the nations . . . He will not fail . . . till he
has established justice on earth."

After liberation, we know that not all of the Hebrews joined
the caravan back to their land. Many elected to stay in the wealthy
city under their Persian protectors, while others set their eyes
east, journeying to the royal capital of Susa, high on a bluff over-
looking the immense Mesopotamian river valley. Jewish commu-
nities, legend says, also founded the Iranian cities of Isfahan and
Shiraz. Generations later, in the imperial palace of Susa, the biblical heroine Esther weds the Persian king Ahasuerus. Another
perilous tale of collective survival begins. Young Esther must do
battle with Haman, a dastardly Macedonian Greek vizier calling
for Jewish blood. Interceding for her people, she tells her uncle
Mordechai, "Go gather all the Jews to be found in Susa, and hold
a fast on my behalf." Then she swoops into action. Employing

her considerable charms to influence her husband, Esther out-
foxes her adversary and seals for him the same fate he had planned
for her people. And in synagogues around the world each year,
the Feast of Purim celebrates the courageous Persian queen.

How ironic, I thought, that across the entire Middle East, it
was the people of Iran who held the most ancient link with the
Jewish people. Theirs was a sacred bond over two millennia old.
And how strange now that, in just twenty years, the mullahs had
turned Israel into their *bête noir*, the symbolic enemy of the Islamic Republic. Cyrus, I had decided, could teach them more
than a few lessons about moral enlightenment.

Sandra Mackey, in her book *The Iranians*, speculates on the luck
of timing. In a "momentous twist of fate on which history sometimes hangs, one of the most significant religious figures of all
time and one of the greatest political-military geniuses ever to
stride across the human landscape both occupied the cradle of the
Iranian nation in the same era. Their creations — one religious,
the other political — blended. Zoroaster gave Cyrus's earthly
realm a soul and Cyrus gave Zoroastrianism a body."

Zoroaster remains one of the great enigmas of world history.
So little is known of the Iranian prophet, called in Persian
Zardusht. The average man on a Western street, if asked about
Zoroaster, might think fire worshiper, or perhaps mention Nietzsche's *Thus Spake Zarathustra*, but after that, all you would get is a
glazed look. His birth? Only scant estimates. Suffice it to say that
he was born earlier than Confucius, Buddha, Jesus and Mohammad. Zoroaster's poetry, the sacred *Gathas*, are the earliest compositions in Persian literature. Written in Avestan — a language
closely related to Old Persian and Vedic Sanskrit — the surviving
scriptures, prayers, rules and traditional stories anchor the holy
book *Avesta*.

Most scholars place the date of Zoroaster's birth sometime in
the sixth century B.C. The place? Some say Azerbaijan, others
claim Iran's eastern province of Khorasan. Yet an amazing coin-

cidence shadows his life. Spiritual masters across Asia were spawned within a generation after his birth: in China, the wise sage Confucius; in India, the prince Gautama, later to be known as the Buddha.

Zoroaster's prophetic vision of an ethical God was shaped by the battle on earth between light and darkness, good and evil, *Ahura Mazda* and *Ahriman*. But man does not stand by and watch the cosmic forces. For the first time in history, Zoroaster preached the doctrine of free will. In his powerful new religion, man holds the balance. In fact, he says, we are all "angels" descended to earth to help in this struggle against evil, to save the world. That is why we are here.

On ethical duty, Zoroaster's message is simple: pure thoughts, pure words, pure actions. At life's end we return to heaven, but there is one small hurdle: our final judgment. When you cross the bridge, Mithra, god of the sun, greets you and measures your life on his scale of justice. If the scale tips toward the good, then a heavenly angel appears to guide you into the light of Paradise that awaits you. If the scale balances equally, then the destination is the Place of the Mixed Ones, where one leads a gray existence without joy or sorrow. Purgatory. However, if it tips in the other direction, the bridge narrows to a razor's edge and a witch, haggard and worn, wraps her arms around the soul, pulling it off the bridge, dragging it into the depths of the underworld, where the wicked endure a "long age of misery, of darkness, ill food and the crying of woe."

Zoroaster's influence on Western religious thought is decidedly underpublicized. Few realize that his pioneering innovations supplied Judaism with the notion of the messiah. I reviewed a list I had scribbled in my notebook before leaving New York. From the exhaustive *Cambridge History of Iran*, I had written down beliefs and concepts born on Iranian soil, borrowed from Zoroaster's faith:

- the belief in a savior
- the dualism of good and evil, light and darkness

- the belief in angels and archangels
- Satan as the epitome of evil and the adversary of God
- the doctrine of an afterlife and the immortality of the soul
- the last judgment
- reward and punishment by divine justice
- the notion of Hell, Purgatory and Paradise
- the resurrection of the dead
- apocalyptic beliefs
- millennial periods
- destruction of the wicked and the renovation of the world at the end of time.

Not a bad list, I thought. Mary Boyce, in her book *Zoroastrians*, explains that, well before the birth of Christ, "These doctrines all came to be adopted by various Jewish schools in the post-Exilic period, for the Jews were one of the peoples, it seems, most open to Zoroastrian influences — a tiny minority, holding staunchly to their beliefs, but evidently admiring their Persian benefactors, and finding congenial elements in their faith."

When Zoroaster's lips first spoke of *Soshyant*, "the coming messiah," who would redeem the world, few of his followers could have expected that his prophetic vision would pass into two other faiths — first the Jewish, then the Christian. Fewer still would have believed that six hundred years later, in Judea, a traveling couple, homeless and exhausted, seeking any lodging, would sleep wedged between a cow and a donkey on a bed of straw. The pregnant mother, we are told, bore her child while curious shepherds lingered outside. Days later, over the eastern hills, regal visitors arrived to view this child, much like Tibetan priests seeking the reincarnated Dalai or Panchen Lama. A divine search.

According to old Iranian beliefs, when a savior is born, a bright sign will shine in the sky. Zardusht's prophecy was unwavering. For centuries, magi studied the stars. On a mountain in Sistan, there was a special temple where they scanned the heavens. Although Marco Polo insisted that they came from the town of Saveh, Iranian folklore tells us that the three priests who went to Bethlehem first saw the star in high Sistan, then followed the star west.

One paleoastronomer, Mark Kidger, pieced together clues from two-thousand-year-old Roman, Chinese and Korean manuscripts, searching for an unusual astronomical event that would have stood out to the naked eye. To his surprise, he writes in *The Star of Bethlehem: An Astronomer's View*, he discovered — in the Asian texts — four unique stellar dramas that lit the heavens.

Beginning in 7 B.C., a strange series of conjunctions occurred in Pisces. First the royal planet Jupiter and Saturn aligned and separated three times, from May to December. A year later, three planets united: Jupiter, Saturn and Mars. But that was not enough. In 5 B.C., a pairing of Jupiter and the moon occurred on February 20. All this would have piqued the curiosity of any astronomer, Kidger suggests. The final sign came with a glowing light.

Asian records describe a bright nova that burned in the dawn sky quite low on the eastern horizon for at least seventy days. New stars such as this carried royal prophecy: the coming death or birth of a king. This would have triggered the attention of the magi astrologer-priests, who saw it hanging in Pisces, long known to be the constellation of the Jews. Did it announce the death of the hated Herod, or did it herald the birth of a new king? "On sighting the nova," Kidger writes, "the Magi would have known their wait was at an end. The occultation told them the new king was the Jewish messiah." The journey to Judea would have taken seven weeks. The star would illuminate the sky for another two weeks.

As Zoroaster was the first to prophesy the coming savior, perhaps it is only fitting that his magi paid homage to the child and confirmed this messiah's arrival. Then, after Christ's death and resurrection, a freshly converted Saul cast his net for Christian souls in the Mediterranean lands, while Peter planted seeds for the mother church in the heart of imperial Rome. The new religion's foundation stones were gifts of two ancient faiths: one Semitic, the other Persian.

The Christian faithful have long celebrated their Judaic roots. Yet I can't help thinking that an unrecognized debt to Iran remains. The Shia mullahs, along with their fundamentalist Christian brethren, are more than happy to keep this quiet. The laws of their holy books do not readily accept new syncretism. And so, in Archibald MacLeish's badly constructed concert hall of history, this patrimony of Zoroaster still hovers in a dead spot where it can't be heard. Without a name. Without gratitude. Unspoken.

This rich legacy seemed so distant as we left Cyrus's tomb. I looked across green-streaked plains, this heartland of Persia. To the west, snow-clad peaks had faded in the mist. We all boarded the minivan and slowly drove back to the clustered mud-packed walls of the village. After the Revolution, it is said that the mullahs wanted to change the name of this historic place, known for millennia as Pasargadae. The locals simply said no, carrying on their stubborn tradition of loyalty and independence.

Along a dusty street, we passed a large mound of rubble. "That's the tomb the Shah built for himself!" Akbar said. "It was never finished. People destroyed it. They don't want him back — better if he stays in Cairo."

Mohammad Reza Pahlavi, the last Shah, had ambitious plans to be buried here, close to his superhero Cyrus. He ordered his own majestic tomb to be erected. As we drove by, Akbar pointed at the inglorious heap, now only an interrupted construction site, covered with sand and broken brick, left in ruins after the Revolution.

In 1971, during his magnificent spectacle celebrating two thousand five hundred years of Iranian monarchy, the Shah, in full regalia, had the temerity to stand in front of Cyrus's tomb and speak across the ages, surrounded by clicking cameras, foreign dignitaries, visiting royalty and the press. His hand rose to silence the festive crowd, then he proclaimed: "Cyrus, you may rest now. I am awake, standing vigil."

Today, one thousand miles away, in Cairo's pulsing human beehive, medieval, befouled and grim, plagued by pollution and endless traffic jams, the last Shah can be found. Within the dust-covered walls of Hussein Ali Mosque he lies in state, a prisoner of his own making, trapped far from the original homeland of the Persians. Pasargadae's broad green plain, it seems, has no room for impostors.

5

# Lords and Ladies of Persepolis

There is no nation which so readily adopts foreign customs as the Persians.

— Herodotus, *The Histories*

O N A STREET in Shiraz, my mother was struggling with her Islamic *rusari*, her headscarf, which would not stay in place, when a sudden gust of wind lifted her dark blue cape like a kite into the air, exposing more than just her ears — beyond any acceptable modesty. I cringed. Her hands darted out, trying to control events. My brother Chris blocked her unveiling from public view by flapping his open arms.

"Stoning or cursing," Chris muttered. "Take your pick."

"Oh my God." Kevin rolled his eyes. Her hair was in full view.

While all her men proved hopeless, a passing young woman stopped to help her. She introduced herself as Mahnaz, a medical student at Shiraz University. "Madam, have a good stay in my country," she said politely after wrapping my mother up again.

A small crowd, I noticed, had gathered nearby to watch some street performers whose strongman, in a scene out of *La Strada*, promised to break his chains. They paid no attention to us. Freshly reassembled, we steered clear of the crowd. We had left my mother's wheelchair in the van. With patience and courage, testing her tender ankle, she walked now arm in arm with my father and, in the waning afternoon light, we all crossed the threshold and passed through the gates of the Vakil bazaar.

Dark shadows swallowed the sunlight. Before us spread a lofty arched central arcade with the vertical spaciousness of a Gothic cathedral. This main pedestrian walkway is where all roads begin and fan out for a mile in each direction. Passing breezes lend an airy feel. Secret courtyard pools and tree-encircled cloisters lie in wait off tributaries for those wanting a break from the rushing action of the bazaar.

Bright cartoon posters of the Shia founding fathers, direct descendants of the Prophet — doe-eyed Imam Ali, sword in hand, and his son Hussein on horseback, bearing the sacred emerald-green flag — all painted in flashy colors, livened up the merchants' dingy, soiled walls. Where once the Shah's image hung, now black-and-white government photos of the regime's bearded leaders adorned the shops. At an intersection of the labyrinth, a huge ayatollah with watchful eyes stared down from the domed ceiling: it was the Supreme Leader, the all-powerful Khamenei. Strings of colored lights drooped underneath his chin like a pearl necklace, ready for future feasts. Richard still couldn't tell the ruling trinity apart: Khomeini, Khamenei, Khatami. He had given up trying and simply called them "the three K's."

Luminous shafts of light slipped through elevated arabesque-carved windows. I touched the thick, cool medieval walls. The rat-a-tat pounding of coppersmiths rang down a corridor to my left. Echoes of bustling shoppers hummed along dimly lit tunnels. Shirazi boys walking hand in hand, mothers and daughters fondling silk scarves, turbaned Afghanis with carpets under their arms, a Turkoman haggling over a teapot, Qashqai nomads fresh from mountain pastures, their women wrapped in vibrant-colored finery.

We felt exposed, vulnerable and self-conscious, but the shoppers were completely oblivious of us. My eyes adjusted to the darkness. Lamps and light bulbs lit each shop and its dangled wares: hand-stitched lace, silks and cottons; copper trays and serving bowls; tribal weavings, saddlebags and carpets; tea glasses and porcelain; leather shoes and sneakers. All to entice customers. And, of course, there were no price tags.

Memories of our long walks with Hassan in our neighborhood bazaar, hand in hand, to buy fruit and vegetables came rushing back. Each shopping journey, then as now, was full of uncertainty. The national sport of bargaining has a firm code of conduct and is not for the faint-hearted. "One should think of it as improvisational theater," my father used to say. "High drama colors every purchase." Two words of caution pertain: *caveat emptor.* The merchants, called bazaaris, are known to be the craftiest of adversaries. I recall how the verbal jousting matches in Tajrish always began with Hassan's question, "For that, how much?" Followed by the response of an inflated price. After a moment's pause, Hassan would roll his eyes and flash feigned indignity, as if insulted.

It always surprised me how rapidly these exchanges could deteriorate. Each new offer by Hassan would be countered with a stiff rebuff. The vocal flurry — interspersed with calls to God, pleas of poverty, accusations of being swindled or swearing on ancestors' graves — moved to a rhythmic beat. Each comment escalated the volume. Finally, before they breached all decency or collapsed in exhaustion, the bout would be declared a draw and, dignity restored, the deal was struck. Hassan would take our newly bought eggplants, tomatoes and plucked chickens and hand me a bag of oranges and pomegranates to carry.

How shortsighted, I thought, to let a simple price tag, rudely scribbled, eliminate all dialogue between buyer and seller. This rapport held the secret of all bazaars. Over a lifetime, one returned time and again to the same stall. Loyalty was rewarded. "*Babajan*, my dear father, I give this one special, only for you." And so, friendships are forged.

Obeying his primal instincts, Richard had already plunged in. Chris followed right behind. Silver Baluchi bracelets — for their wives at home — were calling them.

Deep in the shrouded market, my father and I found ourselves before a storefront gleaming with fine engraved metalwork. Behind the window, bronze hammered trays of proud Achaemenian kings and queens and stiff imperial soldiers were displayed next to silver trays of embracing lovers from Omar Khayyám's wine-drenched *Rubaiyat*. "I don't believe what I'm seeing," my father whispered. This bacchanalian pageant of parading royals, romantic trysts and belly dancers glowing under spotlights took us aback. Two central taboos of the regime — vainglorious Shahs and explicit love scenes — were openly being flouted. When I asked the heavyset owner about it, he answered, "These designs aren't for everyone. Some prefer more conservative, just calligraphy." He pulled out a tray with Koranic script. "Which do you prefer?" He grinned.

I stumbled down an arched colonnade, following my brothers through a portico and out into the sunlight. A courtyard circled by storefronts held a soft green pool and beguiling orange trees. As I blinked in the bright light, a young man with a pompadour sidled up to me.

"Gudday, mate."

"Hello."

"'Ope you're enjoyin' Shiraz. Can I 'elp ya with somethin'?"

"No thanks. But where did you pick up that accent?"

"Sydney, ya know. Down Under. Grew up there until me da decided to bring us back 'ere."

"How're you enjoying it?"

"Not so bad. Now it's home. Met some nice German lassies the other day."

"Really?"

"Look, if ya need to change your dollahs, I'll give a swell rate."

"Perhaps tomorrow."

"No worries, mate. You'll find me 'ere next to the pond. Gudday!"

His "St. Louis Thirty-niners" basketball shirt, torn-at-the-knee Levi's and Air Jordans were decidedly hip. As he walked across the courtyard with his homeboy attitude, I realized I was watching a veritable walking billboard for Generation X. It was all a bit confusing. I had expected a much firmer Islamic clampdown on the MTV global culture. This "decadent" American vogue had not been stamped out, as we had been told repeatedly over the years. The heavily guarded borders of this land of taboos seemed as porous as a sieve.

Shiraz — fabled city of poets, wine, roses and *amore* — felt more like a Mediterranean port than a landlocked oasis behind stony Zagros citadels. A healthy river ran through the center of town. A break in the mountains, opening a passage out of the city to the north, bore the triumphant name Allah al-Akbar. The other ridge, which Akbar called Sleeping Man, lounged across the city's western flank with its round potbelly rising to the sky. Adrift in the ocean of desert wastes that stretches from Syria to Pakistan, Shiraz floated on a rare pocket of naturally irrigated green fields.

This region called Fars is the Tuscany of Iran. Epicenter of ancient Persia, it is also the birthplace of the Shiraz wine grape that flourishes now in Australia. And as Fiesole, above Florence, was once a stronghold of the Etruscans, Shiraz gave shelter to the first Aryan tribes. Over the centuries, it earned a reputation for producing learned scholars, artists and the country's two most celebrated poets: Hafez and Saadi. Another renowned Shirazi son was Ostad Isa, the architect who designed the Taj Mahal.

I knew we had begun our journey in the right place.

It was still dusk as we walked up to the Nasir al-Mulk Mosque, the first pink architectural creation I had ever seen. Here, a Qajar Shah of the nineteenth century surely ordered color-mad craftsmen to breathe life into the bland Dutch-blue-and-white porcelain themes of country life. Meticulously hand painted, thousands of glazed tiles mixed hot rose-petaled images with sunflower yellow.

The entrance was chained shut. We searched for the guardian of the keys, and a balding, half-bearded *haji* popped out of a closed door embedded in a mud wall across the small square.

"*Salam, agha.* Peace, sir," we greeted him.

"*Khosh amadid,* welcome," the caretaker said.

"Why is this *masjid* closed?"

"People don't come anymore. There are no prayers."

"Why?"

"Maybe because the mullah has been sent away."

"Sent away?"

"Maybe he spoke too much devil politics."

Ecclesiastical struggles pitting mullah against mullah, reformers against hard-liners, had brewed to a boil here.

"Some mullahs have their turbans taken away," continued the caretaker. "They become like the common people. That's the penalty. They're lucky to be alive."

The mosque was empty. Walking across the courtyard, I felt the tiles offered awkward patterns, ones that did not belong there: country homes, Dutch windmills and northern European riverscapes. Fawning over Western styles spawned such Iranian experiments. *Gharbzadegi*, intoxication with the West — a term quite popular with today's regime — clearly was alive and well in the Qajar period. The dominant color was not the cool, sacred turquoise that one normally associates with Iran's Islamic mosques; rather, it was splashed with warmth — sizzling pink and bright yellow.

At sunset, dark clouds gathered overhead and a soft rain began to fall. We looked up from the glazed courtyard at the blackened sky. Chris pointed out a double rainbow arcing over the dome. Color prisms cast by the dying sun were even more daring than the florid tiles that encircled us. We took it as an omen.

That evening, our hotel manager assured us that we should be content here at the Apadana, a low-budget rival of the five-star Homa across town. The name Homa had been borrowed from the Persian winged griffin that once sat atop Persepolis's columns and still graced the tails of Iran Air planes as an obedient mascot. But I wanted to believe that the name might have been a corruption of *hoama*, the euphoria-inducing beverage of choice for Zoroastrian priests. Aldous Huxley, in *Brave New World*, modeled his narcotic Soma after the ancient recipe. I was imagining a hotel chain with a similar theme — the Guinness Magic in Lagos, the Vin Santo in Florence, the Mouthful of Qat in Sana'a — when the manager raised other concerns with my father.

"Mr. Ward, excuse me, the other hotel where you were going to stay, please, is not good."

"Why? It has five stars."

"In lobby, they are hanging very big sign. It is in English. 'Down to Amrika.'"

"I see."

"But under these English words it is also written in Farsi, *'Marg bar Amrika.'*"

"Doesn't that mean 'Death to America'?"

"Yes. They are hoping if guests can't read Farsi, then it won't hurt feelings so much."

"So tell me, just what *does* it say at the Homa Hotel? 'Down to' or 'Death to'?"

"Both. Is better you stay here instead." The manager winked at Dad. "We are private hotel, not government. Much more friendly. No politics."

I admired his ingenious marketing. Not missing a beat, my father shot back, "Well, if it says 'Down with America,' we'll turn the other cheek." He flashed a mischievous grin.

In the lobby, I noticed a group of five Italian ladies wrapped in brightly colored headscarves. If this were a movie set, Fellini would have had his camera rolling. A guide held their attention with his story.

"During Moharram, I was with Italians who walked by a holy procession and they wanted to do filming with their cameras. And there was a very good-looking girl among the group."

The ladies giggled.

"Her hair was uncovered, and one religious guy saw her from the crowd and came up to her. Of course, she was very afraid. She expected him to be angry. But then he told her, 'You are sooo cute, I just like to kiss you.'"

*"Ah sì,"* the ladies burst out. *"Che carino!"*

\*　　　\*　　　\*

More than a century ago, Victorian travelers passed freely through Shiraz. Edward Granville Browne, in his book *A Year Amongst the Persians*, found the inhabitants "amongst all Persians, the most subtle, the most ingenious, the most vivacious, even their speech is to this day the purest and most melodious." Harry de Windt also described the city, in *A Ride to India:* "Shiraz has been called the 'Paris of Persia,' perhaps from the beauty and coquetry of its women." And in 1870, H. M. Stanley, the controversial explorer who searched for Livingstone along the Congo, noted, "The Shirazi are a people whose thoughts dwell upon passionate love, and shades of trees. They are a people of sleepy eyes."

It took me a long time to fall asleep that first night; an eerie tingling of pleasure came over me. It felt surreal to be back, to hear Farsi being spoken, to hear the wind rustling through the trees' new leaves outside my window, to see a huddled figure walking home under the lamplight, and to think that somewhere out there over the mountains, maybe, was Hassan. Richard, slumped over, had fallen asleep, leaving his reading light on. His face held a faint smile of contentment. I wanted to thank him for his brainstorm that brought us here. The youngest brother had made it all possible.

Breakfast offered flatbread, sour-cherry jam, butter, honey and yogurt spooned into bowls. Buckets of tea were poured. My father spoke of a rooster's call that lifted him vertically out of bed. My mother had woken to the smells of fresh baked bread. Chris's eyes had opened to cries of "Goal!" from a nearby schoolyard. "I felt a cold sweat. It got my blood running," he said. A semiprofessional goalie, Chris cringed whenever he heard roars of a scored goal. Kevin had dreamt of our old garden in Tehran.

Suddenly the door was flung open and Avo entered the fluorescent-lit room. He sat down and poured tea.

"And so, who is this Hassan?" he demanded with his peculiar upturned eyebrow.

Silence. He had been listening in on our conversation.

"A school friend."

"Ahhh." His eyes rolled.

Slowly, we got up from the table one by one.

As we walked outside, my father warned us quietly. Avo, he said, was the perfect spy for such a low-level training mission.

"But there's no way around it," Richard said. "Foreign Ministry rules. Unfortunately, we're stuck with him."

"Just watch what you say," said Dad.

I looked back. Avo was still eating. Pointy chin, sunken cheeks, pinched nose and piercing eyes behind his John Lennon glasses, this Armenian was a mystery to me.

While we regrouped in the lobby, Avo repeated his story about working in Toronto as a night cashier. He never got a promotion, so he returned to Iran and adopted a new work ethic. "When I got back to Tehran, I used to give it one hundred and ten percent, but they didn't care. Actually, they want much less. Now I only give it twenty percent. Sometimes thirty."

Perplexed and suspicious, he had developed an entangled survival strategy. Each day, he told me, was a new day. The truth was flexible. Whatever had been said could always be denied later. All his statements ended with "more or less."

"Well, Avo," I said, "remember one thing. When it's time to board the minivan, there's only one truth. When it's time to leave, we will leave, with or without you."

That morning, with our fierce driver Nasrollah at the wheel, we drove through the Allah al-Akbar gate going north out of Shiraz. An hour later, over tawny rolling hills, we reached the pine forest that blankets the entrance to Persepolis. Tucked into the vertical folds of Kuh-e Rahmat, the Mountain of Mercy, rose the mighty creation of Darius.

In biblical and Greek texts there is no mention of Persepolis. But that's understandable. It was never a city, only a ceremonial sacred site used once a year by Persian kings. However, Vita Sackville-West, of the Bloomsbury set, did jot down her first impressions: "The space, the sky, the hawks, the raised-up eminence of the terrace, the quality of the Persian light, all give to the great terrace a sort of springing airiness, a sort of treble, to which the massive structure of bastion and archways plays a corrective bass. It is only when you draw near that you realise how massive that structure really is."

And huge it was. A shadow of its former glory, Persepolis rose fifty feet high on an immense limestone platform stretching about three hundred yards across. Towering over an evergreen pine forest — planted during the Shah's day — the imposing vertical wall of blocks dwarfed a crowd standing underneath. Around the grand ceremonial double-ramped staircase clustered dozens of visiting schoolgirls clad in obligatory black, ready to begin their climb to the top. From below, I could see only a few slender coral-white pillars piercing the azure sky. My mother called it a colossal birthday cake, its columns rising like candles.

At first glimpse, it reminded me of Epidaurus, the great open-air theater in Peloponnesus, tucked into a similar encircling hill and chosen for its sweeping vista across a valley to the rising peaks in the north. But where Epidaurus was carved into a hillock, Persepolis boldly extended out from the Mountain of Mercy on a constructed stage that once supported the palaces of Darius and Xerxes, the royal harem, paradise gardens, baths, the imperial treasury and the grandiose Apadana Hall.

Giant hand-cut stones rivaled the work of Inca master builders. Where Epidaurus is poetic, Persepolis is audacious, a daring feat of levitation, raising man above nature. And these days you ascended by climbing the staircase. Holding my mother's arm, I followed the schoolgirls.

At the top, a small, lonely kiosk selling drinks appeared on the left, and I turned to face the Apadana Hall, one of the world's great spaces in monumental architecture. As we passed through the Gate of All Nations, two Asian centaurs — mammoth curly-bearded faces on torsos of horses — stared down on us with Ozymandius's gaze. When we turned around, my mother gasped as we looked back across the plain that spread to mountain-fringed horizons. We stood in silence. There were no surrounding walls, no defensive perimeters, no fortifications, no scent of fear. This palace was clearly designed to face the broad panorama of the Plain of Palms as a showcase for dazzling spectacles. The view was simply staggering.

I was wary of certain descriptions I had read: "Barren and dusty like all ruins." "Abandoned, far from water, like petrified fossils." "An insignificant echo." "All destroyed." "Imagination has to work in overdrive to populate the once powerful site."

Robert Byron, in *The Road to Oxiana,* dismissed it all with a flick of the wrist, repelled by the gray stone that shone like an "aluminium saucepan." Disillusioned, he particularly resented the German archaeologist Herzberg, who ruled the ruins as if they were his fiefdom, offering visitors a booklet with "a code of academic malice compiled from Chicago." These scholars, he wrote, struck a mood like "that of a critic at an exhibition." Today, all foreign archaeologists have long since fled. Byron would have been pleased.

I realized that the best time to visit Persepolis is when the ancients did. Then it all makes sense. During *Nowruz* — at the birth of spring and the Persian New Year — the sprawling plain is streaked with young green wheat, the mountains flecked with wildflowers, crocuses, poppies and herbs. White-blossoming almond and pink-splotched cherry trees bud at this turn of the season. Rebirth and regeneration are all around. Life returns. The emerald vistas are vibrant and inviting.

The ceremonial site of Persepolis was chosen carefully, strategically placed in the Persian heartland between Ecbatana, the summer capital, and Susa, the winter capital. The surviving walls are incised with trees of life, the lotus and solar rosettes that represent fertility. Inscribed prayers welcome the Zoroastrian god, "Ahura Mazda, who has created this Earth, who has created Heaven, who has created man, who has created good things for man." Built by Darius the Great in 500 B.C., Persepolis served as his empire's pilgrimage abode during the sacred New Year festival.

\*　　　\*　　　\*

Before us flowed a chatty gaggle of high school girls, picnicking families of three generations, curious university students led by professors, and rambunctious running children, their huffing grandmothers in hot pursuit. All flooded in as if pulled by ancient collective memory. This was the time, in spring, to pay tribute.

A dozen teenage girls swarmed the ruins ahead of us. I watched as some lingered to touch the stone faces of lost Achaemenian rulers carved in the amber-streaked blocks. One girl looked over her shoulder self-consciously before caressing a bas-relief of a soldier. She brushed some dust away. Suddenly she turned and caught me watching her moment of intimacy with a long-lost ancestor.

As I looked away, she rearranged her scarf and slipped behind a half-fallen column. A voice called out. One of her friends fiddled with an antiquated camera. Focused on her ancient world, she studied the composition and moved closer to the stone figures. Her finger snapped the shutter and she looked up with a smile. Wasn't taking pictures of these ancestors *haram*, forbidden? For decades the Islamic Republic had denounced Iran's pagan past with great fervor. Evidently, some faint music still resonated from these empty chambers.

During the golden age of the Persian Empire, lords and ladies, dignitaries and ambassadors gathered here in Persepolis from the far reaches of Asia, Africa and Europe to pay homage to the Achaemenian king of kings, Darius. From distant realms they hailed — the mighty Danube, the immortal Nile, the azure Aegean and the Indus — all loyal subjects spread across the *oecemene*, the one world.

Bas-reliefs carved in the grand stairway proclaimed the story of their arrival: Egyptians in horse caravans bulging with tribute, Greeks from Lydia proffering gold and precious gifts, Libyans leading antelopes, Babylonians with buffaloes loaded with embroidered garments, Pakistanis offering weapons and mules, Ethiopians bearing ivory on horseback, Arabian camels laden with spices and incense, Afghanis bringing sheep and textiles. I studied a repetitious frieze of a powerful lion sinking its teeth into the haunches of a bull. This announced the summer sun overcoming winter's rain: the triumph of good over evil. Astronomers who re-create the skies of antiquity submit that on the vernal equinox at Persepolis, the constellation Leo was at its zenith while Taurus was setting.

Ascending the stairway, each delegation filed through the Gate of All Nations, and on their way to pay tribute to their great king, they passed near the Apadana Hall. It must have been an overwhelming sight to peer inside the largest auditorium ever built, able to accommodate ten thousand people, reserved for Median and Persian nobles attending the ceremonies. Proceeding farther, they entered the Hundred Column Palace, advancing slowly with their gifts in dim light toward the golden throne, where the awaiting king sat in dazzling splendor amid dignitaries in brilliant robes while incense burned.

After each gift was suitably acknowledged by the king, it was transported to the treasury. At day's end, as Darius walked back to his private palace, he could see thousands of smoking campfires on the plain below, stretching westward, keeping vigil until dawn.

When Pietro della Valle, an Italian merchant visiting Persepolis in 1621, walked the length of the Apadana Hall, he counted twenty-five columns still erect out of the original seventy-two. Today I counted thirteen. Earthquakes, fire and poor maintenance have left little standing.

In *The Iranians*, Sandra Mackey, with the guidance of her mentor, R. K. Ramazani, described the national character as "two warring psyches: one which evolved from the cosmopolitan, worldly culture of ancient Persia, the other from a conservative, emotion-laden Islam."

While modern Iranians may patriotically admire their distant ancestors, they can't escape their clergy's judgment: simply pagans. Mullahs in Tehran speak in unison: those ancestors have no role in our lives. The ancients were born before the true revelation of God, before the prophet Mohammad. Nothing can change that fact. The stigma will stand forever. They are divorced from Islam. Today's black-robed guardians of the faith have tried to sever the past cleanly. The sharp blade of heresy silenced protests.

It was no coincidence, then, that Hassan, Fatimeh and their children were all named after the Prophet's sacred family, heroic figures of Shia Islam. Hassan's older brother bore the name of the great martyr Hussein. None of their children carried the great "pagan" name of Cyrus or Darius. The ghosts of Persepolis, the sun-washed glories of historic Persia, rich and magical, were too removed from their world.

In the twentieth century, the pendulum of national identity swung between Islamic culture and Persian heritage. The short-lived Pahlavi dynasty of fifty years overreached for the Achaemenid Empire of Darius and Xerxes. The Shah resurrected and flaunted it at his own peril. Ayatollah Khomeini ended all that. The "hand of Islam" violently pushed the pendulum away from the royal heathen ancestors back to the holy heirs of the Prophet and the Koran.

Thank God for Akbar, the local guide from Shiraz who had joined us at Rich's insistence. Iranian history was his passion, Persepolis his love. Where Avo was vacant, Akbar was urbane, well versed, spiritual. We followed him into Darius's Hundred Column Palace.

"The darkest area was in here," he explained. Not a single column was still standing. The sun shone brilliantly. We had to use our imaginations. "The king would sit on his throne exactly on this spot." He made a circle in the dirt with his foot.

"But why in darkness?" asked Rich.

"In Eastern countries, the leader must be surrounded by mystery. Even today, we have never seen the wife of Imam Khomeini in public. The same holds true for the wife of Ayatollah Khamenei, our Supreme Leader. We never get to see their families. Those in power don't show themselves in their daily life at home. In our society, the leader acquires a charismatic holy identity, and people look up to him. If you obey me, they say, you obey Allah. So they keep their distance from the people, and their regular life is a secret."

"No photographers, paparazzi?"

"No, absolutely not! For thousands of years, common people have been governed by one ruler, the king. Now we have President Khatami. Patiently we wait for decisions of change. For instance, according to the constitution, mayors should be elected by the people, but this has not happened and the mullahs still choose all city mayors. People want new political parties that will try to improve the economy. The majority of mullahs in government are conservative villagers who spend their time studying *shari'a* — Islamic law. What do they know about economics? To save the economy you need specialists, economists, businessmen. This is the main problem nowadays. Schools, hospitals, roads, electricity and all the great things that have been done for the people after the Revolution are no longer enough. One thing we all agree on, Iran must build a strong economy."

While Akbar was holding forth, I spotted a young girl in a black chador spying on us from behind a column. Sensing her curiosity, I drifted in her direction, pretending to admire the view. As I walked past her, she called me.

"May I ask you a question, Mister? Why do you take pictures?" She pointed to my camera.

"Because we used to live in your country, and we want to remember this trip."

"I know. I spoke to your parents before. Your mother told me she always wanted a girl."

"Of course, because she has four boys."

"I also want to have only boys."

"Why do you say that?"

"A boy is free to come and go without this." She touched her headdress. "Nothing is written in the Koran about wearing it. But tell me, what would you like to have, a boy or a girl?"

"Both."

"I want only boys, so they can be free," she repeated.

"Maybe change is coming," I said, speaking about the new elections.

"No. This is all the mullahs have ever cared about. They just want to keep us covered." She shook her head. Then a voice called out, "Maryam, Maryam."

Her eyes darted around to see whether her teachers had noticed her talking with me.

"Please say my goodbye to your mother." She smiled fleetingly, then quickly moved away.

My mother had been watching us, and walked over to me with her slight limp. She sighed. "Poor baby, she really feels trapped."

I took my mother's hand and we sat down on the base of a column that once helped support the gigantic ceiling of precious Lebanese cedar. Broken pillars were strewn everywhere around us in the sand. A small dust devil swirled up the hill.

Kevin asked the million-dollar question: "What about the burning of Persepolis?"

Akbar related his version of the holocaust, when the Macedonian victor feasted and flames leapt sixty feet to lick the cedar beams and silver roofs. "Alexander, when he invaded Persia, wanted to put his hand on the heart of the country." Akbar raised his hand and made a fist. "He wanted to show the people his power. That's why he set Persepolis on fire. This was the heart and soul of the Achaemenian Empire."

In the autumn of 331 B.C., golden-maned Alexander the Great rode onto these plains at the head of his half-starved troops and saw the roofs shining brightly. Parmenio, an adviser, argued that if he burned it, he would be destroying his own heritage. Already his soldiers had sacked the capitals of Susa and Ecbatana, but Persepolis was the sacred city, the seat of holiness, as venerable as the Acropolis. Only ten miles away lay the cliff-face tombs of Xerxes and Darius at Naqsh-e Rustam. With half the empire still unconquered, Alexander could not leave Persepolis standing. Out of political necessity, this symbol was destroyed.

The Elizabethan playwright Christopher Marlowe described the tragic moment in *Tamburlaine the Great:*

> Alexander, Thais and the Macedonian soldiers,
> Reeling with their torches through the Persian palaces,
> Wrecked to flaring fragments pillared Persepolis.

Richard offered a defense of Alexander, describing the classic version of the bacchanal. Feasting with wine in the banquet hall, the drunken Macedonian prince and his generals watched Thais, the dancing courtesan, cry out for vengeance with torch in hand. She set fire to the heavy gold lace curtains, "and, like another Helen," Marlowe wrote, Thais "fired another Troy."

"When Alexander sobered up and everything was burned to the ground, did he really weep?" Richard asked.

"Of course, he was angry," Akbar replied. "When you study history in school books, you hear only great things about Alexander, but if you look at the other side, you'll understand why in Iran we call him *gostakh*. The important thing about traveling is that you can see two sides of the coin."

"*Go-stakh,*" I said, and wrote it down.

"It's a word from Old Persian."

"And it means?"

"Well . . . son of a bitch."

I stopped with my mother at the tin-sided kiosk next to the former royal ladies' quarters, now a museum. A line of boisterous girls climbed up the stone path of nearby Kuh-e Raghbat, the hill that led to honeycomb tombs carved into the rock face. I asked the fellow behind the counter if it was like this every day.

"Do many Iranians come here?"

"What do you think?" He smiled. "This is *Takht-e Jamshid,* the Throne of Jamshid." He extended his hands, palms up, as if taking personal credit for the entire site. "*Baba,* the whole world must come, like you and Mother, to *Takht-e Jamshid.*"

That name struck me. I had forgotten it. Iranians have always called these ruins the Throne of Jamshid, not Persepolis. If Alexander's hand erased the past, as Akbar said, then the past had been rewritten as myth. The mythmaker was Ferdowsi, the tenth-century bard whose epic poem, *Shahnameh* (The Story of Kings), is four times longer than the *Iliad*. With a stirring cadence, Ferdowsi charted Iran's pre-Islamic history, from its origins to the last heroic Sassanian kings, who ruled before the Arab Muslim conquest. His *Shahnameh* is Iran's national epic. Because of Ferdowsi's mighty pen, for centuries Iranians have attributed Persepolis to Jamshid, a mythic king of whom there is no historical record. Jamshid, glorious son of Kauimers, Ferdowsi tells us, sat here on the Persian throne as master of the world and reigned for seven hundred years in a time when death was unknown.

Reclaiming the past can be tricky business. In 1925 Reza Shah proclaimed his dynasty Pahlavi, after the language of the Sassanian dynasty, which ruled before the birth of Allah's prophet. Reza Shah Pahlavi's heir, Mohammad Reza, eventually wrapped himself in the robes of Darius, resurrecting all things Achaemenian with glossy *son et lumière* productions and Hollywood-style sets of ancient Persia. His peacock throne glinted in the sun. The young Shah named his soldiers the Immortals, after the ten thousand elite warriors of Xerxes. Dreaming of his Persian Gulf empire, he financed a military second to none. Children's names at birth reflected the new epoch: Cyrus, Darius, Jamshid and Manijeh. All goods that were modern and Western, coupled with the new identity of pre-Islamic Persia, were the rage. Like the Greeks who resurrected the Parthenon and Pericles for their new national identity, the Shah tried to do the same.

He knew the Persian mystique would play better for Western audiences than the Islamic identity. A Swiss schooling ensured that the Shah spoke French better than Farsi — his grammatical errors in his mother tongue were embarrassing. Blindness reigned in his lavish Niavaran Palace. He and his advisers ignored the people's Islamic faith; they denounced and persecuted mullahs and curtailed the mourning rituals centered on Hussein's martyrdom during the month of Moharram. Iranians slowly learned to be ashamed of their own culture. Something was bound to snap.

Akbar led us to the edge of the broad terrace. We stared into the distance. He pointed at a huge collapsing tent structure in the pine forest below and spoke of a more recent gathering. In orotund, mocking tones he recounted the Shah's 1971 extravaganza to mark the 2,500th anniversary of the Persian Empire. Champagne flowed freely, and the food was flown in by Air France from Maxim's. Celebrities, royalty and jet setters adorned the Cecil B. De Mille pageantry: nine kings, three ruling princesses, thirteen presidents, ten sheiks and two sultans flocked to Persepolis for the $200 million fete. An emperor was present: Haile Selassie of Ethiopia. Even Imelda Marcos came. Vice President Spiro Agnew represented the United States.

"Every Iranian knows that the Shah's father was a corporal with a Cossack brigade, and the Pahlavi dynasty lasted only fifty years!" Akbar laughed. "So silly for Shah to speak of Cyrus as his blood ancestor." He then described Empress Farah's avant-garde artistic spectaculars in Shiraz and one infamous incident in 1975: "Imagine a French troupe of stark-naked performers romping in broad daylight through the Vakil bazaar!" Shirazis were scandalized. Royal credibility reached a new low.

Five years later, the Shah sat poolside in permanent exile in a Panamanian island hideaway, the guest of President Manuel Noriega. As the pineapple-faced general eyed the sad empress, her husband was lost in conspiratorial thought about the CIA, the MI-6 and his demise. The Shah's last ride was nearing its end. David Frost arrived for his long-awaited interview with the deposed monarch, accompanied by a young BBC reporter, Andrew Whitley, who had covered Iran during the Revolution. Recognizing him, the Shah became hysterical and shouted, "You are the reason why I lost my country!" He was convinced that even the BBC had a hand in plotting his overthrow.

At the same moment, halfway around the world, on the dusty

Margh Dasht plain, the notorious Ayatollah Khalkali, who was responsible for sentencing thousands of people to death for violating Islamic law, commanded a column of bulldozers to drive straight for Persepolis. His dream was to plow the Achaemenian monuments into the earth, a cultural cleansing for the Islamic Republic. The bulldozers stopped a kilometer from Apadana Hall. "A mob of angry villagers shouting and throwing stones turned them back," said Nasrollah proudly. Miraculously, the site was spared.

6

# Nightingale Gardens, Sufi Poets
# and a Tavern

Let sound once more in me the Persian's verse . . .
— Jorge Luis Borges, *Rubaiyat*

A T SUNSET, we arrived in Bagh Eram, Paradise Garden, where we met a group of college students thrilled to find willing guinea pigs with whom they could practice their second language. The University of Shiraz, set on a tawny hill above the garden, has a medical faculty that lectures solely in English. My brother Chris, having put his fears to rest momentarily, joked with one blond inquisitor. Other coeds thronged around him, asking where he was from.

He answered, "I'm from the Great Satan."

They broke out in laughter.

"Where is your home?"

"Philadelphia."

"Pheeel-dul-phya?"

"Exactly."

Avo looked terrified. "Don't say 'Amrika,'" he warned, his eyes flitting back and forth like a nervous sparrow waiting for a hawk to pounce. "It's not funny, Chris. You never know who's listening."

As the students practiced their English, asking the usual questions about how we liked Iran, I noticed a budding Chinese hawthorn nearby. Its familiar pungent scent held Kev spellbound. I could almost hear him purring. An Ivy League dreamer who never fully recovered from the abrupt loss of the sights and smells of his childhood, Kev closed his eyes in rapture, his nose plunged into the blossoms like a drunken hummingbird. I mimicked him, bending my neck to the white petals. The sweet scent, I recalled, had saturated the air around our Tajrish house each spring. Now it was pulling us back to our original garden.

In the autumn of 1960, my mother rented Mr. Jalali's red-brick villa because she fell in love with the garden. Eight years of Saudi Arabia's sand dunes had fortified her longing. Turquoise-tiled fountains stretched into the distance, framed by columns of tall pines, climbing vines, bursting flowers, pergolas and pools. At the end of the shaded waterway stood a neoclassical Italianate pavilion. Under it, you could gaze into a Neapolitan grotto with stalactites gently dripping water. Two white statues, set inside the cave on rocks, faced each other, locking eyes, transfixed: a handsome shepherd serenading with his flute and a reclining damsel, swooning. Her graceful forefinger brushed her upper lip. His toes curled with excitement. Frozen in time, the piper was seducing the nymph. It was my favorite hiding place. Especially when Kev took to stalking us as the "Phantom Killer," disguised in his black cape. Hunting season officially opened when the red iron gate slammed shut and my parents drove off into Tehran's nightlife. Younger brothers, as usual, were fair game. Too small to question Kev's favorite pastime, we ran for cover. Seeking refuge, I would sneak into the cave, behind the shepherd. Panting under my shirt to quiet my breathing, I listened to the stalactites' drops of water hitting a shallow pool at regular intervals. The mysterious love of the shepherd and the nymph seemed eternal. I was terrified of being discovered here. Heart pounding, a scream, then mad scampering into the shadows again.

Those evenings spent as fugitives taught us patience and resilience. We never thanked Kevin for this gift. When Hassan heard our pleas, he encouraged Kevin to retire his Phantom Killer cape, and Kev obeyed.

Our landlord, Mr. Jalali, was a leftist journalist who lived in California, where he helped organize underground activities against the Shah. His politics, like my dad's, had sent him into exile. Each had used the other's country for safe refuge. However, Jalali's garden was anything but proletarian. Pure fantasy, this Oriental "Garden of the Finzi-Continis" reached for a higher level.

One twilight hour, when the sun's rays softened and faded and breezes blew, my father powerfully confirmed my suspicions about the garden's spirits. He pointed at a few glowing lights, fleeting down the mulberry tree and then along a magenta bed of snapdragons. "See them, Terry?" I looked up. Flickers like gossamer alighting from leaf to leaf, pulsing for a few beats, then moving on. He bent down and turned toward me, staring into my eyes.

"Green-eyed people are close to the fairies," he said. "One day I'll be taking you to their native land, behind Mount Erigal in Donegal. Look over there, Terry. The garden's full of them!" I watched the lights brighten and fade. "Shy little fellas," he said. "So far from Ireland, so far from home."

Later that night, I opened the atlas to trace the route of these wayward spirits back to Donegal. First there was the eighteen-thousand-foot Elburz to climb. I imagined them all flapping their tiny wings over the pass at Ab-e Ali through the Chalus Tunnel and then scurrying down into the humid jungles of Sisengan on the Caspian Sea. A steamer from Bandar Pahlavi could get them to Baku. Tramping across the unfriendly Caucasus to the Black Sea, they could stow away on a freighter sailing through the Bosporus, past Gallipoli, rounding the Peloponnesus on their way to Venice at the far end of the Adriatic. Once there, they would huff and puff up the Dolomites, cross the Brenner Pass and float down the Rhine. Somewhere in the Black Forest, I felt drowsy and closed my eyes. When I woke, it was all painfully clear to me: reaching Donegal would be impossible. My father was right. Too far.

I spoke to Hassan about this. "That's why we must be kind to them," he said. The next evening, we placed a bowl of fresh milk out on the kitchen stoop.

Our gardener, Iraj, was a big bear of a man. With his balding head and furry eyebrows atop his heavy torso, he looked uncannily like Popeye's rival, the tough-nosed bully Brutus. Under his stubbly beard, he sported a never-ending scowl. His tree-trunk arms and the dark rings around his eyes spoke of thuggish tendencies. He threatened my brothers and me often, and once barked menacingly at my mother: "This my garden, that you house." Jalali had told him that one day the workers would own all the property. His words were prophetic. Although Jalali spent his whole life fighting for the overthrow of the Shah, in the end, after Khomeini came to power, his garden was confiscated.

Iraj hated Hassan and saw him as an intruder in his world. In a crafty, well-planned move, he tried to sabotage Hassan's position. When a bicycle was reported stolen, the local police dragged Hassan off to jail for questioning. My mother, hearing this, went to the police station and demanded Hassan's release. The captain, an old crony of Iraj, was taken aback by Mother's plea. His usual method of interrogation, "softening up" the accused with a beating, ended before it began. Hassan was freed. Back home, my mother went to Iraj and asked him to take her to his house across the alley. Reluctantly, he opened the door, and there stood the bike, as well as vases, carpets, pottery and tools that he and his wife had "liberated" over the years. "Keep them all and I'll say nothing," my mother said, "but I ask you to kindly look for another job." Iraj never set foot in our garden again. He took his booty and went back to his hometown of Yazd. Hassan was all smiles. A dark spell was lifted.

After Kevin and I pulled our noses out of the hawthorn blossoms, we stumbled in a pleasant daze down Bagh Eram, not taking our eyes off the noble cypresses that stood in rows, framing paths to a vanishing point. Shiraz, I knew, was long known for its cypresses.

Then something else tugged at me. It nudged and pushed until I understood it was the mental imprint of Villa dei Vescovi, the Villa of Bishops, in the cypress-studded hill of Fiesole, where Idanna and I often strolled with a friend. Years ago, when I first walked its paths, I felt a sudden homesickness for Iran without really knowing why. In the Tuscan twilight, it all became clear: the long central avenue of slender cypresses, its quadrants of fruit orchards, fountains set in symmetrical positions, one in the center, the others at each end. This Italian garden design traced its origin to ancient Persia. And here in Bagh Eram lay its original blueprint.

Paradise. Eden. Elysium. Arcadia. Shangri-la. Utopia. Abode of the Blessed. Medieval maps of the world always placed earthly Paradise in the East. Medieval Europe's Paradiso, most famously described in Dante's *Divine Comedy*, was rooted in the Latin word *paradisos*, which in turn descended from the classical Greek *paradeisos*. But to find its true source, one had to look farther east, across the hostile deserts of Asia's gnarled land mass. In ancient Persian, *pari-deiza* meant "enclosed garden." The linguistic roots of the "divine" garden sprouted here.

The walled garden, *pari-deiza*, created history's first manmade oases — fresh, humid microclimates full of colors, fragrances and abundant fruits. Arid stony soil lay just beyond the perimeter wall. Environments, once hostile, became protected, soothing and civilized. Elaborate water systems sprang up fountainheads. Ponds and channels fed the parched land. Broad-branched plane trees and weeping willows cast umbrella-like shade, blocking out the harsh sun, ideal shelter for the nightingale. Inside the enclosures stood palaces or pleasure domes with spaces to walk and talk, to meditate alone or share a romantic idyll. Behind the natural beauty, a meticulous structure of geometrically divided land, irrigation canals and planting seasons held the fragile ecosystem in place. For the Persian nomadic philosopher-kings, it represented a year-round oasis. The sound of ever-flowing water, perfume of tuberoses, double jasmine, violets of all shades, evening primroses, blue hyacinths, rose-scented tulips and precious tea roses, so popular with Iranians, and orchards of peach, cherry, plum, apricot, sweet and sour lemon, fig and mulberry — all composed a new natural harmony and placed man squarely in the cosmos.

Persian gardens represented nature at its finest, celestial heaven on *terra firma. Pari-deiza* entered our mythic landscape. In time, this architectural inspiration migrated west with epicureans and patricians, architects and emperors, to the warm Mediterranean shores of Italy and far Iberia. Hadrian's villa in Tivoli comes to mind.

New landscapes were charted for man's earthly dreams: imperial Rome's country *villa* and Pompeii's *domus*, the intoxicating Alhambra of Granada, Islamic pleasure gardens and medieval cloisters, the lemon tree garden in Naples's Santa Chiara Monastery and the colonial *hacienda* of the New World. From serene Dominican vegetable-garden cloisters in Tuscany to Spanish-style villas in southern California, all have borrowed from a remote Persian tradition — the enclosed garden — that began here in Fars two and a half thousand years ago.

Nasrollah's minivan lurched along bustling Zand Avenue like a bucking bronco, coughing its way to each stoplight. He petted his corroded dashboard, explaining to me, "She likes open country, not city traffic."

"Maybe she needs rest," I suggested.

"*Baleh*, yes."

A moment later, his steed had truly made up her mind and stubbornly pitched to a halt on the boulevard. Embarrassed and flustered, poor Nasrollah asked us to be patient while he fixed the problem. Some oil, she needed some oil, he said. We climbed out while he opened the hood.

Avo told us not to wander away. "Stay close. We have to keep to the program."

"But I wrote that program!" Richard said. "And I'm thirsty."

"We still have Hafez tonight," Avo said.

"I know."

"Tomorrow we drive to Yazd." He began to laugh.

"What's so funny?"

"Imagine crossing the desert in this van?" Avo nodded at Nasrollah. "*Psst*, Richard, don't you think we should get rid of him?"

Nasrollah and Avo each wanted to abandon the other. Richard, who had arranged the travel details, felt responsible for both of them. Akbar chose to stay out of it. The rest of us sided with our bearded driver, except Mom, whose forgiving heart was always bigger than all of ours combined.

Akbar was looking under the hood, trying to give Nasrollah a hand, when he called out to me. "Terry, while we get the engine ready, over there is the Rabizadeh Synagogue. It's the largest in Shiraz. You should try to go inside."

While my brothers elected to bargain for cherry juices from a corner store, my mother and I crossed the boulevard and entered the synagogue. Several old men were reading from books, the pages lit by a chandelier. We stood quietly to one side. A small elderly woman in a long dark cloak, her hair concealed under a scarf, welcomed us. Her name was Esther and she lived in the old Jewish quarter.

"We are preparing for Passover, tomorrow." Her English surprised us.

"I live in New York," I said. "This is my mother."

Her eyes widened. A broad smile crossed her lined face. "America!" She reached out and shook our hands. "Ahhh, are you staying long in Shiraz?"

"No, *khanoum*, madam. We leave tomorrow."

"What a pity. Why so soon?" She shrugged. "My family is spread all over the world. England, Israel, California."

"So many left Shiraz?" I asked.

"Yes, after Revolution. The economy fell down. Only five thousand of us are still here. The young ones only speak of going away."

"And you?"

"I stay," she said. "I'm Iranian. We've been here for so long."

"God bless you."

"You should meet my son, Ramin."

"But tomorrow we're driving to Yazd."

"May I ask why Yazd?"

"We've come to Iran to find an old friend."

"May God go with you."

"And with you, *khanoum. Shalom.*"

"*Shalom.*"

She kissed my mother on both cheeks. As we left, I wondered about Esther and her son — how safe were they under the mullahs? I had the feeling that she was as vulnerable as an exposed pawn in the opening moves of a chess match. Some hard-liners enjoyed the freedom to attack anyone when it served their purpose. The only question was, when and whom would they attack next? Under the Islamic Republic, Israel had served the conservatives as an archenemy, a whipping boy. Iranian Jews risked always being seen as a fifth column. Caught in suspended animation, they could easily be used as political tools.

At the same time, the Jewish minority, I had been assured, was tolerated and respected as "people of the Book." Despite the political vitriol against Israel, back-door communications with the Jewish state had continued for decades. After all, Iran and Israel shared a common enemy, Saddam Hussein. Defending the country against the well-equipped Iraqi invasion in 1980, Iranian leaders made secret arms deals with expatriate Iranian-Jewish middlemen, Israeli ministers, the CIA, Oliver North and even Ronald Reagan. The Shia faithful did not know about these deals until the Iran-contra story broke in Washington. As with most revolutions, the regime thrived on the presence of encircling enemies to justify its rule.

My heart felt heavy. I thought of my fourth-grade girlfriend Sara Haim and wondered if by any chance Esther had known or even heard of her family. Why hadn't I asked? My mother put her arm in mine as we crossed the street again to return to the van. I thought of Esther's ancestors who had chosen to follow their liberator Cyrus east over the high sunburnt Zagros instead of returning west to Zion. Her children were now putting that ancient decision into question.

For a generation, Americans have seen only one side of Iran: televised images of a rigid theocratic rule shrouded in black. Few are even remotely aware that another side exists: the heritage of Hafez's song of the soul that has permeated every Iranian heart for the last six centuries.

Hassan had spoken often of Hafez, quoting his poems. He treasured the fourteenth-century poet's *Divan* and consulted it often for guidance. Shiraz, where Hafez died, was also his birthplace. Hassan would certainly approve of our wish to pay homage to his beloved poet. A good thing to do, he would say, on our long, uncertain journey.

Leaving Nasrollah on Golestan Street with his coughing van, we walked along a path of cypresses that faced a wide, soft-pink granite stairway, festooned on either side with hundreds of terracotta pots of lilacs and yellow pansies, scarlet snapdragons, ruby anemones. Atop the stairs, a cloistered garden lay before us. Budding orange trees anchored the four corners. Two shallow pools, to our left and right, cast an aquatic turquoise sheen. In the center, an umbrella-shaped patinaed copper dome, supported by six slender columns, protected the eternal sleep of Hafez. The poet rested in a translucent sarcophagus in his garden of earthly delights and luminous ponds.

Iranians revere their poets in a fundamental way. Rumi, Hafez and Attar, all three from the Sufi tradition, are as sacred as Dante, Shakespeare and Yeats. These Persian mystics celebrated life's pleasures — nature, wine and love — while singing to their beloved with ecstatic emotion. "Sufi" may come from the Persian *saf,* meaning "pure," or, in Arabic, "wearer of wool," for the humble garments worn by enlightened seekers who wandered over Iran as sadhus did in India. By the twelfth century, they could be seen in every part of the Muslim world. For Sufis, God is the beloved, found in the heart and in every particle of creation. Their poetry is a far cry from the puritanical austerity of the mullahs.

Like opera in Italy, poetry is the all-encompassing artistic passion of Iran. If La Scala in Milan is the site of worship for music *cognoscenti,* then this rose-petaled reflecting pond and carved marble sarcophagus of Hafez is the ultimate place of peace and inspiration for lovers of poetry — that is to say, for almost all Iranians. Long before the medieval English language shook off its clangy Germanic growl, Iranian poets were at work, crafting their verses in Farsi, the language that defined high culture from Ottoman Turkey to Mogul India. For almost a thousand years, classical Persian poetry has mapped the soul of the nation.

This unbroken language of Farsi has long been the country's Rock of Gibraltar, its living monument of identity that survived the Arab and Turkic invasions. All the lands between the Atlas Mountains of Morocco and the Tigris River of Iraq adopted the Arabic of the conquering Bedouins, and in doing so erased their historical past before Islam. Only Iran resisted. Its mother tongue remained intact, even though it assimilated Arabic script and numerous Arabic words. The country's rich heritage acted as an immovable bedrock. All cultural flowerings east of the Zagros Range — whether in Isfahan, Shiraz, Bokhara, Samarkand, Kashmir or New Delhi — bore the stamp of Iranian culture. The Ottoman court in Istanbul also discoursed in Farsi. And many scholars insist that it was Persian culture that actually saved Islam, by reshaping the Arab-conquered lands into a refined universal state.

A sculpted language flourished with its own rhythm, form, sophisticated style and renowned artists. Iran's literary womb gave birth to Rudaki, Ferdowsi, Omar Khayyám, Rumi, Saadi, Nizami and, greatest of all, Hafez. No self-respecting poet would begin to practice his craft without having read all the works of the masters, whose profound legacy was of the tongue, imagination and emotion. But a deeper layer also resonated in the poetic tradition. Many of the masterpieces were inspired by brilliant Sufi mystics and their love of the divine. Poetry became ingrained in the Iranian psyche.

*        *        *

Akbar walked us around the tomb, quietly explaining. "Hafez made a prophecy that this place would become a site for pilgrims."

"And so it is," my father said.

"Since his death in 1390, people from all walks of life have been coming to his grave."

In the soft hues of twilight, I watched men, women and children place their hands on his sarcophagus and whisper his verses. Carved in the stone were two songs from the *Divan* in flowing Farsi calligraphy.

"Yes," Akbar continued, "everyone is welcome, even those who drink wine."

"Drunkards?"

"Yes." Akbar laughed.

"Don't say that," Avo snapped.

"By God, this is what Hafez wrote here." Touching the inscription, he recited: "'On my grave don't sit without wine and musician, so that I may rise up dancing.'"

"Today he would go to jail for this," Avo said.

"In those days, it was the Zoroastrians who were making wine and running the taverns. Only non-Muslims could do these activities," Akbar said. "But Hafez was writing in symbols. Red wine stood for the drunken love of God that all Sufi mystics thirsted for. The tavern was the sanctuary of the soul, and the innkeeper was the revered teacher who guided his disciples on the spiritual path."

"Still, they would all be arrested today."

I watched an old woman gently stroke the marble and move her lips. She was oblivious to us. With her eyes closed, she seemed to be confiding in Hafez as if he were listening.

The word *hafez* means "he who has memorized," and it is a name given to a person who has learned the entire Koran by heart. Named Shamsuddin Mohammad at birth, Hafez also became known as Interpreter of Mysteries, Sun of the Faith and Tongue of the Invisible.

Jorge Luis Borges, in *Seven Nights*, wrote, "I ought to have studied the Oriental languages: I have only glanced at them through translations. But, I have felt the punch, the impact of their beauty. For example, that line by the Persian poet Hafez: 'I fly, my dust will be what I am.' In this there is the whole doctrine of transmigration."

Goethe, in his poem *Hegira*, called him "Holy Hafez." While Federico García Lorca spoke of "the sublime amorous *ghazals* of Hafez," Goethe was so moved by the poet that he raised him higher than all others in literature. "Hafez has no peer," he wrote. "In his poetry, Hafez has inscribed undeniable truth indelibly."

Ralph Waldo Emerson read Goethe's translation of Hafez in German. In 1858, in his essay on Persian poetry, he described Hafez as "the prince of Persian poets." His mystical insights staggered him. The founder of American transcendentalism began to translate the master's poetry into English. "Hafez fears nothing," Emerson said. "He sees too far; he sees throughout; such is the only man I wish to be." Criticizing English poets — Wordsworth, Tennyson and Byron — he wrote: "that expansiveness which is the essence of the poetic element they have not. It was no Oxonian, but Hafez who said, 'Let us be crowned with roses, and let us drink wine, and break up the tiresome old roof of heaven into new forms.'"

Even Walt Whitman, whose poetic voice heralded a new America, wrote in a style influenced by Persian poets. In his final days, he honored the debt in the poem "A Persian Lesson," which was originally titled "The Sufi Lesson."

Seated in the outdoor teahouse at the far end of the cloistered garden, my brothers and I sipped tea from miniature gold-rimmed glasses and puffed away on water pipes. I wondered how much Hafez had really influenced the American transcendentalist movement. His poetry tapped into Zoroastrian and Platonic roots, drawing from the wisdom of the ancients. His vision challenged the mullahs' strident dogmas. Kev opened the *Divan* that Akbar had been carrying and read aloud:

What is the meaning of the water of life and the garden
of Eram,
but delicious wine and the edge of this stream?

Since the upright man is kin to the stumbling drunk,
to whose sultry glance should we give our heart? What is
choice?

What do the heavens know of the veiled secret? O impostor,
be quiet. What is your quarrel with the veiled keeper?

The ascetic thirsts for the wine of Heaven's fountain,
Hafez wants his glass refilled. Whom will God prefer?

Always a positive humanist, Hafez never accused the weak; he
excused them. He defended the downtrodden, reaching out to lift
them up. He rehabilitated the *rend* with his uniquely Persian
traits slightly decadent, charmingly vague, a free spirit with
savoir faire. He portrayed the *rend* as a seeker devoted to the path
of love whose quest is the ultimate act of liberation. For Hafez,
the flexible and imaginative Persian character held the key to survival in any troubled time. Proclaiming himself a *rend*, he defied
the *zahed*, the morally righteous:

Do not judge us, you who boast your purity —
No one will indict you for the faults of others.
What is it to you whether I am virtuous or a sinner?
Busy yourself with yourself!
Each in the end will reap the seed he himself has sown.
Every man longs for the Friend, the drunkard as much as
the awakened.
Every place is the House of Love, the Synagogue as much as
the Mosque.

He dismissed public postures of piety and despised religious
hypocrisy. He openly challenged the mullahs' blind obsession
with the letter of the law. By staring at minute details, they missed
out on the grandiosity of God. However strong his poetic attacks,
Iran's clergy has never dared to tamper with him or try to banish
his voice from the Iranian home or heart.

Today his verses are sung by popular traditional musicians, heard in bazaars over the radio, read at home and transmitted from one generation to the next. His poetry resonates with such power and poignant meaning that every listener or reader takes it personally, as if it had been written just for him or her.

"When you hear his words, it's like he's speaking to you right now," Akbar told us, shaking his head. "This is what's so amazing."

A young boy holding a birdcage passed by. Inside, a green parakeet was singing.

"We also believe that Hafez can see into the future. He has a solution to all our problems. Open his book and read. The answer is always there."

"I just turn the page?" Rich asked.

"No, you must first close the book and then open it at random."

"Like this?"

"*Baba*, no, you must close your eyes first, clear your mind, and call to Hafez."

Rich closed his eyes and opened the book. Akbar began his recitation: "Our webbed world's future lies knotted like closed buds; so float like a spring breeze unfolding new blooms." The melodious notes of a *tar* gently sounded around us.

"We Iranians," Akbar said, "turn to him whenever we feel lost, in pain, or of course in love. His poetry communicates with people of all levels. I can't really say why, but it's perfect. Everyone, man or woman, has private conversations with him."

Iranians seek advice from the *Divan* much as some of us consult our horoscopes, the *I Ching* or even the Runes. It was well known that Queen Victoria sought answers from Hafez.

The fourteenth century was a chaotic and violent age. Hafez watched as warriors on black-clad horses threatened his beloved Shiraz time and again. But only rarely did any of this political turmoil seep into his poetry. Instead, his focus was fixed on his love of God.

When the Turkic conqueror Timur loomed on the horizon, ready to sack the city — he had just annihilated every living soul in Isfahan, erecting a tower with seventy thousand skulls — legend has it that he confronted Hafez face to face. He was known as *Timur-e lang*, Limping Timur, because of his short leg, and in the West his name came to be Tamerlane.

Hafez had written in a poem that he would gladly trade away both of Timur's royal capitals, Samarkand and Bokhara, for the affections of a slender Turkish beauty. The rash warrior-emperor had taken these words as a grave insult against his native cities. Hafez calmly offered this explanation: "Sir, because of my reckless extravagant excesses, you can see how poor I am." Tamerlane's rage was defused, and Shiraz was spared. Instead of being decapitated, the poet was rewarded.

"Who's that?" My father noticed a colorfully clad, shaggy character who had just arrived in the teahouse.

"Don't point," said Chris.

"That fella. The one with the long white hair and tattered clothes."

"He's *darvish*, a Sufi," said Akbar.

I turned to look. Under his white bushy beard and eagle nose, he beamed a broad grin my way. His torn heavy coat was a handwoven paisley patchwork in bright orange and deep reds. His lambskin boots had walked many miles. Avo glanced up for a moment, then slipped back to his hubble-bubble pipe.

"What an amazing outfit," my mother remarked.

"That's his uniform," Akbar said.

"He's just showing off," said Avo.

"Do Sufis have their own mosques?"

"No. They have nothing," Akbar said.

"They're nowhere and everywhere. Like your gypsies," said Avo.

"Don't listen to him," Akbar said. "This one is an old-style *darvish*. But today Sufis are no longer wanderers — they're merchants, farmers, policemen, students and housewives. You may meet a Sufi and never know it."

On a Sufi journey, the teacher is the guide. He tells parables, riddles and stories to gently enlighten his devotees. The goal is to dissolve the ego. Just as a Zen Buddhist monk seeks to empty the ego completely, a Sufi aims at emptying his inner vessel. But in the world of *erfan*, the Persian path of mysticism, one empties the vessel so it can be filled with the bliss of divine love. Huston Smith, an authority on the history of religions, wrote, "The Sufis are the mystics of Islam. Every upright Muslim expects to see God after death, but the Sufis are the impatient ones. They want God now — moment by moment, day by day, in this very life."

As he poured our tea, Akbar told us that the Farsi word *divaneh*, crazy, has a double meaning in the Sufi lexicon. "It can also mean madly in love."

"I sign all my letters like that," said Kevin. "Madly."

"And our word *divaneh* is where you get your English word 'divine.'"

Once touched by the divine, Akbar assured us, one feels the illumination that Hafez described:

> If, like Jesus, stripped of everything, you ascend to Heaven,
> From your lantern a hundred rays will reach to light the sun.

"And this," said Akbar, "is exactly what many mullahs don't want. They say, 'No, we are the teachers. You have to follow us.'"

I looked up to see if anyone was eavesdropping.

Akbar went on. "Many people now are turning to the Sufi path. They are looking for a gentler Islam, a softness of the inner heart, for God's blessing. This is what President Khatami seems to be saying. Many people feel, when they hear him speak, that his words carry that *ishraq*, illumination."

Perhaps the simple act of paying our respects to Hafez was more rebellious than we had understood. Our teahouse under the stars, surrounded by honeycomb walls, bustled and hummed with fleeting glances. Couples sipped their sweet tea, students ate pistachios and rosewater ice cream, friends shared tobacco water pipes that burbled steadily away. It felt like a collective act of defiance.

A young woman with lovely almond-shaped eyes confidently strode over to our table and introduced herself to Kevin. He grinned and chatted away in his usual disarming manner that gave way to laughter. Heads turned to stare. Then the woman handed Kevin a note. Somewhat befuddled, he took it and she left.

"What's that?" I asked.

"She invited us to her home. It's her address."

"So you know her a long time?" asked Avo.

"No, I met her just now."

"Wow, I'm impressed," Avo said. "You work fast."

"Her name is Farinaz. She says she's a med student."

We nervously debated visiting our first Iranian home.

"But how can you trust her?" Avo said. "You don't know her."

"What if we're followed?" asked Chris, lobbying for a safe way out.

"Maybe they'll rob you," Avo added. "It could be a trap. You never know."

"I'd love to meet her family," said Mom.

An hour later, in the dark, we were lost in a suburb of Shiraz. Driving in circles, Nasrollah cursed while Akbar coaxed him right and then left. Lonely streetlamps dropped small pools of light on deserted sidewalks lined with high brick walls. There was no one to ask for directions. Avo advised us to turn back.

"You know . . . we tried. What if we can't find it?" Rich asked.

"No, no," my mother protested.

"We can bag it," Dad said.

Kevin said, "They may have dinner for . . ."

". . . ten people," my mother added.

"We don't want to have the next group be 'Death to Americans' because we left such a stellar example in Shiraz," Chris said.

"I said no seventeen times," Kevin insisted.

"And now we've got to go," my mother concluded.

"Think it'll be a big party?" I asked.

"We won't know," Avo said, "until we get there."

Finally we found the alley. Our van pulled over in the shadows and our engine stopped. A dog's howl sent a shudder up our spines as Kevin found the door and rang the bell. Farinaz opened it and greeted us, smiling, in blue jeans and no chador. My mother and father went in first, then all the brothers followed. Rising from the spacious carpeted floor, the entire family welcomed us.

We all shook hands before sitting down on the carpet, cross-legged with our backs braced on cushions against the wall. Tea was served. On the wall hung a small picture, silhouettes of a loving couple, cut out of delicate white lace. They were holding hands. We spoke of the warm weather, the gardens of Shiraz and the upcoming U.S.-Iran World Cup match. Instead of skipping over the potentially explosive subject, my dad, an avid soccer fan, pumped Farinaz's father about Iran's team. With a few players in Germany's Bundesliga, he told Dad, it should be a strong side, although his colleagues at the post office weren't as confident.

"And who do you want to win?" he asked.

"Iran, of course," Dad replied.

"Or maybe a draw?"

"Ah, yes."

Both laughed heartily at their diplomatic answers.

"Mr. Patrick," Farinaz said, "you should have been here when Iran qualified for the World Cup! The game was in Sydney, so we were up watching late at night. Then all Shiraz woke up! The streets were full of cars beeping horns, and people danced in traffic. The police could do nothing." She smiled. "They just watched."

"Sorry I missed it."

"Our next match, Mr. Patrick, against Amrika, will create big delirium, I promise!"

A warmth had settled over the room. Rich and Chris befriended the younger children and chatted away, telling jokes and getting responses. After our third round of tea, *santur* music with a bouncy rhythm played from a tape deck hidden from view.

Farinaz's precocious little brother and sister, in her Minnie Mouse T-shirt, got up to dance. We clapped softly to the beat until the boy pulled Chris up to join him. Blushing at first, Chris began to dance. He extended his arms with palms turned up. Soon they were flapping like storks in flight. It was his signature piece, perfected from childhood, one that showcased his fluidity.

Farinaz's siblings tried hard to mimic him but looked like frantic chickens and fell into giggling fits. Before long, Chris was twirling like a dervish. The children followed suit, spinning like tops before falling to the carpets in hysterics. By then, Kevin too had gotten up and was earnestly trying to teach some Fred Astaire footwork to another enthusiastic little brother. Then Farinaz hopped up and joined in, as if dancing were second nature to her. Each dancer circled the room miraculously missing the parents' legs. All were surprisingly agile. As I mirrored my own little partner's movements, I recalled how on feast days Hassan used to guide our feet to dance with abandon.

*Dan* is a Sanskrit word for religious behavior. From this root, apparently, the word "dance" entered our language. Sufis often used dance in their rituals to reach a higher state. Our harmless spectacle in Farinaz's house was anything but sacred, but we all felt a sense of liberation. Our cheeks were flushed red, we were panting, our eyes glowed. Apart from the odd World Cup victory, dancing occurred only behind closed doors, in the privacy of home. I was beginning to understand the country's two faces: inside and outside, *baten* and *zaher*. Intimacy and public face. Levity and austerity.

Dates as big as plums and more tea were brought out as we caught our breaths. I asked Farinaz about her medical studies.

"Very difficult. We must work very hard. Under the Shah, villages had few clinics or doctors. But now," she said with emphasis, "everyone has medical care. We know how important it is to serve the people."

She represented a new generation, dynamic and idealistic. I asked if many of the students had voted for Khatami.

"*Hameh*, all!" she answered. "Especially the women. Our president has promised he will make changes to improve society, and he talks about women's needs for the first time. He talks about a different Islam. He speaks about the God of love."

"Like Hafez?"

"Yes, exactly. And our president is also very handsome." She blushed as she filled Kevin's teacup. I sat down next to Farinaz's mother, who was discussing religion with Mom.

"Can you tell me, *khanoum*," she asked, "why do Christians and Muslims fight so much?"

"I don't know." My mother sighed.

"Why do they fight if there is only one God?"

"It's politics, always politics."

Farinaz nodded and asked, "And what is your religion?"

A silence filled the room. Then my mother replied, "The same as Hafez!"

All applauded except Avo.

As we stood up to leave, Farinaz offered my mother a gift: a copy of Hafez's *Divan*. Moved by the kindness, Mom touched the cover, closed her eyes, whispered his name and opened the book at random. Farinaz read from the page in her melodious Farsi, translating the lines as she went on:

> I have learned so much from God
> That I no longer call myself
> A Christian, a Hindu, a Muslim,
> A Buddhist, a Jew.
> The Truth has shared so much of Itself with me
> That I can no longer call myself
> A man, a woman, an angel, or even pure soul.
> Love has befriended Hafez so completely
> It has turned to ash and freed me
> Of every concept and image
> my mind has ever known.

"Blind luck, Mom," said Kevin as we stumbled outside into the darkness. We had to wake up Nasrollah, fast asleep in the van.

\*       \*       \*

Back at the Apadana Hotel, I sat down in the empty bar, elated and tired. The lobby was quiet. A lone concierge looked up and offered me a copy of the *Iran Daily*, a new English-language paper. I read the headlines of April 11:

> Mayor Questioned for Six Hours at Evin Prison
> 118 Pilgrims Die in Mecca Stampede
> UN Human Rights Commission Faults Iran: Admits
>     Improvements in the Khatami Era
> Russians Dismiss Israeli Claims over Warheads
> Yeltsin and Nazarbayev Discuss Control of Caspian Sea

On the back page I found a promising column, "What's Up," which contained a number of short news items, including:

- **Human Rights Watch** called on Iran to hold a fair and public trial for Tehran's mayor, Gholamhussein Karbaschi, who was arrested on corruption charges. "We feel this is a politically motivated act," wrote Hanny Megally, director of the group's Middle East and North Africa division, in a letter to the Iranian judiciary. The issue has polarized the Islamic Regime, with moderates accusing the conservative opponents of seeking to destabilize President Khatami's Administration.

- **The Satanic Verses,** which prompted Iran to impose a death sentence on British author Salman Rushdie over its alleged insult to Islam, is to be published in worldwide paperback. The book sold more than 250,000 since it was published nine years ago. The Guardian quoted Rushdie, "While this is, of course, a satisfying final step, it's really scarcely more than a reprint." The author has been in hiding since the late Ayatollah Ruhollah Khomeini issued a *Fatwa* on the author's life in February 1989. He later backed up the decree with a $1.6 million bounty.

- **The Jerusalem Post** reported that Iran "with Russian help will soon pass a critical milestone in developing an engine for a medium-range missile capable of reaching Israel . . . Israel has been using its friends in the US Congress to press for sanctions against Russian companies participating in Iran's missile program. The Shahab 3 will reportedly have a range of 1,300 kilometers with a

payload of 700 kilograms — capable of carrying conventional or
non-conventional warheads as far as Israel."

- **German Foreign Minister Klaus Kinkel** said on Wednesday
  that Bonn had failed to secure a pardon for a German businessman condemned to death in Iran for having sexual relations out
  of wedlock with a Muslim woman.

Prayer times were also listed: Dawn, 5:16; Sunrise, 6:43; Noon,
13:07; Evening, 19:52.

Under a column called "Hotline," a Mr. T. Shiralilon complained about the absence of a hotel in Maouleh village, a charm-
ing spot in the Caspian forest of Gilan that attracts a large number of visitors. Another citizen, P. Mehrjouei, discussed Iran's
"brain drain" and how the lack of facilities and incentives pre-
vented scientists from pursuing careers inside the country. "It is
no less than the flight of national treasures," he wrote, implor-
ing the authorities to learn from countries that successfully attract foreign talent. Yet another reader wrote the paper simply to
ask that officials provide more telephones in Karaj, a city near
Tehran.

On the entertainment page, a headline trumpeted: "Holly-
wood Returns to Iran After Two Decades." During the two-week
*Nowruz* holiday, it was reported, more than a dozen American
films were shown on state television's five channels, including
Charlie Chaplin and Buster Keaton movies, Steven Spielberg's
*E.T.*, and *Robo Cop*.

The sports page featured color photographs of Michael Jordan
soaring to the basket and Tiger Woods blasting out of a sandtrap
at the Masters in Augusta, along with reports of the Tour de
France and Michael Schumacher's Formula One victory.

The *Daily* offered more entertainment and healthy self-criti-
cism than any other Middle Eastern newspaper that I could remember. Mayor Karbaschi's arrest and trial were of foremost
concern, and several articles described this political litmus test
signaling the long-awaited public battle between moderates and
conservative hard-liners. One headline advised caution: "Ayatol-

lah Emami Kashani Calls for Keeping Society Free from Tension," a plea for calm heads after Karbaschi's arrest.

I had expected a news blackout of the depraved West, or at best a tainted journalism with a pro-government slant. Instead, I was reading direct quotes from the *Jerusalem Post*, the *Guardian*, the U.S. State Department spokesman James Rubin and his boss Madeleine Albright. Incidentally, the *Iran Daily* reported that Secretary of State Albright offered a cryptic apology to Iranian wrestlers, invited for a tournament in Oklahoma, for the rude treatment they received from U.S. immigration officials, who fingerprinted the athletes when they touched American soil.

In the throes of revolutionary change, the press here seemed much more open than I remembered during my years in Sadat's Egypt after the signing of the Camp David peace accords.

I put down the paper and noticed a man sipping a Zam Zam cola in a corner of the bar. I invited myself over and we began to talk. He was a Frenchman, and his interest was oil. Always oil. Iran's blessing and her curse. My father walked in, sat down with us and began to speak about the first place in Iran where black gold was struck in 1908, the British camp at Masjid-e Suleiman, in the foothills of Khuzestan. By the site of an ancient Achaemenian temple, later renamed the Mosque of Solomon, lay the unrefined origin of British Petroleum, once known to the world as the Anglo-Iranian Oil Company.

My father described flying into Masjid-e Suleiman in 1958. "I'd never seen conditions like that in my life," he said. "Grim and hopeless. Everyone still living in tents like refugees in a bad dream. Brits from India waiting to do their five-year service before getting a paid trip home. They were all out of their minds. A pathetic raj in miniature. Different pay scales for each nationality: the English supervisors on top and then the Indian accountants. The poor Iranian laborers were given nothing. The only incentives they got were tiny bonuses. I remember there was even one for catching rats."

"*Alors*, this is terrible. Rats?" the Frenchman, Philippe, said.

"The rat catcher's allowance," my father told us, "was a bonus given for each dead rat, half a rial. Clever way to keep the place clean, they thought. I remember a bright young Iranian had received the most bonuses by far. I went over to his barrack and discovered that he was actually breeding them in cages behind his tent, just to make a little extra from those cheap Brits. Couldn't blame him."

"Despicable, those English," sneered Philippe. "We French would surely have treated them better."

"Like in Algiers?"

"But Patrick, that was different. Algérie was zee France."

"At any rate, the British had been pumping oil in Iran for fifty years and there wasn't a single trained Iranian technician. It was a scandal. In Arabia, where I had been working, a whole generation was being trained."

The Frenchman rolled his eyes, nursed his thoughts, puffing on his Gitanes. He was that odd dapper foreigner who can be found in every Near Eastern country, a self-appointed expert on all things, who always explains why the local regime is worthy of support. He praised the mullahs, with whom he'd been negotiating oil concessions. "They're quite amusing, you know. Some have a fine sense of humor."

It was just the three of us sitting in what had been a swinging bar before the Revolution. A sleepy concierge served us a round of Zam Zams. A photograph of turbaned Khamenei stared down from the wood-paneled wall. A travel poster advertised the sunbleached columns of Persepolis; its arabesque turquoise script read, "Islamic Republic of Iran."

Having recently returned from the Khuzestan oilfields in the west, Philippe was now surveying the refinery in Shiraz for possible business opportunities. He put down his Zam Zam and sighed. "You speak of history? *L'empereur* once had great plans for this country. Iran missed her big chance. Napoleon's grand army could have marched all the way to Calcutta. Then, no more British." He slapped his thigh.

"*Bolshaya Igra*," said Pat.

"'Zcuse me?"

"The Great Game."

"Ah, yes. Well, that would have changed many things."

I had first found Philippe insufferable, with his pinched mustache and darting eyes. Yet he had a point. What if Napoleon had made it all the way to India? It's not often, I realized, that a Frenchman abroad gets to relive the joys of Napoleon's aspirations.

"*L'empereur*, ah yes, on the Neiman River they divided the world. But the czar wanted Istanbul. Napoleon refused. First we take India, he said, then we'll see."

"So they planned to march across Iran?" I asked.

"Of course. Well, look here, in those days one didn't ask permission for that sort of thing."

Philippe's eyebrows twitched. He lit another cigarette. The murky intrigues of the Great Game filled the smoky room. He sketched out the route along the coffee table, navigating around our Zam Zams. His finger traced Levantine ports, then passed through the cedars of Lebanon and across the napkin that served as the Syrian desert.

"*Voilà*, now we go down zee Euphrates and up over the Zagros. It must be in spring, for the good weather. Then we cross the plateau to India." He was panting with excitement. I noticed beads of sweat on his brow. It felt surreal, in this darkened lounge, to be marching like this. I looked over at my father, who winked at me.

We both watched as Philippe's finger made its way through the treacherous Hindu Kush, another crumpled napkin, stained cola-brown on the far side of the table. The sleeping plains of India lay below. Finally Dad leaned over to utter one word, "Moscow." It all ended then and there. Philippe came crashing to earth with his Zam Zam. The entire Syrian desert was covered in dark, sticky soda.

In a Baltic town, there is a plaque. Peter Hopkirk describes it in his book *The Great Game*. It sums up the Russian winter. On one side is written, "Napoleon Bonaparte passed this way in 1812 with 400,000 men." On the other, "Napoleon Bonaparte passed this way in 1812 with 9,000 men."

"Ah, Napoleon," Philippe moaned, wiping at his spilled Zam Zam. "Why did he have to go to bloody Russia? Why?" I helped mop up his mess.

When Philippe's partner entered the tavern, we all stood up and shook hands. Reza wore a trimmed beard and the kind of tieless suit so popular in Iran today. His eyes shone like dead moons.

Yes, he told us, he had overheard our comments. But it was not the French or the Russians that Iranians feared, and not even the Americans. It was the British.

"The British hand has been in everything. Even taking down the Shah and bringing back Imam Khomeini."

Listening to Reza, I remembered Hassan's joke: "When a neighbor is talking rough, insulting his wife, the English must be behind it." For centuries, Anglophobia had explained virtually every vice in Iran.

"Let me ask you something about the British," Reza said. "Didn't they force their way into Iran from India? And didn't one Englishman, D'Arcy, buy the concession for everything that lay under the soil? How in God's name," Reza asked, "could the Shah sell the right to all our oil to an Englishman? But he did. And didn't another Englishman, Reuters, buy the rights to the national railroad and the national bank? And wasn't the entire tobacco crop given to the British for nothing? And didn't all this begin the constitutional revolution of 1906?"

Reza went on to remind us why it failed. In 1907 the Russians and the British secretly divided up Persia, with the north going to the czar and the south going to the king. But in 1917 the British occupied the country with the intention of making it a protectorate. And with the long-awaited fall of the hated Qajars, he asked, wasn't the new Shah Pahlavi really chosen by General Ironside? "Of course, he was," Reza sniffed. "And during the Second World War, in 1941, when England and Russia invaded us, wasn't the Shah unceremoniously bundled off?"

"To Johannesburg," I replied.

"And by whom?"

I ventured a guess. "The British?"

"Of course, *baba*." He smiled warmly.

I told Reza that George Bernard Shaw once wrote, "An Englishman does everything on principles: he fights you on patriotic principles; he robs you on business principles; he enslaves you on imperial principles."

"Yeeees! Exactly." He was beaming.

The refrain "The English, of course" lives on in the Iranian psyche of conspiracy theories. Its literary epicenter is one of the best satires ever written in Farsi, *Da'i-i Jan Napuli'un*, or *My Dear Uncle Napoleon*.

Published in the early 1970s, Iraj Pezeshkzad's howlingly funny bestseller also aired as a highly successful series on Iranian television. Its cast of much-loved characters lampooned the inbred belief that every detail of Iran's destiny has been manipulated for the last two centuries by the "hidden hand" of the British. Yet the comic character of Uncle Napoleon did more to confirm longheld views of English manipulation than dispel them. "Satire," Jonathan Swift wrote, "is a sort of glass wherein the beholders do generally discover everyone's face but their own."

*My Dear Uncle Napoleon* takes place during World War II, behind the walls of a leafy garden estate in northern Tehran, where the fidgety megalomaniac Uncle Napoleon, a retired colonel, holds court with his extended family, repeating tales of exaggerated bravery in inflated battles as the invading British troops approach the capital. Comic household intrigues move among love stories, mistaken identities, henpecked husbands, family rifts, and Uncle's obsession that Churchill's agents are plotting night and day to seize him.

Uncle Napoleon, the neurotic patriot, steals our hearts. He has earned his nickname through an undying admiration for the French general, whom he quotes with passion. Pezeshkzad, a cultivated, worldly and long-serving officer in Iran's diplomatic corps, masterfully weaves Uncle Napoleon's imaginary battles with windmills as the narrative builds to a fever pitch.

The family's collective Anglophobia reaches a climax when Uncle accuses Mash Qasem, his faithful servant, of being a British agent. Uncle points a rifle at him, and Qasem confesses to plotting with the enemy, yet the reader knows he's never met an Englishman in his life. Qasem is so consumed by his master's delusion that he actually believes he has unwittingly become a spy. Such are the powers of the British that they are capable of making anyone a spy, even without him knowing!

When I uttered the magic words "Uncle Napoleon," Reza broke into laughter. Philippe perked up.

"'Zcuse me. Napoleon, you said?"

"Is a very famous story. Very funny too," Reza said.

Philippe was thrilled to hear the story. "*Voilà.* I knew the Iranians would have loved our *empereur.*"

"Of course," sighed Reza, playing Mash Qasem.

"I'm not so sure," I said.

"Of course they would," Philippe insisted.

"*Baba,* it's true. Anything but the English. Anything."

The two partners gleefully shook hands.

In 1941, when British and Russian forces seized the Iranian lion by the throat and occupied the country, Reza Shah's young Swiss-educated son, a playboy, was thrust upon the peacock throne. The old Shah was sent off on a British warship, first to Mauritius and then to the Transvaal — surely not the retirement spot he had in mind. And there he died.

By 1951, all eyes had turned to oil and the Persian Gulf. A newly elected prime minister, Mohammad Mossadegh, had shocked London and Washington by nationalizing Iran's oil, ending all of Britain's claims. No wonder. He had discovered that Iran's royalty income was less than the taxes paid to the British treasury. And that was the end of that.

Overnight, Mossadegh became the darling of Third World leaders. *Time* made him its "Man of the Year." The London press labeled the defiant leader "Mossy." Meanwhile, the world's most powerful oil companies — Standard Oil, Shell, Socal, Socony, Texaco and Gulf — rallied round the Anglo-Iranian Oil Company. These "seven sisters" refused to load a single drop of Iranian crude onto their tankers. Their collective boycott worked.

Two years later, Iran's economy lay in shambles. Mossadegh's popular dream of national sovereignty was in grave danger. The young Shah, fearful of being stripped of his monarchical powers, secretly fled to Rome. Sulking in his Via Veneto haunt, he waited for news from British agents in Tehran directing an archetypal cold-war coup that would end "Moussy's" bold experiment. U.S. dollars are said to have flooded the bazaars and financed mobs that surrounded Prime Minister Mossadegh's home in northern Tehran. In 1953, the Shah returned on a magic carpet stitched together by MI-6 and its eager new partner, the American CIA.

The year of the infamous coup, Freya Stark, the indomitable Middle East traveler, looked out over the skyline of Abadan, the focus of Britain's interests in Iran that drove both nations to the brink of war: "I am sitting contemplating the beauties of civilization — a forest of tall chimneys, an expanse of iron aluminium-painted tanks, a belching column of smoke which burns year in and year out — the Anglo-Persian oil port . . . Looking south the great river flows quiet and flat between palm groves just as the Sumerians saw it; and north it might be Glasgow except for the sun."

All for the oil. With the Shah back on the throne, CIA operatives strutted into the spotlight, taking more credit than was due, though everyone in power knew that British intelligence ran the operation. Such grandstanding helped divert public and congressional criticism from American fiascoes in Guatemala and the Bay of Pigs. Kermit Roosevelt, the Middle East CIA station chief and grandson of President Theodore Roosevelt, spoke proudly and openly about the newly formed agency's first successful coup. The British were only too happy to see him do so.

Unabashedly, he chronicled the glamorous plot line in his book, *Countercoup: The Struggle for the Control of Iran.* Roosevelt detailed numerous highlights: his original summons to London by the British secret service, flying into Iran in disguise, hiding in car trunks, sneaking into Golestan Palace, paying hundreds of thousands of dollars to street toughs, staging popular demonstrations and, finally, welcoming the Shah back home at Mehrabad Airport. At that historic moment when his feet touched the tarmac, the Shah shook Roosevelt's hand and said, "I owe my throne to my God, my people — and to you."

In time, Iranians would transfer their suspicion and anger from the British to the brash Americans and their eager pupil, the Shah. Conspiracy theories were fueled for generations to come.

We heard a bang on the glass door and looked up. The door opened and Avo was holding his nose as he entered the bar. He was in obvious pain. He had been listening when his nose got caught in the motion of the swinging doors.

"Mr. Ward, you forgot to talk about the Trilateral Commission of Jimmy Carter and Henry Kissinger? Or the Freemasons who want to dominate the world?"

No one replied. It was too late. Philippe was tired and Reza was yawning. We had become pleasantly exhausted of conspiracy talk. We all got up to leave.

But what about Avo, I wondered, walking past the sleeping night guard before climbing the stairs with Dad. Was he simply a translator randomly assigned to join us from Richard's travel agency? Just who was Avo really working for?

7

# Every Place Is Kerbela

Every day is Ashura, every place is Kerbela.

— Ayatollah Khomeini

A HUNDRED MILES north of Shiraz, on the way to Yazd, the desert road was blocked by a Qashqai tribe migrating to higher pastures on frisky horses and mules. Barking dogs herded flocks of sooty white and black sheep, scruffy plump mutton wagging their drooping tails — fortunes of *kebab* on the hoof.

"Turks . . . barbarians," Avo muttered under his breath.

"They're Irani, Avo," said Rich.

"Not really."

"Sure they are."

"You don't know. They're dirty and uneducated. The Shah settled them down and built cement houses for them. For free."

"And what happened?"

"They pitched their tents in the middle of the courtyards and slept outside."

"So who slept inside?"

"Their sheep. They put them in the rooms. You call that civilized?"

"In a Qashqai kind of way."

"Richard, come on, I thought you were a modern guy."

"But their permanent homes were short-lived. In the chaos of the Revolution, they packed up and hit the road," Akbar added, pulling out his map of Fars and pointing to a valley wedged deep in the mountains. He called it "hidden heaven." In the summer, the Qashqai pitched their tents by the River Kor, high up on the green-flecked Zagros, where their sheep grazed and their campfires blazed under the stars. "One day we must go there," he said.

Our journey continued through hostile landscape. Nasrollah weaved his unwieldy van over a heartless pass known as Couly Kush, Killer of Gypsies. In winter, he said, even the toughest nomads could not cross it. Stretches of scrub desert opened across the eastern horizon. Blue snow-capped mountains rose to the west. Crows flew overhead, gray wings and bellies with black heads and tails. We stopped at a roadside checkpoint. A bored-looking policeman began his search.

"They're looking for *taryak*, opium," Akbar told us while Nasrollah was being questioned. "Many smoke *taryak*. It comes in from Afghanistan. They are the biggest opium producers, thousands of tons a year."

Above us on the flanking hill, I could spot Qashqai freely moving ahead in a thin line. A bald, grumpy soldier in ill-fitting khakis asked where I was from. He looked far too serious for my usual answer, "The Great Satan."

"Amrika," I replied, using my best Farsi accent. He nodded and then shouted at a waiting truck packed with young Afghan men. Illegal immigration was as much a problem here as in southern California. The Soviet invasion of Afghanistan, a brutal civil war, and now the fundamentalist Taliban had forced millions of refugees into neighboring Iran. Once across the border, they found work and safety instead of hunger and fear. But after two decades, their hosts' welcome was wearing thin.

"Better than them, *bah*." He spit. "You tourist?"

"Yes."

"You come to Iran, you leave, *insha'allah*."

I looked at his gun. "*Insha'allah*." I laughed nervously.

"Then you are better than them."

"Why?"

"They come, never leave."

Tipping his plastic-brimmed cap, the soldier squinted to study the ridge line above us. The faint tinkling of sheep's bells could be heard. The Qashqai had crossed over to the other side of the hill and were far from any checkpoint.

"And they," he sighed, "they came long time ago and never left."

In Iran there has always been tension between farmer, city dweller and nomadic shepherd. It is an age-old rivalry. Over the centuries, waves of tribes from central Asia rode into the country, searching for grazing land. Still today nomads herd their flocks to pasturelands with the changing seasons. Forever on the move in the mountains, their two contributions to the Iranian economy are carpets and mutton. Townspeople and peasants view these wandering sheepherders in the way that many Europeans view Gypsies. Few admire their proud nomadic tradition.

Iran emerged as a complex, ethnically rich mosaic of Farsi-speaking urban dwellers, making up only about half of the population, and Turkic-speaking clans and tribes of Azeris, Baluchis, Kermani, Turkomans and Qashqai.

"Imagine my village only fifty years ago," Hassan never tired of saying. "Mud walls and four towers. The wooden gates closed at night, and outside, robbers roamed freely. Travel was dangerous business, like a time of cowboys and Indians."

Each village was its own walled island. Beyond was a cruel ocean with few ports for shelter. Any journey was filled with fear and uncertainty. Few brave souls risked it. And they never traveled alone. "When my father went out in his caravan with twenty or thirty people," Hassan told us, "he knew he might never come back. That's why each time he said to his brother, 'I have this much money. If I don't come back, then give it to my family.' "

At night, under the stars, Hassan used to tell us how his village was protected by mud walls fifteen feet high, pierced with holes for lookouts. At sunset, all the sheep and camels were herded inside and the gate was closed. But everyone knew it was their hero, the crack shot Haj Ali Jamail, and not the high walls that kept the roving Qashqai raiding parties at bay. So sneaky were the Qashqai that they would strap bits of carpet on their horses' hooves to quiet their advance in the dead of night. Each evening, as Hassan drifted off to sleep as a young boy, two guards on watch would cry out to each other, "Be ready there!" and "Hey you, pay attention!"

Armed with British-issue rifles and riding on horseback, Qashqai tribesmen would burst into sleeping villages in search of booty: bronze plates, carpets, dishes, money, sheep, anything of value. When the raiding season began, Hassan hid the family's bronze tray inside a hole in their mud wall. It was the only valuable possession they owned. "Thank God for Haj Ali Jamail," he would tell us. Once a notorious bandit, Haj Ali later in life went to Mecca on pilgrimage and found redemption and God. Upon his return, Haj Ali offered his marksmanship to his defenseless village. Qashqai raiders knew of his keen eye and rifle, so they left Tudeshk in peace. And each night, the voices on the ramparts echoed in little Hassan's ears: "You there, stay awake." "Hey you, don't fall asleep."

Under the Qajars, the British armed the tribes, and the Germans funneled in weapons too. The logic was simple: the stronger the tribes, the weaker the Shah. The great chieftains of the Qashqai and the Bakhtiari hosted diplomatic emissaries from Britain in their mountain grazing grounds under royal red tents, feasting on roasted mutton, watching feats of bravery and horsemanship. Agreements were signed. Treaties forged. The Shahs seated in Tehran could do nothing to prevent these independent tribal leaders or Khans from doing whatever they wished, even becoming pawns of British agents in the struggle for power. But that all changed when Reza Shah Pahlavi took the throne in 1925. From then on, a ruthless pattern emerged. The Shah invited tribal leaders to the capital and later did away with them, emasculating the great families of their anarchic chieftains. Then he unleashed his troops. Hassan remembered those days well. "One night, from my village, we saw two hundred soldiers. So we killed four goats for them. Praise God, they were chasing the *Turki*."

The banditry and mayhem of the Qashqai and Bakhtiari subsided and their weapons were confiscated. Forced settlements locked them in place on the land under the close watch of the army, and the lawless tribes were decimated in attacks by armored cars and planes.

Only years later, well after Hassan came to work in Tehran at the age of seven, did Tudeshk's mud towers and high walls come tumbling down. They were dismantled by hands that knew that the marauding days of the raiders were finally over. Slowly, all over Iran, villagers and townspeople poked their heads out of their homes and tasted the forbidden view of the horizon.

The sun beat overhead as I thought of Hassan's old nemesis, the Qashqai, trekking in the hills beyond us. Not slowed down by police checkpoints, they moved faster here than any truck on the road.

I heard a groan behind me. Kevin, in the back of the van with a splitting headache, had covered his eyes with a black scarf, and my mother dabbed his forehead with a moist cloth.

"On journeys like this," Rich explained to Akbar matter-of-factly, "odds are someone always has to fall." My father nodded while I passed him some water. Moaning quietly, Kev was our sacrificial lamb for the long drive that lay ahead, across the desert in the direction of Hassan's Tudeshk.

A passing truck sprayed a cloud of diesel fumes that snuffed out our view, spilling its petro-stench through our windows. When the gray fog lifted, an overloaded bus packed with passengers roared past, tilting heavily on its right side. On the back window were bold English words in red: *Don't Forget God.*

"Glad we aren't riding on that bus," said Mom, covering Kevin's face with her scarf.

"*Al-hamdulillah*, praise God," Akbar said.

"*Al-hamdulillah*," I instinctively echoed.

"Why is it written in English?" Chris wondered.

"That driver's just trying to be chic," answered Avo.

Although the message felt old-fashioned, the font was decid-

edly modern: a spiritual billboard for the new theocracy and a reminder of the Almighty.

In the past few days, I had noticed that God — *Allah* in Arabic, *Khoda* in Farsi — was never far from people's tongues. "By
God," *Be Khoda*; "Praise God," *Al-hamdulillah*; "If God wills,"
*Insha'allah*; "God protect you," *Khoda hafez* — these phrases are
sprinkled into conversations with the same frequency that Americans use "Have a nice day." They are common forms of speech
in ancient cultures with strong traditions. Throughout Asia,
whether in Iran, India or Indonesia, God is continually evoked
in daily life. And for travelers, these expressions serve as a gentle
form of insurance. After all, only that morning, in Shiraz, the
concierge of the Apadana had waved us off with the classic Persian saying *Mosafer aziz Khodast*, "The traveler is beloved by
God."

Each of us was uniquely suited for this journey: fellow travelers. Chris flashed lightning strokes of fear at the oddest moments
with his high-pitched confused questions. His confidence was
frayed, pulled tight like piano wire. Kev chose to counter Chris's
shrill outbursts with a Zen-like silence, as if patient observation
were the only antidote. Unruffled Rich was neither silent nor
anxious. Overly concerned with detail, our younger brother meticulously tracked our slow, plodding, step-by-step advance. My
mother's mending ankle had been strengthened by the unusual
reunion with her four sons. And Pat, ever the patriarch, kept
firing one-liners just to keep us straight and Avo off guard.

At the roadside village of Sarmaq, stunning swatches of sprouting green wheat fields added a brief flash of life to the bleached
landscape. Just as I spied a forlorn dirt road heading into the distance, Nasrollah wrenched his wheel to the right, and we spun off
the comfortably paved north-south highway and rumbled into
the desert. A dense cloud of dust billowed around us. We quickly
lost sight of what lay behind. Our direction now pointed east, to
the ancient Zoroastrian stronghold of Yazd, a city in the geographic heart of Iran.

The van bounced along the rutted waves of packed clay that rolled before us. We flew into air: I cracked my head on the roof, Chris ended up in Richard's lap, Avo lost his glasses, Kev slid onto the floor. The van filled with a chorus of instant howls. Startled, Nasrollah pulled his heavy foot off the gas pedal. He turned around and offered his profuse apologies to one and all. When he saw my father, he put special emotion in his "*bebakhsheed.*" Dad was dripping wet, liberally doused by my flying bottle of water, but he took it in stride, laughing at the chaos.

"It's OK, *agha!*" he said. "It really woke me up."

"And your wet shirt should cool you down, dear," my mother said.

She gently dabbed his neck and ears with a dry cloth. His eyes gleamed as if he had been anointed by an archbishop's sprinkle of holy water. A boyish smile crossed his face. Flushed from the high altitude, his apple-rosy cheeks had already caught enough of the sun's rays to turn a color that was naturally Irish — bright red. He turned to look at my mother with tenderness.

"We must travel," John Berryman once advised, "in the direction of our fear." But I could see that my parents carried none. Together they stared ahead with wonder.

A hellish drive faced us: ten hours across a wasteland and over two mountain passes to reach the grim Dasht-e Lut, a desert that blankets the center of the country in chilling silence. There, our path east would end abruptly at Yazd. Beyond this city, the hostile terrain competed with Saudi Arabia's Empty Quarter, China's Gobi Desert and the Libyan Sahara as the most terrifying land on earth. This desert supported no life. And no illusions. It was, quite simply, impassable.

On my map, I studied our route. It was a thin red line, faint and fragile — not that healthy thick blue line that we had just abandoned. It traversed mountains that appeared to rise out of no man's land. Only one village, the map predicted, lay astride this road. Broken lines of dry riverbeds and creatively colored elevation zones filled large empty spaces. A rumpled backbone of an alpine ridge cut north to south across our path. The highest peak was Sher Kuh, Lion Mountain, elevation 13,036 feet.

Our gait slowed to a teeth-rattling pace until the road began to flatten out and the blacktop unfolded like a welcome mat before us. Shark-tooth ranges tipped with ice loomed in the distance. A debate on the color white began.

"Beautiful snow," said Rich.

"What do you mean?" asked Avo.

"What do I mean? It's snow." Rich pointed at the towering peaks to the west.

"That's not snow."

"Of course it is."

"It can't be," said Avo. "It's too dry here."

"So then what is it?"

Avo thought for a moment. "Salt."

"You can't have a salt deposit on a mountaintop."

"Why not?"

"Geologically, it's impossible."

"You know, Richard, in Iran many things are possible."

Rich threw up his hands. "You're crazy."

"I may not be that smart," Avo said, "but I'm not that stupid. You see, I work a little bit in between."

"Convenient," muttered Kev under his scarf. "The world according to Avo."

Over millennia, the snow has helped Iran to survive. Cursed with little rain — only a few inches annually — the countryside's water source lies in the last place you'd look. Cloaked each winter with snowfall, the high mountain summits act like giant reservoirs. During the hottest months of summer, slow dripping snowmelt filters through the bedrock. Trickles of the precious liquid are coaxed by gravity through ingenious manmade underground canals called *qanats* into desert cities, towns and farms miles away. When the ice caps disappear, everyone fears the drought.

Kevin wasn't enjoying the view. He was still groaning, defeated by a bug that had gripped his throat all the way from New York. He lay sprawled across the back seat, our first casualty.

"Ahriman's got me," he muttered, cursing the Zoroastrian god of evil. Mom's scarf shielded his eyes from the sun's glare. She took my bottle and nursed him with the little water we had left. Yes, our spirits were willing, but our bodies were still learning how to travel.

With each passing hour, the desert unfolded with sandswept monotony. Unexpectedly, I thrilled to see this landscape. Nasrollah's erratic driving shook loose more recollections. Adrenaline staved off sleep amid the engine's roar. Long-forgotten images flashed by. A lone hut with a sleek poplar. Warm smells of dry land. The raw beauty of desolation, so welcome in its bleakness, so firm in its severity. And so liberating, with no billboards, motels or shopping malls.

The pre-revolutionary "Mad Max" driving frenzy that we remembered so well had been truly calmed. Apart from a few close calls, the roads had been quiet, orderly and well paved. The hulks of cars that I remember rusting at the bottom of chasms and riverbeds were no more. Draconian laws and checkpoints had tamed flamboyant driving habits.

My mother recalled a brush with death that almost hurled her and her boys over a cliff after an afternoon of skiing, thirty-five years ago in the mountains above Tehran.

"Remember coming back from the Noor Club by Ab-e Ali, when we almost ended up in the valley below?" she asked.

How could we forget? I shivered at the memory of her driving along those switchback alpine roads above the yawning chasms that dropped thousands of feet.

That afternoon, an out-of-control truck skidding on ice careened around a corner and toward us. My mother pulled over to the asphalt's edge as the truck fishtailed. Pressing our noses to the window, Rich and I helplessly watched. Its bumper missed our left door by inches. After the danger had passed and the truck gained control again, we all jumped out and stared at each other as if a true miracle had spared us. My mother was shaking. Our right wheels clung to the farthest edge of the pavement, inches from a sheer drop. One gentle nudge and we would have been killed.

"After Abarqu, there is nothing," Akbar reminded us, "between us and Yazd." A quick cup of coffee was not an option. Nor was a glass of water. "The desert is an ocean on which we can walk," wrote Napoleon. "It is the image of immensity." If he had tried to march his army across these limitless wastes to India, it certainly would have been swallowed up more completely than in Moscow's snows.

Yet Marco Polo had passed this way seven hundred years ago. After tromping over this forbidding land, the wandering Venetian must have been exhilarated to reach utterly remote Yazd and find sprouting wind towers, fire temples and a cool bazaar with honey-dripping sweets. The remoteness had always been the city's protective barrier. Lonely Yazd was one of the few Persian cities spared by the galloping Mongol hordes. Genghis Khan simply couldn't find it.

Richard's curiosity about Yazd's Zoroastrian heritage had sealed our route. In any case, no one else in the family had taken the time to study the map. With an Irish fatalism, they surrendered to the road ahead. Only I knew the precise details. One hundred thirty miles beyond Yazd lay Tudeshk, Hassan's village.

Italo Calvino described the curious effect of travel on memory: "Arriving at each new city, the traveler finds again a past of his that he did not know he had: the foreignness of what you no longer are or no longer possess lies in wait for you in foreign, unpossessed places." What were we going to find in the end? A past we didn't know we had?

Abarqu was a half-abandoned mud-brick town in pitiless solitude. We drove into it at midday. Camouflaged by sand, the empty streets showed no signs of life. But just south of town we came upon a cypress tree that stood like a wondrous minaret. Towering like an ancient redwood, its massive trunk was as thick as the tropical banyan, which the Balinese wrap with sacred cloth and worship as an abode of the spirits. Branching out with needle-clad arms, reaching vertically to the sky, it soared alone. Akbar told us that this immense tree had first shaded migrating Aryans from the northern steppes. With her bright saffron parasol, my mother also sought shelter under its welcoming branches.

John Berger, the English writer, wrote of origins spawned by such trees. "Long before any numerals or mathematics, when human language was first naming the world, trees offered their measures — of distance, of height, of diameter, of space. They were taller than anything else alive, their roots went deeper than any creature; they grazed the sky and sounded the underworld. From them was born the idea of the pillar, the column."

A pitted, rusty turquoise sign hoped to explain the tree's long pedigree in Farsi and English, but the sand-scoured lettering left me guessing. This sacred cypress of Abarqu was some sort of monument, but there was more.

"Look at this design," Akbar said, pointing to the paisley pattern on his scarf. "It's a cypress, the symbol of my country. And why do you think it is bending?" he asked rhetorically. "From the weight of Arab invaders. It's bending, but never broken."

"A silent witness," my mother said from the shade. "Imagine how many invasions it has seen."

"Too many, Mrs. Ward."

So the famed paisley, synonymous with Indian prints, was actually a drooping Persian cypress from Iran. Perhaps the pattern had come to India with the invading Farsi-speaking Afghan armies who founded the Mughal dynasty. Or even earlier, with the Parsees of Bombay, who had fled Muslim persecution and carried Zoroaster's fire into exile with them. Whoever carried the cypress to the banks of the Ganges, the symbol was a protest. Woven and sewn into carpets and fabrics, the paisley served as a silent reminder of Persian suffering under Arab subjugation. Bent, but not broken.

\*       \*       \*

Arabia Deserta, the historic name for Saudi Arabia, had always been a parched, marginalized land, a depressed cultural backwater in antiquity. Along the Red Sea coast stood a few ramshackle trading towns dotted with palms. In the scorched interior, Bedouin tribes fought, raided and squabbled over camels, possessions and women. At night, tales were spun over campfires in the poetic tradition of their fathers and the fathers before them.

But in the year 610, the life of these Arabic-speaking desert nomads forever changed. In Mecca on a humid night, a pious forty-year-old spice merchant retreated to a cave outside the city to meditate. There, while in prayer, a ball of fire came to him. From this fiery vision he heard the word "Recite." Mohammad was stunned. Then the voice spoke again: "Recite!" Mohammad's encounter with the archangel Gabriel was his first divine revelation.

Soon, jealous rumors threatened Mohammad, forcing him to flee Mecca with his small group of followers and take refuge in nearby Medina. This flight, known as Hegira, marked the first year of the Muslim calendar, 622. The literal meaning of the word for the new faith, Islam, is "submission," to the one and only God, Allah. Believers were called Muslims. Mohammad was viewed as the last prophet of the long biblical line that included Abraham, Moses and Jesus. God's very words, revealed and transmitted to his chosen messenger, later gave birth to the holy Koran.

The Prophet died in 632 without appointing a successor. Soon after, Islam was ripped apart by a central question. Who was his rightful heir? Who should become caliph, defender of the faithful?

Mohammad had only one child, his beloved daughter, Fatimeh. She had married Ali, the Prophet's first follower, and gave Mohammad two grandchildren, Hassan and Hussein. For many Muslims, the Prophet's lineage was clear.

Yet power politics caused deep rifts in Islam. The patriarchs of the largest tribes bypassed Ali and chose their leader — the first caliph, Abu Bakr — through tribal consensus. These multitudes, their descendants and converts would call themselves Sunnis, derived from *sunnah*, the tradition.

Those in opposition looked upon the Prophet's family as the only legitimate heirs, led by his son-in-law, Ali, and his grandchildren, Hassan and Hussein. This branch of Islam came to be known as Shia Ali, partisans of Ali. Because of his nonviolent nature, Ali accepted the first three community-appointed caliphs. But growing resentment exploded into a bloody uprising against the decadent third caliph, Uthman, in Damascus. Finally, Ali was chosen as the fourth caliph, yet five years later he was assassinated. With his death, the corrupt son of Uthman proclaimed his rule over the Muslim world from Damascus, founding the Umayyad dynasty.

Since then, Ali's Shia followers have rejected all caliphs as usurpers. For this reason, the Arab Sunni, who now comprise 90 percent of the Muslim world, came to view the Shia as a dissident sect — revolutionaries to be persecuted and subjugated. Iran and southern Iraq remained Shia strongholds.

From the blazing sands of Arabia, Islam swept into Iran only five years after the Prophet's death. Under the fearful command of Omar, the second caliph, sun-baked men in rags, riding camels and flashing lances, appeared on the southern horizon. In 637, on the battlefield of Qadisya, the vaunted Sassanian imperial army of Persia was smashed. It was a humiliating finale to the glittering four-hundred-year dynasty that had even humbled Rome. Almost overnight, twelve hundred years of Persian rule on the plateau came to a halt. In the patriotic epic of Ferdowsi, the invasion is lamented as "a national catastrophe." Henceforth, Iran became a subject nation of foreign conquerors, a piece of the Islamic mosaic that would stretch from stormy Atlantic breakers to frigid Himalayan snows to the South China Sea, along an archipelago called the Ring of Fire.

Omar's brutal conquest of Iran was followed by a migration of Muslims to the city of Kufa in southern Iraq, which soon became a refuge for Ali and his followers. Wandering Shia poets, merchants and other dissenters escaping Sunni persecution spilled into Iran, sowing Ali's teachings and the legitimacy of Mohammad's sacred bloodline. Ali came to occupy a special place in the hearts of Iranians. He preached social justice and respect for truth. His exemplary life is still a clarion call to faith.

Ali's heroic son Hussein took as a bride the last Sassanian princess, the Shahbanou, who had been captured by Omar's troops. Their union symbolically tied the Prophet's family to Persia's royal lineage. Over the centuries, Shia opposition became the rallying cry for the politically and socially discontented in the Muslim community. A revolt in 760 led by Abu Muslim, from the eastern Iranian province of Khorassan, finally destroyed Umayyad power, giving birth to the glittering Abbassid caliphate in Baghdad, with its heavy Persian Sassanian influence. But another eight hundred years passed before the Shia faith was officially embraced by Iran's ruling elite. Today, Iran stands as the only Shia nation in the world.

As contentious as the historic rivalry between the Catholic papacy and Luther's Protestants, the Sunni-Shia religious divide has fueled great bitterness over the centuries. Standing at opposite poles, each still views the other as the antagonist. Sunni Arabs will tell you that all Shias are heretics.

While Shias condemn as illegitimate all caliphs after Ali, their faith is grounded in their belief in saints, called imams, all descendants of the Prophet. Ali and his two sons, Hassan and Hussein, are the first three imams. Various Shia schools differ in the number of recognized saints: five among the Lebanese Druze, seven for the Ismailis, led by the Agha Khan. Iranians believe in twelve imams. The twelfth, Imam al-Zaman, or the Saint of All Time, mysteriously disappeared in the tenth century. He is the Shia messiah, or *madhi*, living in hiding, who will reemerge on judgment day to restore justice on earth. Throughout Iran, silent prayers are offered for his return.

Sunni Arabs consider this sheer apostasy. For all Western fears of Muslim unity, in the end Iranian Shias will always stand in direct conflict with the more numerous Arab Sunnis. Ultimately, it is a chasm that can never be bridged.

*        *        *

Like most Iranians, Akbar, with his passionate spirit, could not hide his distaste for Arabs.

"Ignorant and uncultured," he said emphatically. "The Arabs sent by Omar were true barbarians." He scoffed at those ancestral Muslim brothers who had destroyed all Persian books and libraries. "Illiterate camel drivers, they couldn't read, and so they tore all the books and threw them into rivers."

"No," gasped Mom.

"And as an intellectual, I protest," Akbar said.

"Hear, hear!" said groggy Kevin, wrapped in a red scarf now moistened with water. Nasrollah lay outstretched in his van, the doors left open to catch the desert breeze. Rich and Avo carried on their debate about snow and salt. Avo still wasn't budging.

"You can never trust Arabs," Akbar went on. "All they want is our carpets and our women! Barbarians, they are only barbarians." His face turned red. "Today the Arab sheiks laugh and say, 'We have the money. We can buy anyone, and let *them* do the thinking.'"

"Amen," Richard said.

In Dhahran, Saudi Arabia, my younger brother had already endured five years of frustration with a tempestuous boss who shamelessly took credit for all of Rich's ideas. In return for his acquiescence, Rich received a healthy salary and a suburban split-level house close to an oil-soaked dirt-brown golf course.

"Imagine, they destroyed all the books." Akbar's eyes flared. "Barefoot lizard eaters!"

His voice became more shrill as he quoted the conquering caliph Omar: "If the books agree with Islam, then we don't need them. And if they don't, they are *haram*, forbidden."

"What a huge blunder," my mother said. "Unforgivable."

"Our prophet Mohammad told us, 'Seek knowledge even unto China.' He truly valued learning. But Omar was so blinded by his fanaticism that he ordered all books to be destroyed here and in Egypt."

When Arab troops rode into Alexandria, the famous library was seized. Legend tells us that seven hundred thousand papyrus scrolls went up in smoke, stoking the city's bathhouse fires for six months. Some scholars believe that rampaging Christian zealots may have done the senseless act two centuries earlier. Mysteriously, in Iran, Omar's legions missed one library.

The medical university of Jundi Shapur, in the southern region of Fars, held perhaps the world's greatest treasure trove of Greek scientific and philosophical manuscripts. The collection was discovered over a hundred years after Omar's invasion. Caliph Mamun, whose enlightened reign was considered the Augustan Age of Islamic literature and science, quickly ordered translations of all the texts into Arabic. Stored in Baghdad's famed Bait al-Hikma, House of Wisdom, these precious works slowly made their way west.

One surviving first-century classic serves to illuminate that perilous journey. The *Syntaxis* of Ptolemy, the renowned Greek-Egyptian astronomer, listed 1,022 stars observed by him in Alexandria. A papyrus copy of his collection of stars later traveled from Baghdad across Africa, through the Pillars of Hercules and into multicultural Muslim Spain. In Toledo, King Alfonso the Wise ordered the work translated yet again, this time from Arabic into Latin.

By the mid-thirteenth century, the *Syntaxis* had reached Europe. Navigators adopted it as an essential tool. Armed with the astrolabe, another Islamic invention, Portuguese argonauts sailed south across uncharted seas in their cannon-loaded carracks filled with Madeira wine. They rounded Africa's Cape of Good Hope and dropped anchor off Persia's southern coast, only a few miles from Jundi Shapur. It was the dawn of the Age of Discovery. These were the first rumblings of the global economy. Multinational trading companies and colonial powers would soon divide up the world.

We were sitting in the shade when a wiry, energetic little boy suddenly appeared holding a deflated soccer ball.

"Let's play!" Rich called out. Seconds later, the boy was kicking the ball and running with my brothers. Two stones marked each

*above* Hassan and Fatimeh Ghasemi in Tehran, 1963. Their son, Ali, smiles from the arms of his grandmother Khorshid, Fatimeh's mother. With only this photograph in hand, the Ward family returned to Iran in 1998 to begin our search. *below* In the garden of our Tehran home, Rich, Chris and I sit with Fatimeh and her children, Ali and baby Mahdi, and a brood of newly born puppies.

*All photographs © Terence Ward*

*above* At Persepolis, a young woman in a doorway of Xerxes Palace.
*opposite* My father, Patrick, stands dwarfed before the 2,400-year-old
tomb of the Achaemenian king Darius II.

Touching the marble sarcophagus of the mystic poet Hafez, pilgrims whisper his verses as if in prayer.

*above* We stop to ask about Hassan's whereabouts among baffled villagers of Tudeshk. *below* Hassan's mother-in-law, Khorshid, welcomes us with homemade cookies.

*above* Omnipresence en route. *below* After twenty-nine years, my mother, Donna, and Hassan meet at last in Isfahan as my brother Kevin looks on.

The Ghasemi and Ward families are reunited in the courtyard of Hassan's house in Isfahan. Chris, Kevin and I are in front. Behind, left to right, are Fatimeh, Donna, Hassan's grandchildren Masoud and Saeed, my brother Richard, Hassan, his son Majid, Patrick and Ahmad. The figure in shadow is our eccentric guide, Avo.

*above* One of Hassan's scrumptious dinners.
*opposite* An ecstatic Isfahani carpet dealer who's just closed a sale.

*above* The Safavid dome of Sheik Lutfullah Mosque, a masterpiece of Islamic architecture, rises from Isfahan's Imam Square, rimmed with a shopping arcade. *opposite* Two boys in Isfahan's Friday Mosque.

*above*  The caretaker of the Isfahan Synagogue and his wife.
*below*  The tomb of Ayatollah Khomeini, in south Tehran.

goal. They booted the ball to and fro, and then my father joined in. While the ball spun between cartwheeling legs, I remembered the day when Hassan first brought us out onto the lawn and presented us with a small yellow ball he had found.

Since that spring afternoon, we had played with kids in many places: on the beaches of the Caspian, in the Tivoli Gardens of Copenhagen, on the meadows of Central Park and in the bush of Kenya. In this universal game, we all made the same head fakes, bad passes and wild scrambles. Raw enthusiasm coupled with the grace of ballet tossed off flashes of elegance that could elevate the most rustic sandlot into the clouds. Chris's skill as a goalie had won him national acclaim at Cornell, first as all-Ivy, then as all-American.

The boy scooted out to the left. Richard let him slip by. With a gift pass from my dad, the boy dribbled, then booted the ball toward the goal. A generous Chris leapt in slow motion, deliberately letting it go through his arms and between the two stones.

"*Gooo-aallll!*" the boy called out triumphantly, rushing over to my father to give him a hug. "*Gooo-alll!*" Avo cheered.

Mom, Akbar and I watched the game while Kev sat with his eyes closed as if in deep meditation. A long kick sent the ball flying down the hill. The boy and Avo chased after it.

This simple game of kicking around a single ball has captured the imagination of the world, even in remote outposts like Abarqu. This scruffy ball has connected more people than any cellular phone. It has reached every corner of the earth. It is understood in every language and more global than a Big Mac.

"Sure hope we can see a match in Tehran when we get there," said my dad. The World Cup countdown and Team Iran's debut were soon on everyone's lips. Akbar, though, was sulking.

"Mrs. Ward," he asked, "why do Americans keep mistaking us with Arabs? When will they understand we are not the same people?"

She sighed. "Akbar, America is like an island, cut off from the world," she replied. "Most don't know any better."

I shrugged my shoulders. "And don't seem to care."

But to label Akbar an Arab was not only a blunder. It was an insult. Like insisting that an Irishman is the same as a Brit, or calling a Greek a Turk, or thinking that a New Yorker is like a Texan. Divided by history, culture, language, cuisine and, above all, by their branch of Islam, Iranians and Arabs have never been friends. While Greece and Turkey are neighbors, all Greeks will remind you that the border is all they share with Turks. So it is with Iranians and Arabs.

"How can Americans get it so wrong?" Akbar asked again.

"The reasons are many," Mom said. "Arrogance, smugness, narrow-mindedness, naiveté. They get all their answers from CNN and the Internet. You should know, Akbar, you lived there. It's Fantasy Island."

"So," Kevin asked, lifting off his bandanna and wiping his brow, "what actually is an Arab?"

The definition, I told him, was simple. "A person whose mother tongue is Arabic."

Only a handful of Iranians living along the Persian Gulf fell into that category. The other sixty million citizens did not.

"You see, Kevin," Akbar said. "We are *not* Arabs."


We strolled along Abarqu's empty streets with Akbar. We entered a small grocery store, where a raven-beaked shopkeeper lazily tried to interest me in a few onions, cigarettes, two bags of rice and his plastic bowls. I bought some bottled water and an apple, and complimented him on his town. He spoke of the weather. He called it "the month of heaven." Cooler now, he said, but wait until summer. Asphalt melts, tires explode.

"When were you last in Tehran?" I asked.

"I've never been, *al-hamdulillah*. They tell me to go. But I say no thank you. Not even to Paris would I go!"

He hated big cities — too much traffic. Here, a car passed every half hour, just the right pace. There was little hope of increased movement any time soon. One could read all of Tolstoy certain that nothing and no one would ever bother you.

Across the square stood an impressive adobe mosque, whose

two domes mirrored the pleasing shape of a Bactrian camel's double hump. I admired the pure geometric harmony: the absence of lines, the clean rounded corners, the tan-colored domes, the circular walls blending into the roof.

Akbar and I went to have a closer look. The door swung open wide. Inside, we took off our shoes. I ran my hand along the wall, a cool membrane of gold-red clay smoothed by human touch. The light was dim, the silence palpable.

In the far corner, a black-robed mullah nodded slowly, facing the *mihrab*, a small marble arch that points, in every mosque, toward Mecca. A sleepy old man sprawled on a reed-thin mat lifted his head. He gave me an encouraging grin, then rolled over to continue his nap. Stress was not an endemic problem in Abarqu.

We sat in the coolness of the mosque, and Akbar described the profound appeal of the Shia faith for the ever-suffering Iranians.

"Our patron saint, you know, is Imam Ali."

"Of course," I replied.

"Yes. In all our hearts, Ali lives on like a hero. He lived simply, in poverty, following the words of the Prophet. He did not fight for power, he fought for social justice. You see, he loved and defended Iranian converts who had been cruelly treated by Omar's Arab conquerors."

Through Ali, Iranians were welcomed into Islam, he told me. In him they found their spokesman, their defender, their martyr. As partisans of Ali, they could mourn their historic tragedies and pray for justice.

"Ali would ask his Arab followers battling the Zoroastrians, 'Have you read their holy book, *Avesta*? They have their own faith and worship only one God just as we do.' He even tried to stop the Bedouins itching to wage war against us," Akbar whispered.

"Then what happened?" asked Rich, who had joined us in the mosque.

"His Arab brothers turned against him. 'He loves the foreigner,' they said. They killed him first, then his sons, Hassan and Hussein. Terrible deaths."

The Prophet's bloodline was savaged.

"Ssshhhhh," Akbar admonished Rich, whose curiosity about the early days of Islam had provoked yet another question. The dozing man had now awakened, and he stretched into a kneeling position. Time for *namaz*, prayer. He turned his hands upright, seeking to receive Allah's grace. A silent offering. Eyes closed. A breath. Then his body bent over, his head gently touching the carpeted floor.

"Remember Hassan's *namaz?*" Rich asked me.

How many times had I watched Hassan kneel in prayer? One afternoon, he and I were coming home from Tajrish bazaar, his bicycle loaded down with bags of eggplant, cucumber, yogurt and lamb, and long loaves of hot fresh bread. We stopped by the *Imamzadeh Saleh* — the mosque and shrine — attached to the bustling market next to the Darband River.

"Terry *jan*, wait for me here. I must go in and pray." Hassan handed me the plastic sacks before slipping off his sandals and padding across the rugs to find his special place for meditation.

Peering inside, I sat next to the rows of shoes, nibbling on the warm bread, guarding the shopping bags and his sturdy black bicycle. The warm carpeted floor, turquoise-colored walls and glancing mirrors enveloped his simple act of devotion. Hands turned upward to the sky, he knelt in quiet recitation. He lowered his head to the floor, in obeisance to the Almighty, his forehead touching the small disk believed to be made of earth from Kerbela that Shias use in worship — Kerbela is the place, in southern Iraq, where Ali's son Hussein was savagely murdered. He rose and kneeled three times.

Later, walking home along the tree-lined streets, he spoke. "It was for baby Mahdi," he murmured. "God must help us, he's so sick."

After visits to the doctor with my mother, the child was still in jeopardy. When we came home, Fatimeh lifted her little coughing Mahdi and passed the frail child into Hassan's firm hands, then rose from behind her loom, washed and silently moved to her mother Khorshid's room. There, she prayed.

In Abarqu's mosque, the kneeling old man lifted his head again and the mullah rose to stand.

"Quick, let's go." Grabbing my arm, Akbar gestured for us to exit. In the fierce sunlight, we stumbled down the steps and put on our shoes. An enormous wooden structure in the shape of a dome rested against the mosque's clay walls. Some young men stood next to it, testing the planks.

"On *Ashura*, the tenth day of the month of Moharram, many young men will carry this platform, where someone in the role of Hussein will be dying," he explained excitedly.

"*Baleh*, yes." I remembered the vivid scenes as a child.

"Everyone watching will be crying."

In eastern Bali, where my wife and I had lived under the sacred volcano Gunung Agung, every funeral features a procession led by musicians in which a lofty tiered platform is carried by dozens of young men. In a heated drama, invisible forces try to thwart their advance to the cremation ground. Raucous shouts and passions seize the marchers. Some are overcome with emotion, and the platform shifts and buckles as if gone amok. Fearful cries pour out from the crowd. Many forces are at work, and everyone knows it. Each participant becomes an actor in a timeless struggle.

A similar spectacle of mourning happens all over Iran. "It's almost time," Akbar said. "*Ashura* is just five weeks away."

Every year, a passion play called a *taziyeh* is reenacted during the first ten days of Moharram. It's the timeless Shia tragedy that centers on the martyrdom of Hussein, the Prophet's grandson and the son of Ali. This event anchors the faithful. It is played out not by professional actors but by local people in a kind of theater in the round.

The crowds of spectators know the plot by heart. Women surround the stage, shrouded in black. Tears welling inside, they know they will weep long and hard. The actors are divided into good and bad characters. Green and white are the colors for Hussein and his followers, who sing their parts. Red is the color reserved for the hateful general Shemr and his savage warriors, who recite their lines.

The play begins with a lonely caravan traveling east. Trudging across the desert of Arabia, noble Hussein is on a holy mission to the city of Kufa, in southern Iraq, which has beseeched him to return and rule like his father as the rightful heir to the Prophet. His small caravan numbers seventy-two, including women and children.

The legacy of the Prophet is at stake. The caliphate is now in the hands of a usurper, the tyrant Yazid. Hussein knows that Yazid plans to kill him, and yet he does not turn back. His act of defiance is harrowing. Hussein is prepared to die to save the purity of Islam.

Tragedy strikes on the tenth day of Moharram. The year is 680. Hussein and his followers are mercilessly slaughtered under the blazing sun at Kerbela. The few surviving women and children are dragged to Damascus along with Hussein's head to be shown to the caliph Yazid. This butchery lives vividly in the Iranian psyche. It symbolizes the nobility of martyrdom, the never-ending fight against tyranny and injustice. It echoes the Jewish martyrs of Masada and Christ's Passion.

The theater director Peter Brook described, in *Parabola Quarterly*, the intensity and immediacy of a *taziyeh* drama he once witnessed in Iran:

> I saw in a remote Iranian village one of the strangest things I had ever seen: a group of four hundred villagers, the entire population of the place, sitting under a tree and passing from roars of laughter to outright sobbing — although they knew perfectly well the end of the story — as they saw Hussain in danger of being killed, and then fooling his enemies and then being martyred. And when he was martyred the theater form became a truth — there was no difference between past and present. An event that was told as a remembered happening in history, thirteen hundred years ago, even-

tually became a reality that moment. Nobody could draw the line between the different orders of reality. It was an incarnation: at that particular moment he was being martyred again in front of those villagers.

The young men testing the platform outside the mosque had begun wrapping their heads with black bandannas as if preparing for *Ashura*. They were joking around, giggling and having fun, unaware that we were watching them.

In Tehran during the black month of Moharram, the mood even in our household changed. It was a ten-day buildup. A strange darkness settled over the city. Smiles disappeared. Tension filled the air. Fatimeh became surly with us, as if a cloud of melancholy covered her loom. In the evenings, Hassan would emerge in his black shirt bound for *rowza* — performances where the suffering and deeds of the Shia martyrs were narrated in the mosque or in private homes — and in the chanting congregation he would beat his chest with open palms in rhythm. As the days passed, Hassan and his loved ones plunged into sadness. He let his beard grow in a sign of mourning.

"Terry, it's so sad to watch Imam Hussein and his children," Fatimeh once said about the *taziyeh*, "when you know they will die."

She described the tears that always flowed as Sakinah, Hussein's youngest daughter, cries out in thirst. Holding a full lambskin sack of water, a young man called Abbas is seized by Yazid's bullying soldiers. His hands are hacked off, yet Abbas bravely tries to carry the water by lifting it with his teeth. Young Qasem, who marries on the devastated plain, puts on a white cloak with his wife's help. At that moment all gasp, for white is the color of martyrdom. Then it is Hussein's turn to die by the sword. A headless figure appears and falls. Most painful of all, Fatimeh confessed, was the crying from the handful of orphaned children who survived.

At noontime on *Ashura*, Tehran exhaled with Hussein's death. The mourning was over, but the intensity of the collective grief and guilt quietly lingered. For several days, Hassan was drained.

Pious Fatimeh kept silent. It was no coincidence that the Ghasemis were named after Mohammad's family: Hassan, Fatimeh
and Ali.

This defining moment of *Ashura* rivals the agony of Christ. But
unlike the Christian ordeal, for the Shia there is no resurrection,
no deliverance, only suffering and tears. Iranians will never forget
or forgive evil Yazid for his crimes. Yet the Sunnis do. This is why
the divide between Shias and Sunnis is so irreversibly profound.

In a singular stroke of genius, Ayatollah Khomeini tapped into
the potent symbolism of *taziyeh*. As early as 1963, when rioting
first rocked the streets of Tehran, the future Supreme Leader
broke with tradition and openly attacked the monarchy using
the drama of Kerbela. Over the years, Khomeini had branded
Mohammad Reza Pahlavi as none other than the ruthless caliph
Yazid. This illegitimate Shah, he had said, embodied corruption
and evil on earth. The suffering Iranian people had to rise against
injustice. Like Hussein, they too had to prepare to fight for a noble cause. Yazid must go, he had demanded. The Shah must go.

And behind Yazid lurked, of course, evil incarnate: America,
the Shah's longtime backer, perfectly cast in the role of the "Great
Satan." Iran, Khomeini declared, had to be cleansed of plunder-
ing imperialists who acted with impunity, sucked away God-given
oil, cultivated immoral pleasure and corrupted society. No com-
promise! This Shah, this puppet of America, must go!

In a nation scarred by centuries of foreign capitulation and hu-
miliation, Khomeini's words struck a sensitive chord. In 1964, the
Majlis passed a law forbidding courts to prosecute American military staff charged with a crime. In return, Iran was promised a
massive infusion of U.S. aid. Ayatollah Khomeini spoke out defiantly against the diplomatic immunity: "If the Shah should run
over an American dog, he should be called to account, but if an
American cook runs over the Shah, no one has any claims against
him . . . I proclaim that this shameful vote of the Majlis is in con-
tradiction to Islam and has no legality."

This criticism went too far. The government sent him into exile, first to Turkey, then to Iraq's holy Shia city of Najaf, shrine of Imam Ali, and finally to France. But Khomeini did not relent. His tape-recorded sermons, along with those of the fiery Islamic nationalist Ali Shariati, were smuggled into Iran and were heard in homes, buses, taxis and mosques across the country. This was music to the ears of the former prime minister Mossadegh's followers, persecuted leftists, intellectuals, nationalists, Communists, students, traditionalists and the clergy. All these opponents of Pahlavi found their rallying cry in Khomeini's uncompromising stance. United by their hatred for the "American-manipulated" Shah, the broad alliance needed a spark to light the fire.

The match was struck in January 1978 when a slanderous article denouncing Khomeini was published. Outraged theological students in the religious city of Qom marched in protest. Police responded by firing into the crowd. Several students died. According to the traditional mourning period, forty days later a procession was held for the fallen protesters. At the same time, in Tabriz, a similar procession took place and violence erupted. Again, the soldiers opened fire and riots broke out. More were killed, spawning mourning marches in other cities: Isfahan, Shiraz, Mashhad and Tehran.

Over the summer, wildcat strikes hit the oilfields and bazaars, and more processions brought temperatures to a boil. Rising discontent sent thousands of demonstrators into the streets. By December, events reached a climax during the month of Moharram. On *Ashura*, two million people paraded in downtown Tehran, shutting down the city. The lead marchers wore white, signaling their readiness to become martyrs. Many young women from the chic northern suburbs chose to wear the veil in protest. One month later, in January 1979, the Shah fled overseas as he had done twenty-seven years before, when Prime Minister Mossadegh nationalized Iran's oil. Repeating the same pattern, the Shah abandoned his supporters to their uncertain fate. This time no foreign-inspired coup would rescue his rule. Khomeini would return in triumph from Paris. The Kerbela cycle was complete. Yazid was gone.

The politicized *taziyeh* became a living theater. Mobilizing the ardor of the crowds, Khomeini and his revolutionary *Komiteh* committees turned on the wealthy Westernized Iranian elite, calling them idolaters, polluters, enemies of the people. Then he turned on his nationalist and leftist allies. When the dust finally settled over the land, his dream of an Islamic republic had become an unassailable reality.

On November 4, 1979, a few students penetrated the U.S. embassy and seized their hostages. For a moment, the revolutionary leaders were uncertain about the next step. But Khomeini understood the symbolic nature of their act. The hostage taking, the Revolution, the "Great Satan," all were linked to the Kerbela epic of Imam Hussein. In the two decades since 1979, the Islamic regime's moral role has centered around the clergy's divine mission to purge the "Great Satan" and the "evil Yazid" from Iranian soil and soul.

In 1980, another event further fueled the Kerbela paradigm. Lightning assaults, missile bombardments on the southwestern oil province of Khuzistan: Saddam Hussein's Iraqi armies invaded Iran by way of the Shatt-al-Arab. Imam Hussein's martyrdom was so potent in the Iranian psyche that Khomeini invoked it to rally the nation with his new battle cry: *"Kull yawm Ashura, kull ard Kerbela.* Every day is *Ashura,* every place is Kerbela."

"Yes, we lost many young boys," said Akbar, glancing at the youths jostling the platform. "So many volunteered and never came back."

The fighting reached a stalemate early on, but for the clergy that war was a golden chance to capture the shrines of Najaf and Kerbela in southern Iraq. The dream of liberating these hallowed pilgrimage sites where Ali and Hussein were martyred turned into a holy crusade. After centuries of grieving, it was time to punish the shameless Arabs and to avenge the historic crimes. Iraq was invaded.

Six years of unspeakable carnage followed, leaving more than a million dead and crippling Iran's petroleum centers of Abadan and Khorramshahr. The bitter stalemate ground on and on, like the horrific World War I trench warfare. Volunteers charged across no man's land into a deadly haze of poison gas, minefields, barbed wire and raking machine-gun fire, often without any bullets to fire back. The cycle of martyrdom fueled their hearts and filled the cemeteries. Fierce patriotism silenced all internal critics of the regime. Streaming out from war-ravaged Khuzistan, millions of refugees trekked their way into slums and shantytowns, seeking safety in Shiraz, Isfahan and Tehran.

Finally, in 1988, Ayatollah Khomeini announced his greatest disappointment: "I drink the chalice of poison." With those words, he ended the war.

We stopped at a coffeehouse. Rich ordered a *dough*, a thirst-quenching yogurt drink with sprinkles of mint. Looking knack-ered, Avo lumbered in with the panting little soccer player, covered with dust. The boy carried his ball like a trophy. The old man walked over from the mosque and Akbar motioned for him to join us. He did so with the usual Iranian courtesy, offering us tea and shaking all our hands save my mother's. Soon he was telling Akbar about his trip to Mecca.

These days, Radio Iran had ceased broadcasting its revolution across the Gulf's waters. All the ruling families from Bahrain to Kuwait slept much better, no longer fearing the twitch of their necks on a wooden block. Harsh words had been toned down. For the mullahs, access to Mecca was more critical than spreading revolution. And our *haji* had just returned from the holy city of the Prophet.

By now, the Islamic Republic had made up with its Arab neighbors, even with the despised Saddam Hussein. After all, the most sacred Shia shrines were still in his territory. Ironically, many nationalists now accuse the regime of being Arab-intoxicated, or *arabzadegi*, for pushing Arabic language, music and culture on its people, to cement the Islamic identity on Iran for future generations.

\*　　\*　　\*

In the 1970s, V. S. Naipaul witnessed a cultural shift in the opposite direction. Iran, he noted, was afflicted with "West-mad inanity": "Everywhere are the spivs, the young men in tight trousers who call you Meestah, and who, in late afternoon, loiter outside the cinemas, gawking at the near-naked, lasciviously posed women festooning the posters advertising Western films. 'They get very weird ideas about us,' an English secretary complained."

Tehran in those years, with its avalanche of oil wealth, fashioned a high-flying hybrid society with its foreign advisers and technicians, which ran counter to the traditional social fabric. Instead of stabilizing, it spun out of control. Norman Smith, my father's colleague, gave us his description of the last days before the Revolution: "It's one thing to be hit by a car every time you step into the street, but when it's always a Mercedes, it simply adds insult to injury."

"The new elite wanted to believe 'they were part of Europe, that only a ghastly accident of geography had placed them in Asia,'" Naipaul wrote, quoting a bitter intellectual he had met in Iran.

When the Iranian writer Al-e Ahmad coined the now famous term *gharbzadegi*, or Euromania, it was soon on the lips of critics of the imperial regime. In his 1965 book, *Occidentosis: A Plague from the West*, he described the term:

> An occidentotic who is a member of the nation's leadership is standing on thin air; he is like a particle of dust suspended in the void . . . He has severed his ties with the depths of society, culture and tradition. He is no link between antiquity and modernity . . . The occidentotic is effete . . . [He] hangs on the words and handouts of the West . . . Western products are more essential to him than any school, mosque, hospital, or factory. It is for his sake that we have an architecture with no roots in our culture.

"By the seventies classical Persian music had collapsed," an ardent musician, Gholam Hussein, said. "Western notation was the rage. The tradition of learning from the master was cast out the

window." Persian musical technique and its rich textures had influenced Arabic and North African music, flamenco, the Indian
raga and even the melodic muezzin's call, heard from Morocco all
the way to Indonesia. "Orders came from the court," Gholam
added. "'Only Beethoven, please. Fly in those violinists from Vienna. Inaugurate Rudaki concert hall with Mozart.'" Meanwhile,
one of the world's oldest and most sophisticated musical systems was classified as embarrassing folklore. Traditional musicians found themselves no longer in demand.

In the end, most Iranians began to feel like strangers in their
own land. Leading dissident intellectuals openly called for a return to their roots. But what were Iran's true roots? Ali Shariati
made it clear: "For us a return to our roots means not a rediscov-
ery of pre-Islamic Iran, but a return to our Islamic, especially Shia
roots."

This prophetic call positioned him as one of the leading ideologues of the revolution to come. And in the wake of that revolution, all pre-Islamic and Westernized emblems and symbols
vaporized. Iranian culture stood cleansed, indigenous and alone.
Some even argue that this was the developing world's first back-
lash against American-led globalization.

A few years ago, a correspondent of the Parisian daily *Liberation* asked a celebrated filmmaker, "What did the revolution give
you?" The filmmaker, Mohsen Makhmakbaf, replied, "Pride and
images."

The words *arabzadegi* and *gharbzadegi* embodied the minefield of
Iran's identity. One needed a kind of Geiger counter to detect the
trip wires, the booby traps, the explosive forces.

A friend of mine, a Berkeley graduate, passionately shed light
on Akbar's anti-Arab rhetoric, labeling many such arguments as
simply conflicting emotions. Before I left New York, Mansur and
I met for lunch in a Greek diner around the corner from Gramercy Park.

"What's so great about pre-Islamic Persia?" he asked. "To be
frank, it just doesn't interest me."

"Why not?" I asked.

"What's there? Where is the literature? Nothing," Mansur said. "They wrote in Aramaic, for God's sake, not even Persian. Don't forget, the Arabs gave us an alphabet. All these Iranians in America are lashing out at Islam, claiming it has no role in their Persia. What are they talking about? Look at the history — how can they be so stupid?"

"They speak of patriotism, nationalism," I offered.

"Of course, Iranian intellectuals always go back to the pre-Islamic period. But if you're denying great Arabic poetry, you're an idiot. What's so great about pre-Islamic Persia? Everyone speaks about it like it was a golden age. They're full of baloney. They just want to hang on to everything Persian. But the Arabs brought a beautiful language and a faith and a world empire.

"Western scholars in love with Iran have fallen under the spell of Iranian nationalism. It's stupid! Look what happened to Spain after the Muslims and the Jews were expelled. A disaster. And no one ever mentions that for the last two hundred years the best Iranian literature has come out of New Delhi and Lahore. Mixing is important, so is new blood. Tamerlane opened up roads to China, and so in came all sorts of goods. Everything that we are now has been borrowed from elsewhere.

"I don't consider myself an Iranian," he then announced. "Who cares who did what? I call myself a Middle Easterner. I'd like to see us unite culturally, like in times past."

Discounting the hypernationalism of most Iranians, he dreamt of the golden epoch, between the eighth and ninth centuries, when the Abbassid caliphate ruled the civilized world from Baghdad, the city of *The Thousand and One Nights* that lay upstream from the old Sassanid Persian capital of Ctesiphon. The enlightened caliph Harun al-Rashid — Charlemagne's counterpart in the Islamic world — and his son Mamun oversaw the birth of great centers for translation and the study of Greek, Syrian, Persian and Sanskrit literature. This cosmopolitan state, staffed with scribes, intellectuals, artists and scientists, fueled Islam's brightest flame. This was a time when the acquisition of knowledge was one of the highest ideals of the tolerant world religion.

I thanked the *haji* for his gracious hospitality and asked the owner of the coffeehouse for the check.

"*Befarmaeed*, please," he said, demurring.

In the traditional style, three times he declined my offer to pay, then finally he accepted my rials. Chris poked his head inside. Fine dust still coated his pants from the frenetic soccer game. The kid tossed his ball to the big American whom he had vanquished with his mighty goal. A grin stretched across his little face. Chris rubbed his close-cropped head and laughed. From the van, Mom called: "Don't forget to bring some water for Kevin." He was flattened out again on the back seat. It was time to leave. Holding on to his ball, the boy waved us out of Abarqu.

At a bus stop across the street, a man slept soundly in the shade lying on a weathered tin bench. One of his feet dangled over the side. Nothing could stir him. A large billboard hung above the snoozing man. Avo laughed, pointing out the scene to us. He translated the sign's words. "It says, 'The Islamic Revolution is always vigilant, always awake.'"

In the distance, taller than the town's highest minaret, the great cypress of Abarqu, alone in the expanse, stood in silent watch.

8

# Towers of Silence, Temples of Fire

The prisoner will eventually be released, but the prison-keeper will be forever in prison.

> — Carved on the wall of a solitary-confinement cell
> in Iran, from V. S. Naipaul's *Beyond Belief*

Our desert has no bound, our hearts and souls no test
World within world has taken Form's image, which of
these images is ours?
When you see a severed head in the path rolling toward
our field,
Ask of it, ask of it, the secrets of the heart: for you will
learn from it our hidden mystery.

> — Jalaluddin Rumi

W E RODE ACROSS an ocean of glistening waves of sand. The dull droning of our tiny van roared on. Cooling gusts blew through the windows. My parents dozed off. Chris read Freya Stark's *Valleys of the Assassins* while Rich gazed out at the stark terrain and Kevin lay sprawled in the back. Thank God it was only April, Akbar said. Three months from now, this land would radiate like a furnace.

Since leaving Abarqu, our long hours on the road had offered few glimpses of life. Each patch of green appeared shrill to the eye. Each dash of emerald paint on the tawny earth canvas looked downright shocking. Each blade of grass seemed out of place and startling, like a hallucinatory mirage. The *qanats*, or water networks, still baffled me. Trapping precious water under this desert and ushering it to the surface of these barren, forsaken wastes took such courage, such tenacity, such audacity.

"Fields of dreams," my father said as we passed.

An almond grove next to a solitary mud-walled house took on new meaning. A lonely field of parsley became a revelation. Any sprig or leaf of chlorophyll seemed miraculous, as if sprouting from God's hand.

In this boundless expanse, the fate of tiny settlements encircled by the relentless desert looked grim. As quickly as a green field came into view, it disappeared as if by a magician's hand. All that was left was the eternal sun, wind, rock and sand.

Little had changed since Marco Polo's caravan passed this way. The account of his travels, strangely entitled *Il Milione*, The Million, was transcribed by a Pisan named Rustichello, who shared his prison cell for three years. It shocked readers of his day as outrageous fantasy. Surprisingly, Marco Polo revealed little of his Chinese experience and offered few profound reflections. Mostly, it read like a merchant's guide, a how-to-get-there-from-here inventory. Written for commercial agents, each chapter served up a dry ledger of goods found en route, an accounting journal obsessed with costly spices and practical information. About this terrain en route to Yazd, he wrote:

> Merchants who in traveling from one province to another are obliged to pass extensive deserts and tracts of sand, there is no kind of herbage to be met with and on account of the distance between the wells or other watering places, it is necessary to make long journeys in the course of the day. In some of these districts, the people are savage and bloodthirsty, making a common practice of wounding and murdering each other.

When we were children, my brothers and I passed long summer days romping in our swimming pool, shouting out the Venetian's name. With my eyes closed I would cry out, "Marco!" as blue water splashed around me. Ours was an aquatic game of tag. Across the pool my brothers would echo "Polo!" before diving to escape my blind grasp. For countless hours we called his name into the heated Tehran sky. Only later did I learn that if it wasn't for a certain love-struck Persian ruler living two hundred miles west of Tehran, Marco Polo's name would never have crossed our lips. The Venetian would have died in China in total obscurity.

Arghun, a Mongol of the Il-Khan dynasty, made Marco's return journey to Venice possible. Or, more to the point, it was Arghun's wife. On her deathbed, she made Arghun promise that her place as queen would be taken only by a bride of similar royal Mongol blood. When Arghun's emissaries rode through Peking's gates for an audience with Kublai Khan, the nervous Venetian seized on his long-awaited chance to return home.

More than twenty years had passed since Marco, his father and uncle had ventured east from their native city. He had been trapped in the service of the Mongol emperor, and each plea for permission to leave had been denied. But when the Khan of Khans decreed that Lady Kokachin would be sent across Asia to heartbroken Arghun in Persia, the Polos offered to lead the mission. Kublai Khan relented.

In a fleet of fourteen ships, their voyage took two years. Their sea route circled Java, then Ceylon, passed through the Arabian Sea and ended in the Persian Gulf. Marco does not tell us about any of the disasters en route. Indeed, there were more than a few.

Out of the six hundred who sailed from China, only eighteen survived to set foot on Persian soil, among them the three Polos and their Mongol princess. After enduring the treacherous journey, they arrived to tragic news: Arghun had died.

Evidently, what killed him was an elixir of life. In those days, alchemists concocted potions with mercury and sulfur as key ingredients. The secret was in the combination, and often the balance was off. Like many omnipotent rulers of the age who sought immortality, Arghun died of slow poisoning. One of his sons gladly swept up the beautiful young woman. The Polos returned to Europe with their precious gems, exotic tales and a debt owed to Iran.

*       *       *

I fought off sleep. Avo was pleased to spot a camel nibbling on scrub. Alone, the beast cast a surreal image. Not a person was in sight. Hobbled by ropes, the camel couldn't run away. Kevin was uninterested. He was still flat on his back, and his propped-up knees rolled with the bumps. Black gauze drooped over his face. Mom slept with her head resting on Dad's shoulder while he and I tried to keep alert.

Curious about Akbar's school days in California, Chris quizzed him on Santa Barbara hot spots. His favorite, Pancho Villa, overlooked the beach and the pier.

"So, Akbar, did you like your time in the States?"

"Of course, Chris."

"So why didn't you stay?"

"I'm not like those Iranians living in L.A. You know, all the Shah's people with their stolen money. Look what they did. They turned their backs on their culture, their religion, their land. All they think of is clothes, whiskey, movies and money. That's not a life for me."

Like Robespierre's assault on white-wigged Louis XVI, the Islamic Republic waged a slash-and-burn war against the Shah's regime. Merciless vengeance lashed out at the *taghouti*, those debauched lovers of the high life noted for drinking, gambling and womanizing.

In this class warfare, the extravagant rich lost dramatically. They were labeled arrogant, uncaring and immoral. Their lands were confiscated, factories seized and lavish homes occupied. Those who stayed accepted their fate silently. Those who fled still fear to return. Embargoes crippled international trade. Western business leaders shunned Tehran. Cut off from the world, the country learned to be self-sufficient. But low oil prices, economic mismanagement and runaway inflation, Akbar told us, quickly began to curse the nation.

If you want to become a millionaire, so the joke goes, go to Italy, change five hundred dollars, and you've got your million. The same applies to Iran. We were shocked to see so many zeros on the rial bills. One thousand bought a cup of coffee. Two thousand, a taxi ride. A far cry from the ten-rial fare of years ago. Hyperinflation had taken hold with tiger claws. And at five thousand rials to the dollar — a bit higher on the black market — it was clear that the economy had hit rock bottom.

Akbar was philosophical. "Life is more than the rat race of New York. Who really needs that? I love my country. If I'm away from it, I'm lost. This is where I want to live."

"But —" Chris wanted to list the inconveniences, the privations, but was cut short.

"Well, there are times I miss the ocean and *Saturday Night Live*, you know," he joked. "But my life is here."

He offered Chris some dried melon seeds.

Avo, taking up Chris's cue, asked my mother about Tehran's wild nightlife in the sixties.

"Oh, the nightclubs were marvelous, Avo, with belly dancers from Egypt."

"Yeah," Pat said, "she loved to chat with them."

"Wow!" Avo's eyes lit up.

"All the hotels had clubs," said Mom. "It was such fun. And there were glorious parties."

"But," Pat said, "the villages were very poor."

"Now people look a lot healthier, I must say," Mom said.

Dad went on, "I remember children without pants and shoes, their eyes covered in flies."

"And those attacking dogs," Kev muttered from the back.

Over the rumbling engine, my ears twitched. A familiar voice rose from the speakers. Nasrollah flashed a rebellious wink toward me. Could it be Googoosh?

In the seventies, when the streets of Tehran rocked with booming discos, risqué miniskirts and wide bell bottoms, the reigning diva of pop was a cute, bubbly girl called Googoosh. She sang and danced with fresh sensuality. It was all so new and daring.

Merging a Western pop sound with Farsi lyrics, Googoosh's tunes topped the charts. Her clothes inspired a generation of teenyboppers. Picture Diana Ross, Edith Piaf and Madonna all rolled into one. Unflinching under the spotlight, she defined the youth culture of the elite. For them she embodied the Western craze. Her bouncy style and coquettish charm captivated all the girls, who came to school with Googooshy short hairdos. At lawn parties, the girls copied her dance moves and hand gestures as they danced away under the night sky, bottles of Pepsi left standing in the grass. But Googoosh's coy songs weren't for everybody, least of all the mullahs.

And they surely weren't Hassan's cup of tea either. Hearing her voice on the radio, he would cluck his tongue while nodding his head upward. That meant *nakhe*, a very emphatic no. I knew I had to find another station. Hassan preferred the traditional Persian music that flowed from his *sehtar*, the small stringed mandolin that he used to pull out and play late in the evening. He also enjoyed listening to the crisp, ringing rainfall of notes from the *santur*, the Persian dulcimer, ancestor of the harpsichord and piano. But his favorite was the simple *ney*, the reed flute, with its hypnotic breath-filled tones.

After the Revolution, the new regime imposed strict silence. Singing was deemed non-Islamic. The radio played only the monotonic recitations of the Koran. Stage lights darkened. Theaters and clubs shut their doors. Given the choice of running into exile or being mute, most performers ran. Googoosh chose to stay. She served one month in prison before she was banned from leaving the country. She ended up spending most of her time on the Caspian coast, as a guest of friends.

"Is it really Googoosh?" I asked.

"Yes," Nasrollah shouted. "You like?"

"Where did you get it?"

"What do you mean?" His nostrils flared and he gave me an offended look, as if I had questioned his hipness. Just to show me his true colors, he reached under his seat and waved two more tapes. "In Sivand. I bought four."

"Four?"

"My daughter's getting married soon."

"Congratulations!"

"She loves Googoosh. She's going to dance to it."

"That's great!" I said, giving him the thumbs-up sign. "What's the name of this song?"

"*Hejrat,*'" he bellowed. "'The Journey.'"

Through the moan of the motor climbing at this altitude, I heard a syncopated thump-a-thump of drums and synthesizer with Googoosh's voice lifting above the grinding roar. Avo had drifted off to sleep.

"Safe to play it out here," Nasrollah said, gesturing out the window at the desolate land.

"Not in town?"

"No," he whispered, raising his eyebrows again. "You understand . . ."

Below us lay famed Yazd. The sprawling city blended with the desert, diffused under a uniform tan cloak. No sharp line marked where sand ended and dwellings began. From a distance, a pair of sleek minarets anchored the skyline, while dozens upon dozens of sand-colored towers rose above the flat sun-baked mud roofs.

We had not come here for the immense catacombed bazaar, prized textiles and succulent pastries. With its ancient fire temple, this city had served as a place of pilgrimage for centuries. Yazd was still the world's Zoroastrian capital.

As we descended to the plain, the towers of the tan metropolis reminded me of those medieval Tuscan towers erected by feuding families. But instead of blood feuds, each year Yazdis faced a common enemy: summer heat. Blistering temperatures topping 140 degrees had created the need for these ingenious towers, marvels of architecture. They are life preservers, wind catchers, fishing lines to the sky.

A large opening at the top of the tower traps the hot wind. Gusts channel their way down the shaft, then bounce off a cool pond below. Thus the heated breeze changes into fresh, soothing air. Families sitting in nearby homes rejoice at this ancient natural air-conditioning system that staves off the inferno outside.

*     *     *

Two steep hills dominated the southern suburbs. Each was crowned with a circular stone citadel. Rich spotted them first.

"There!" he bellowed. "The burial turrets."

Perched on rocky crags, these structures stood against the blue afternoon sky. We drove in their direction, bypassing the city's medieval center, until we reached the modern outskirts, sliding onto a gravel road. Our dusty cloud followed us to its end. Piling out and stretching, each of us breathed a sigh of relief. It had been ten hours.

I held my mother, whose stiff ankle was giving her pain. She looked pensively up at the stone turrets. Chris and Rich shared the last drop of water. Kevin had just woken up. My father hailed a white-bearded man passing by on a donkey.

Kev and Akbar were immersed in a discussion.

"Did you know," asked Akbar, "that Zoroaster was the first ecologist?"

"You mean he was a green?"

"For Zoroastrians, earth, water and fire are sacred. When a man dies and the soul leaves, what is left?"

"The body."

"Filthy, dirty. More toxic than even a rat's skin."

"Do they bury it?" asked Kev.

"No, they cannot pollute the earth with a rotting body."

"Do they cremate it?"

"No! They cannot pollute the holy fire."

"So what do they do?"

Akbar pointed up to a circling vulture. "They leave the body on top of these towers of silence. A sky burial. If you think about it, it's respect for the environment."

"Many say that ecology is the missing commandment," Kevin said.

"*Baba*, you're sounding *very* Zorro-astarian."

Kevin loved hearing those words. His face lost its afflicted expression and beamed an angelic smile. His first of the day. The long sleep had done him good. He looked inspired. His chin jutted out with renewed certainty. Already, I knew, he had adopted this new faith. Soon he would fold it into his Celtic-mystic nature. Blessed with Irish exaggeration, he would refashion it in his own image.

He pulled out his copy of Yeats and read aloud what he had circled: "If we knew the Fire-Worshippers better we might find that their centuries of pious observance have been rewarded, and the fire has given them a little of its nature; and I am certain that the water, the water of the seas and of lakes and of mist and rain, has all but made the Irish after its image."

Armed with these words and parched for water, we scaled one of the hills. The wind howled as my brothers scrambled up the rocky path. I climbed slowly with Mom, helping her cautious steps, hoping her ankle would hold up. My father followed after his boys. The sun drifted down in a crimson blaze.

The tower lay abandoned, bare and uncovered. Only a crack allowed our passage inside the walls. We stood in the enclosed courtyard, which was vacant, eerie. Here, for centuries, dead bodies had been placed close to the sky, where birds of prey could pick the bones clean. Later, the bones were pushed into a small pit in the center.

Akbar told us that although the Shah had claimed Achaemenian roots and appropriated Zoroastrian symbols — which infuriated the mullahs — he decreed in 1965 that these towers be closed and a cemetery be built nearby, at the foot of the mountain. On the windswept precipice, Kev stood looking down on the graveyard, so far below the sky. The blurred horizon faded; the city lay in slumber.

On the edge of the cliff, a sheer drop of hundreds of feet, my mother's cape fluttered in the updraft. The sun shone behind her. Elated after her climb to the top on her bad ankle, she threw back her arms like a bird's wings.

"Be careful, Mrs. Ward!" Akbar shouted.

She obeyed. And as she ended her brief moment of flight, her cloak spun back around her body.

"Akbar," I asked, "the chador, when did it become Islamic dress?"

"You know, it was originally Sassanian practice."

"Before Islam?" My mother turned, surprised to hear his news.

"It was a custom of high-class women, the aristocrats. Even Ferdowsi describes ancient Persian women as having covered faces. If you look, there is no law in the Koran that dictates covering the whole body with a veil. But the Arabs, when they arrived, took on the traditions of *our* rulers. And over the years, harem and chador became Islamic."

And a symbolic flashpoint. In the twentieth century, Iranian society had swung back and forth regarding the black body-length chador — which literally means tent. In 1936, Reza Shah ordered it removed. By 1979, Ayatollah Khomeini ordered it to be worn again. This issue became a fault line for Westernized Iranian women. In the nineties, fashion codes had loosened, and manteaus — knee-length raincoats — and flowery scarves were part of everyday life. More significantly, forceful calls for equal rights were being voiced by women, emboldened by Khatami's election.

I remembered that Fatimeh never left our front gate without being wrapped in her chador. And this was before the Revolution. Around the house, she wore a pastel scarf. We never once saw her full head of hair, just her hairline. She was more comfortable like that. We never questioned it. I had no idea until now that her custom was older than Islam.

A tree-lined street led to the Safaieh Hotel, set in an oasis with pleasing white stucco bungalows scattered among pine groves. Pushed by Rich's relentless schedule, we checked in, washed up and rushed over to the nearby *Ateshkade*, the Zoroastrian fire temple. Exhausted, we straggled into the courtyard.

Carved into the white-columned façade, sacred Ahura Mazda flapped his brightly painted eagle's wings. I took a deep breath. A calm peace shielded this place from the bustling street outside. The door of the temple was open. Kev and Rich marched in.

In the center of the long white hall, an immense five-foot bronze urn spouted flames behind an opaque pane of glass. A priest dressed in white walked over and spoke to us in fluent English.

"This fire was first lit one thousand four hundred years ago, then it was brought to Yazd."

"You mean it has been burning nonstop for all these centuries?" We looked at it in disbelief.

"Yes," the priest said, "someone is always here to feed the flames. Generation after generation, the fire is never alone."

Behind the glass, a young girl in a robe placed more wood on the fire.

"But there are so few of us now." He sighed heavily.

"How many Zoroastrians in Iran?"

He looked over his shoulder to see if anyone was eavesdropping. Then he turned. "In Yazd, ten thousand. Some mullahs call us heathens and stir anger toward us. What can we do?"

Pilgrims, he told us, came from all over the world to visit the twenty-two temples in the province of Yazd. They arrived by the planeload from Bombay, home to the world's largest Zoroastrian community. The wealthy Indian Parsis — whose name derived from their Persian origin — worshiped here at the fire temple.

Chris asked his usual question: "Do you ever think of leaving?"

"No. I must remain. Who will keep the sacred flame going?"

"And what about your children?"

"I pray for their future," the guardian said. "Many of our people are old. Life is very hard. There should be more tolerance. After all, Imam Hussein married a Zoroastrian princess, the Shahbanou. In Tehran you can see her tomb, but still some insult us and call us fire worshipers. But we only look to the light, our god. It's not just about fire."

The term "fire worshiper," mentioned by Marco Polo, was pejorative, and this misconception had plagued Zoroastrians for centuries. Of course, like the cross or the crescent, the flame was only symbolic. But zealots did not understand symbols. We said farewell and returned to the hotel.

While the family rested, I walked out the gate past the trees. And from there I spotted three figures on the summit of the hill next to the towers of silence. Moments later, I found myself climbing to the top again, where I had a sweeping 360-degree view of the plain. Any dust of approaching horsemen could be seen fifty miles away. It was twilight.

I was admiring the vista when I heard a voice behind me.

A young woman in a chador spoke with a clipped English accent. "Excuse me, do you speak English?"

"Yes," I replied.

"I couldn't help noticing your ginger hair."

"It's Irish."

"Pappy! Mummy!" she called into the wind. "I'm afraid they're quarreling again," she said. "You know, there's a common joke about Parsis. Put three of us in a room and there will be four arguments." She smiled.

"And if one is alone?"

"Then a Parsi will look in the mirror and argue with himself."

I laughed. The Parsis are one of the eccentric, perhaps unique offspring of the original Zoroastrian tribe that fled eastward in the seventh century to escape the invading Arabs. They settled in the Indian coastal state of Gujarat and the trading port of Bombay. They amassed great fortunes, lived in palatial grandeur, entertained lavishly and centuries later enjoyed favored status under the British raj. Their pale skin reinforced their position in the caste system. All in all, they had fared well far from home. But nowadays, their inbreeding was a grave concern.

A tall older woman appeared, pink silks fluttering from under a billowing black cape. Her striking face was no-nonsense, firm and handsome.

I introduced myself.

"Ah, so you're an American," her daughter exclaimed.

"Don't be silly, Roshan," the mother said. "He wouldn't be wandering about here in Iran."

"Mummy, don't be unpleasant."

"Roshan, you're arguing again."

An older man in white cottons walked into my view. "Speak up, old boy. Are you really a Yank? What in heaven's name are you doing here?"

"I . . . well, my family . . . we're on a sort of pilgrimage."

"Smashing. So are we!"

"From Bombay?"

"Heavens no, old boy. London. We're Parsi pilgrims, you know."

"Yes, your daughter was just telling me."

"You're sounding like Noël Coward again, Darius, with your 'Parsi pilgrims.'"

The gentleman's well-lined face was unfazed by his wife's snipe. "You see, we Zoroastrians have lived in exile for over a thousand years," he said. "I thought it was high time we came to visit our native soil."

"My son is resting in bed at the hotel," the mother said. "He's simply worn out from all this marching up and down."

"No backbone," Darius said.

"Yes, well now, Darius, enough culture for today."

"Darling, this is not simply culture . . ."

"Here we are, night's falling. Come, let's leave these rocks before I faint."

"Yes, dear."

"Very good to have met you," the mother said. "Darius is hard of hearing, please forgive him." She reached over and shook my hand, something women rarely do in Iran nowadays.

"Perhaps we'll have a chance to speak again at a lower altitude," her husband said with a wave.

And off they went, trudging on spindly legs holding up rather corpulent torsos that spoke of a lifetime of fine dining. Roshan lingered behind. I watched them stumble over the rocks, and Darius reached down to pick up something and put it in his pocket. A memento?

In the most apocalyptic American novel, *Moby-Dick*, Herman Melville portrayed Captain Ahab not as a Quaker Christian but as a Zoroastrian. Harold Bloom, the renowned literary critic, writes that Ahab's "own whaling boat is staffed by Fedallah and other Parsis, the world's last Zoroastrians."

I had already seen Zoroaster's face. In the Vatican, walking slowly with Idanna, passing from one hall to another, we stopped where Raphael immortalized the learned giants of the ancient world. In his fresco *The School of Athens*, Plato boldly strides across the white-marbled agora. Aristotle walks on his left. Satyr-faced Socrates leans stage right. In the foreground, Euclid draws triangles for students.

Raphael's unassuming self-portrait peeks out from a crowd on the far right. And next to him, oddly enough, with a red-trimmed cap and a long, luxurious gray beard, stands the great Zoroaster. The Persian prophet holds a globe lit with stars, the sacred constellations. His eyes are piercing and clear; his smile is knowing. He stares beyond the viewer. Because of the astronomical powers attributed to him, Raphael naturally placed Zoroaster with the scientists, gathered around Euclid. Only he represents the mystical East as ambassador to this summit of classical minds. He alone has straddled both land and sky, and holds the heavens in his hands. All the other visionaries are earthbound.

After dinner, we drove through modern Yazd, with its well-paved broad avenues that offered a few cheery stores still open for night owls. We passed a movie theater and two brightly lit restaurants and almost forgot about the desert. Soon we reached the historic thriving heart, one of the largest traditional city centers in the country. Turning a corner, we unexpectedly confronted a remarkable sight, a display of baroque bravado: an ostentatious bazaar edifice called *Chakhmaq Tekyeh*. Grandly, it opened onto a piazza. The sky vibrated with wondrous pastels of last light and held a full moon hanging low. Two stories of vaulted arches, turquoise and cream, spanned the square. Floodlit in gold, the façade glowed. In the center towered an eighty-foot faienced portal whose steep minarets rose like lances, doubling its height. A large fountain reflected the image.

Originally built to herald the bazaar's entrance, this splendid pleasure was a worthy tribute to medieval Yazd's mercantile patrons. But the bazaar, according to Akbar, had moved soon after its construction. Now it stood as an enchanting folly. I sat with my brothers by the fountain, gazing at the marvel. The long golden structure seemed poised like an archer's bow, ready to launch those two tile-tipped minarets straight into the heavens to pierce the grapefruit moon above.

Surprised to find a copy of *Iran News* at the hotel reception desk, I scanned it to take the pulse of distant Tehran. The headlines said it all: "Karbaschi Has Emerged as a National Hero," "Supporters of Tehran's Imprisoned Mayor Rally to His Defense," "Karbaschi's Release Imminent." The momentum of the reformers was building.

Another paper, the daily *Farda*, reported that a young girl imprisoned in Abadan had hanged herself using her scarf. Her crime? "The girl had been strolling in a public park along with a young man not related to her." And then I read this announcement:

> The Jewish Community of Yazd Province yesterday started celebrating the feast of Passover. Moussa Dodashi said the celebrations will last eight days. While performing their religious rituals, the Iranian Jews pray for the long life of the Leader of the Islamic Revolution, Ayatollah Ali Khameini, the success of the Islamic Republic of Iran and the establishment of peace and tranquillity throughout the globe.

After cups of tea, we sat out on the porches of our bungalows until, one by one, my parents and then my brothers drifted off to sleep. I prepared to say farewell to Akbar. Tomorrow at dawn he would return home to Shiraz.

The dry air left the stars polished, dazzling over us like a grand fireworks display. Bright Arcturus blazed in Boötes; Virgo's left hand held her sheaves of corn marked by Spica, signaling spring. The Greater and Lesser Bears chased each other around the Pole Star. Cassiopeia circled in watch.

My family had agreed from the start not to mention the real purpose of our trip to our Iranian escorts. The three had seemed puzzled about our obsession with the village of Tudeshk. But now I decided to tell Akbar about our search for Hassan. As he listened, his eyes widened behind his thick glasses.

"I don't believe it." He shook his head. "Risking to come back to Iran only to find a cook."

I showed him Hassan's photo.

He studied the picture. "I can see it's a nice family." He raised his head. "And their village?"

"Tudeshk. Between Yazd and Isfahan. We hope."

"Never heard of it."

"No one has."

"You've asked around?"

"Rich even offered the travel agency a thousand dollars for information."

"And?"

"Nothing."

"Terry *jan*, I'm surprised. You really think after all this time you'll find him?"

*"Insha'allah."*

"And what if you don't?"

"Don't know. I guess we'll keep heading north to Tehran . . ."

I was stumbling and had no real answer. Before I could finish, Akbar cut me short.

"Don't worry, my dear friend. Even if you don't find him, something else will happen." He paused, then smiled. "In the end, you will find many Hassans along the way."

Lifting his eyes, he scanned the night sky. He spoke now in a calm *sotto voce.* "You see, the master is God, and if you make a prayer he will listen. God is everywhere. The problem is, we don't see Him. We are too busy with everyday work. We use less than eight percent of our faculties. We're busy making money, working, driving. When you wake up in the morning, for instance, and unexpectedly hear a bird singing in the courtyard, that's His sign. It depends on you to ask, What is the message? If we learn to observe what is really happening around us, then we'll get His answer." He sounded like a Sufi mystic.

He reached over and hugged me. We promised to stay in touch and exchanged addresses. I had come to admire him. His poetic nature, artistic sensitivity, knowledge and humanity, we would sorely miss.

"Very special people, your dear parents, so much love they have," he said. "Good luck and good night."

*"Khoda hafez,"* I said and thanked him again.

He went to bed, and I stayed outside in the night breeze. Passing clouds swallowed the moon's light. A tingling fear came over me. What had we embarked on? In our mobile Ward family cocoon, it had all seemed natural, so straightforward. I tried to push negative thoughts out of my mind.

A gentle wind gusted suddenly, rustling the leaves overhead. I heard a shuffling behind me. I turned and peered into the dark grove, but spotted nothing. Then a lone figure appeared. It was Avo. Had he been eavesdropping on my conversation with Akbar about Hassan? Puffing tensely on his cigarette, he didn't say a word. He swung his leg over the low stoop, sitting down opposite me. I said nothing. We stared up at the heavens. Then he spoke.

"Terry, why didn't you tell me?"

"What?"

"Look." Avo lowered his voice. "You really want us to get into trouble?"

"No," I protested.

"A *baji*, a servant. I don't believe it. It's crazy." He kept his eyes on the stars. "So, this Hassan was your cook?"

"Yes."

"Does he know you're coming?"

"No."

"And you really think he wants to see you."

"Don't know."

*"Baba*, after all these years, he may be dead."

I was silent. He was restless.

"So, please tell me, why are we going?"

"Because we have to."

"Why can't you just be ordinary tourists?" Avo tossed his burning butt onto the marble floor, stomping on it.

I did not reply. If he didn't understand, there was no point.

"Look, you can go back to Tehran tomorrow," I snapped. Rising from the stoop, I glanced over to gauge his reaction. My words were still sinking in. "*Shab-bekhair,* good night."

"*Shab-bekhair,*" he mumbled.

Lighting another cigarette, he stared in the other direction. I slumped back to my room, leaving him smoking under the moon. In darkness and flickering shadows, I tossed and turned. Was I out of my mind? With more than sixty million people in Iran, how could we ever hope to find Hassan? And if by some miracle we did find him, what would he say? Would he greet us with open arms or slam the door?

When I awoke, Akbar was gone. On the porch, sitting on the same stoop, Avo looked groggy, rubbing his eyes in the crisp morning sun before putting on his glasses. Chris was giddily laughing, telling Rich a story that he called "The Night of the 1,001 Beds."

In the confusion brought on by all our traveling, last night Chris had stumbled into the wrong room and fallen asleep in Akbar's bed. When Akbar had turned in, he had found his bed taken, so he staggered into Kev's room and crashed in my bed. When I saw a body in my bed, I crept into the adjoining room and lay down on an open bed, which belonged to Avo. After all his cigarettes, Avo found both mattresses in his room taken and, not realizing Richard's room was half empty, he did the obvious. He slept on the floor.

In the fresh morning light, with my brothers laughing, I overheard Nasrollah complaining to Avo. "That one kept me up all night." He scowled at Chris. "Snoring like a buzzsaw. *Be Khoda,* worse than a train!"

"That bad?" Avo said.

"The worst noise I've ever heard. How am I going to drive to-

day without falling asleep? This was a trick of yours. You sent him
to my room, and you slept —"

"On the floor."

"Just make sure it doesn't happen again."

Unfazed by the driver's diatribe, Avo looked at Chris with keen
admiring eyes. During breakfast of yogurt and honey, hot bread
and fig jam and steaming tea, he commended Chris on his snoring prowess.

"*Bah, bah*," Avo said, shaking his head. "You must be a real professional." He poured Chris a fresh cup of tea. "Only a real pro
could keep a driver awake all night," he said.

"You handled it brilliantly, Avo," said Kev, who looked refreshed. A night's sleep without Chris's railroad engine had done
him well. His eyes no longer had that deadened look. It was
Nasrollah's turn to suffer.

When you wake up in a new city, the prodigious travel writer and
historian Jan Morris suggested two rules: "One is found in E. M.
Forster's guide to Alexandria; . . . to wander aimlessly around.
The second is from the Psalms; grin like a dog and run about
through the city."

Before we could do either, a crisis erupted. A new van mysteriously appeared. A loud argument between Nasrollah and a new,
unwelcome driver obliged Avo to call his boss, our travel agent.
After putting down the phone, Avo was ashen-faced. All of us
wanted to keep Nasrollah at least until we reached Tudeshk. To
make things worse, the new van would not start.

"Call again," my father told Avo. "Rich will straighten it out."

"I can't."

"Why not?"

"You don't understand, Mr. Ward. I have just been fired."

In the end, Rich phoned and saved Avo's job. Nasrollah stayed.

"Rich, I owe you one," Avo said. "Believe me, I know. I've got a
lot of experience in being fired. For instance, in my last job I was
supposed to hold the marker for a surveyor, but I couldn't read his
hand signals from a distance. It was the type of a job where you

don't get dumb, but you get something. You know what I mean? Anyway, I was fired there too."

After all the confusion, I was secretly relieved. With each passing day, it became increasingly clear that our Inspector Clouseau's hard drive had limited storage capacity. He had probably already forgotten about our search for Hassan.

Back in Nasrollah's van, we began to explore the architectural treasures of Yazd. The fourteenth-century Masjid-e Jame, or Friday Mosque, boasted the highest arched portal in the Islamic world, a lofty Timurid design topped with a pair of slender, soaring minarets. Here, Kufic script fired into the toffee clay brickwork blended with multicolored geometric designs and stunning faience that predated the Safavid floral turquoise. This was the raw elegance, the explosive creativity that Robert Byron saluted. In 1934, he was astonished to find no mention of the mosque in any travel book. "Are travelers blind?" he ranted. The spectacular tapered arch stood more than one hundred feet high.

In Yazd's bazaar, we wended our way past coppersmiths and goldsmiths under cool vaulted ceilings pierced with circular holes that let the sun slip through. The dizzying maze of whitewashed corridors was splashed with light. With all the negative news about Iran that we had heard in America, we had not expected pristine highways, clean streets and, above all, these immaculate paths in the bazaars.

"What's going on? You can literally eat off the floor." Kev expressed the same astonishment that he first voiced in Shiraz's Vakil bazaar.

"Where are the beggars?" my mother asked. "Where is the glaucoma, the rickets and polio?" And where was the hopelessness that stripped all dignity away? Where was the despair we had seen in the Shah's day, when crippled children crawled up to a chauffeur-driven Mercedes, beseeching, "My sacrifice, sir. A slave of yours. Forgive me, kindly throw me a blessing." When the oil boom of the seventies flooded the country with petrodollars, beggars swarmed the streets of the Shah's capital. Since we had returned, we had seen neither extreme — neither dejected poverty nor obscene wealth.

Throughout the bazaar, a quiet dignity was palpable. Rarely did anyone approach us. A glance or a respectful look our way in passing, but the shoppers seemed more interested in their own business than in a group of six rather odd-looking foreigners. We wandered past textile merchants selling silk brocade and delicate white lace.

Two young women walked by with lofty hairstyles under elevated gray scarves.

"They must be from Tehran," sniffed Avo. "We call those five stories high."

Cosmetic creams and oils sold well at pharmacy stalls. Cotton and silk shirts in discreetly patterned earth tones attracted Chris. Fashionable vanity, an Iranian trademark, was alive and well. By ostracizing foreigners and the immensely wealthy Westernized class, perhaps Iran had finally reached a balance: the irresponsible rich and the hopeless beggar had truly disappeared.

Leaving the bazaar, my parents had made a new acquaintance, Mr. Jamshid, a schoolteacher whose broadly lined forehead, bushy white hair and rotund belly projected a winning charm.

"He's invited us to come to his home," my mother said. "We can't refuse."

"Excessive hospitality — I was warned about it," Kev whispered to me.

We agreed to come along, and soon we sat in a quaint two-room house, on Mr. Jamshid's carpeted floor, studying a detailed architectural plan of the bazaar that he had painstakingly mapped out for the city. His precocious daughter, Masumeh, brought us pastries and tea. Yazd's medieval shopping mall, which had swallowed us in three hours of erratic navigation, from goldsmiths' shops to the café and back out to our van parked in bright sunlight, was all there, meticulously drawn on rolled sepia-colored paper. The labyrinth had a distinct form and obvious limits.

The design seemed organic. Straight lines curved like rivulets.

No city planner's grid had been imposed on this marketplace. It had evolved naturally. Each pathway had been carved out not by an architect but by random walkers.

Over many years, a consensus of Yazdi footprints established the twists and turns, the right angles, blocked crossings, squares and basements. The bazaar was a living thing. Its interwoven links within the city were as fluid and vital as blood vessels.

"Why does he do all this work?" asked Avo, staring at Mr. Jamshid's map. None of us reacted. "I guess because he's into it," Avo muttered to himself.

"When you look at the form of the bazaar," Mr. Jamshid explained, "it's like a *dastgah*, or collection of musical notes. You see, each store and shop on the route is a note of the melody. And when you come upon an opening, it's like a pause in the musical score. Listen . . ."

He hummed a gay *dastgah mahur* as he moved his index finger from shop to shop. This *dastgah*," he said, "is ideal for the twilight hour." Then he paused, pointing at a courtyard, and, still singing, he circled the covered spaces. "You see?"

"*Bah, bah*, wow!" Rich was amazed.

Mr. Jamshid had deciphered his own unique hermetic blueprint. Intuitively, he had unified the city's medieval brick and mortar, its myriad walking paths, with classical melodies, all connected by an invisible thread. Masumeh too looked just as surprised, before breaking into a nervous giggle.

Could Mr. Jamshid be a Sufi? His upturned generous mustache offered a clue. While the others were devouring homemade ginger biscuits, I sat down next to him.

"Pardon me," I said quietly. "Mr. Jamshid, may I ask you, are you a mystic?"

He answered with a diagonal upward nod of the head and a slight wink. I nodded back as he offered me a ginger cookie. He twirled his curling white mustache tips and snapped his head back. A fire came to his eye. Something had just discharged in his memory. A broad, pleasing grin raised his cheeks like balloons, and he offered us all another surprise.

"Tonight there is *zoor khaneh*, the house of strength," he declared. "Special champions. Be my guests! Come, you must not miss this."

All of us agreed immediately.

"*Kheli khub!* Very good!" He rubbed his chubby hands with delight.

As he rose and went to tell his wife to bring out more biscuits, his words began to sink in. Would this be a trip to the local gym? A stroll down to some hot, smoky men's club to watch heavyweights work out? We debated in hushed tones whether to go.

"Mr. Ward," whispered Avo. "If it's OK with you guys, I think I'll stay at the hotel tonight. I'm not really a big fan of *zoor khanehs*."

"Who is?" moaned Chris.

For centuries, *zoor khanehs* have been places where the Iranian martial arts are performed by heavily muscled men, named *pahlevan*, after renowned Sassanian warriors. In short, these were Iran's sumo wrestlers. Dad wondered aloud whether *zoor khanehs* hadn't turned into premier recruiting stations for revolutionary toughs, a natural breeding ground for zealots.

"Brawn over brains, like football players," he said.

"Bravery over intelligence," Chris agreed.

"With a heavy dose of patriotic fervor."

"A place where emotions run high," Kev added.

"If there's any setting that might be unwelcome for Yanks," said Chris, "this is it."

"So, I'll meet you back at the hotel," said Avo.

"But Mr. Jamshid has been so kind," Mom said.

"So you're really going?" Avo asked.

"I'm afraid so." My father looked us all in the eye.

Hearing Dad's decision, Chris coughed out his tea. His eyes pleaded no. My father's head nodded yes.

Back in the old days, Hassan used to exercise regularly outside his rooms by our cherry orchard. Stocky with strong arms, he had built up his burgeoning chest over years of devoted workouts. With a quick swan swoop, he would lift up two wooden clubs shaped like huge bowling pins the size of tree trunks. No problem. In one continuous motion, he would swing the two behind his shoulders, then twirl them around his head to complete a figure eight. Enthralled, my brothers and I tried to mimic him using smaller branches. When he was finished, he would leave the clubs standing and grab a towel to wipe off his sweat. Red-faced, huffing and puffing, we each tried to pick up the clubs, but they wouldn't budge. Panting, Hassan would smile. "In time, boys, in time."

In Yazd's glimmering twilight, our time had come. Feeling self-conscious, we followed Mr. Jamshid in single file down a narrow, dusty alley. A mother and daughter in chadors scurried past. Two dogs growled in a doorway. Soon we heard the sound of muffled drumming and the ringing of a bell. My mother gripped my arm.

"We're close."

Our host led us around a corner into a small square and stopped before a green wooden door. Obediently, we lined up in back of him when we heard a loud exultation from a crowd: *"Aaaaaahhhh!"*

Mr. Jamshid swung the bronze door latch open, and before us lay a hundred pairs of shoes. Bending our heads to pass under the low doorframe, we quickly added our own shoes to the pile. The air was thick, warm and pungent. Perhaps a hundred men sat in a small theater with ten circular rows that looked down onto a sunken stage.

On the wooden floor, six young athletes moved through their exercises. Perched to our right, a handsome musician sang and drummed into a microphone. Rapid-fire thumping and chants, synchronized motion and sweaty bodies rocked the walls. The charismatic drummer directed events like an orchestra conductor. The crowd was in his hand. On the beat, the assembly responded, *"Yaaaah Ali!"* My mother took Dad's arm and walked inside to find a seat with Mr. Jamshid.

Since medieval times, athletes have trained publicly in *zoor khanehs*. Part calisthenics, part gymnastics, part dance, the exercises were meant to prepare men for battle. The drum, the bell and the cantor's voice set the pace. Group performances were tests of speed, nimble footwork, strength, dexterity, endurance and artistry.

My mother slid onto the bench between Dad and Mr. Jamshid. It was not hard to notice she was the only woman here. This was surely the most private bastion of the country's male-dominated world. Undaunted, Mom gazed on intently. Dad, an ardent athlete himself, was captivated.

The intense crowd, pressed together, raised the temperature. The boys below were in their teens, not heavyset potbellied brutes. Gazelles instead of rhinos, these nimble warriors represented the flower of youth, defenders of the land. The crowd followed every move.

Their exercises had already begun. I could see that pride filled the older spectators' eyes. The old men were no doubt looking nostalgically into some mirror of yesteryear when they had once swung their clubs in the night, when they possessed youth's fire. A fierce bond connected the spectators and athletes. Chanting throbbed through the warriors' circle. The air was teeming with martial spirit.

Rich reached down to pull out his movie camera.

"Don't even think about it," I said, jabbing him with my elbow.

"We'll never get another chance," Rich said.

"Not here."

Over the loudspeaker, the drummer made an announcement: "Our guests this evening have arrived from . . ."

Silence.

"Am-ri-ka."

As Rich put his camera away, all eyes turned toward us. A murmur rose from the crowd. One man nodded at me, then another. A bearded man winked. I nodded back. Then, from the floor, a mahogany-haired athlete tilted his head and quickly raised his eyebrows. Even the drummer turned to toss me a quick grin. With great respect, I nodded and bowed my head slightly at any eyes that met mine.

"Signs of welcome," said Rich.

"Thank God," said Chris.

Meanwhile, some spectators — father, uncle, cousin or friend — seemed lost in their own thoughts, carefully studying the dexterity shown by each athlete. Chris's eyes were bulging as the drum cadence thumped faster and faster. Soon the bleachers were shaking as the drummer chanted poetry from Ferdowsi's *Book of Kings* to a martial beat. His staccato delivery built up charged emotion. His drums danced. *Dom do dom . . . ppiiinggg. Dom do dom . . . ppiiiing. Slap . . . riing. Slapppedy slap!*

Like a jazz concert, each athlete had his chance to improvise and jam. Each worked the stage, flaunting his own moves, strutting his stuff. It was a combination of collective harmonics and solo riffs. Windmill motions of twirling heavy wooden clubs overhead drew spontaneous rounds of applause. The real crowd pleaser was a frantic spin-like-a-dervish maneuver. I had never seen this as a boy, but here in Yazd, these teenagers had nothing to stop them. With the flick of the drum and bell, their feet launched into a frenetic whirl. Rhythm quickened to rapid fire. *Dom . . . do . . . dom, slap . . . slapppp . . . ring . . . be-rinng!* Heads swung back. Arms flung out. Rapturous acceleration grew into a dizzying blur. Around and around they went until thunderous clapping and stomping erupted from all sides. And the human propeller spun back down. Prolonged cheers signaled this as the favorite riff.

On the bright green walls overhead hung the Valhalla of the Yazdis. I studied their shrine of heroes, portraits of sportsmen, past champions and martyrs. I spotted a black-and-white photo of the handsome folk hero and beloved Olympic wrestler Takhti, a silver medal winner in Helsinki. In the sixties, Takhti had been a leader in the National Front Party of Mossadegh, the Shah's rival. After winning the world wrestling championship in Yokohama, Takhti shocked his countrymen by snubbing the Shah when he refused to shake his hand. Soon after, he was found murdered. It was rumored that the Shah's secret police, SAVAK, had murdered him.

Like the mythical warrior Rustam, Takhti and these champions before us embodied chivalry and tradition. Looked up to as role models, they represented patriotism of a powerful and humble sort, and a moral code: strength with generosity. Only a month after Khatami's historic overture, the *Tehran Times* saluted five U.S. wrestlers who arrived to compete in the Takhti Cup, an international wrestling tournament. Twelve thousand fans attended the event, whistling and cheering. Significantly, after two decades the first official hand-to-hand contact between Iran and its arch-enemy America involved athletes.

The drummer had stopped beating his drum, and now he quietly brought us down. All chanted softly, *"Yaahhh Ali,"* and the session ended with a prayer for Imam Ali, the patron saint of *zoor khanehs*. We got up to leave. Hands reached out to shake ours.

"Yazdi bebop, like wild jazz," said Kevin as we searched in the pile of shoes for our own before going out into the dusty street again.

"I loved it," declared Mom.

Smiles greeted us as we followed Mr. Jamshid back through the town's streets in the dim light of hanging bulbs. Our ears still rang with *"Yaaaaahhh Ali!"*

9

# Appointment in Tudeshk

> She is very aware of her looks, so she wears a little makeup,
> not when she goes out in public but in private social gather-
> ings like this. We like to say that God is beautiful and appre-
> ciates beauty.
>
> — Maryam Sadeghi, describing Mrs. Sakineh Ziai, mother of
> President Khatami (*New York Times,* January 15, 1998)

CLEARING HIS THROAT, Kevin addressed us all at breakfast.
"You know, I had no dreams at the Apadana Hotel in Shiraz, but here . . ."

"Did you expect it to be this gentle?" my mother asked.

"The hotel or Iran?"

"Iran."

"I had no idea what to expect."

"I didn't either. I was . . . well, a bit afraid."

"I wasn't scared," Kev said. "These people are amazing. I mean,
the aura I'm getting."

"Nasrollah's a peach," said Mom. "And Inspector Clouseau is
growing on me."

"Oh, totally," Kev agreed. "Once you get what he can do and
can't, he's totally amusing."

"We know what he can't do," Mom said. "He's terrified because
of his lack of self-confidence."

"You know what I feared the most?" asked Kev. "Long drives in
incredibly hot and dusty vans, dirty and smelly . . ."

My father nodded. He had endured many such journeys in his treks to the oilfields years ago.

"... And mean police," added Chris.

"I read in the *New York Times* that President Khatami's family is from Ardakan. That's nearby, isn't it?" Mom asked.

"About twenty miles."

"I'd love to visit his mother. What do you think? Is there any way we can do that?"

"We'll put Avo on the case."

"Yes, he'll have to pick up where Akbar left off."

"No," Kev pointed out. "Now we're on our own."

My mother was determined to pay a visit to Mrs. Sakineh Ziai, President Mohammad Khatami's seventy-eight-year-old mother. She wanted to congratulate Mrs. Ziai and tell her what an admirable man her son was. She felt it only right to want to share her enthusiasm over the recent rapprochement with the world community brought about by her son. Plain and simple Kansas logic.

President Khatami, elected with 70 percent of the vote in August 1997, carried a Kennedy-like aura in Iran. Wildly popular among women and young people, he refused to view the world as Khomeini had done: a clash of East and West. Schooled in pre-Islamic Persian history, Shia Islam and Western philosophy, he was also fluent in English and German, having lived two years in Hamburg. The Internet-literate leader spoke eloquently about women's advancement and dialogue among nations. He was a fresh wind of change.

"And he dresses well. You should see his leather shoes," Avo said, "not those rough slippers that mullahs like to wear. And his beard is always neat. Everyone loves him."

On February 1, two months before we arrived in Iran, the *New York Times* quoted him: "We love all the people in the world and we want them to love us in return. Resentments should be turned into kindness and love." Later, he spoke over Iranian radio, asking the people to stop chanting the Revolution's mantra, *"Marg bar . . . ,"* or "Death to . . . ," during his public speeches.

"I stand for life, not death," he said. "Ours is the God of love." After reading this, my mother was determined to bring her message of praise to his mother.

Akbar was sorely missed. Our calm, poetic patriot had left us squarely in limbo. I studied my map again: Ardakan, twenty miles north of Yazd. As we approached the dusty town, forlorn and dun-colored, my mother asked Avo for his help in finding the president's family home. But he was being difficult again.

"No, no, no! I'm not going to ask for directions to Khatami's house," he said. "There could be secret police, Revolutionary Guards!"

Chris quickly agreed. "He's right. Why stir up trouble? Mom, do we have to? Can't we just keep going?"

"Besides," said Avo, "we don't have an appointment or anything, do we?"

"No," my mother answered.

"So, you see, we can't go."

I leaned over and asked Nasrollah if he could help.

"Yes, of course," he answered coolly and stared straight ahead. Our zealous driver enjoyed my mother's singular challenge. Refusing to listen to Avo's protests, he called out his window to passersby for directions. One young student waved us to the left along a dusty boulevard.

With his flaring eyes, thick mustache and a two-day beard, Nasrollah earned sudden respect from rival motorists. He kept asking as we careened through the town. At a stoplight, a taxi driver shouted back and pointed to the right. We turned down that street and after five minutes came to another intersection. Avo was still protesting, but no one listened. Nasrollah was in charge. One driver timidly pointed back in the direction we had just come. Hearing this, Nasrollah immediately spun us around in a wrenching U-turn.

At the next red light, he leaned out the window and called to an old *haji*, who agreed to help and hopped into the van. He guided us toward the parched fringe of town, to a simple brick house. No trees, no police. The street was deserted.

My mother got out and rang the doorbell. Avo reluctantly joined her to translate. The rest of us remained in the van, except Richard, who slipped out behind Avo.

A green metal gate swung open, and a woman in a black chador greeted my mother. Behind her, I could see a small compound sprouting a modest wind tower. Mom and Avo disappeared inside. The dwelling behind the brick wall looked spartan. Mom had entered the Khatami family's inner sanctum; her wish had been fulfilled, I thought. Now she would speak as a mother who has always loved Iran, and in this moment of openness and friendship, she would extend her heartfelt wishes to the family whose son spoke of breaking the Islamic Republic's isolation from the outside world.

An hour later, when my mother emerged, a desert gust lifted her veil like a sail as she boarded the van. The *haji* guide and Nasrollah seemed quite pleased. Mrs. Ziai, Khatami's mother, was not at home, she said. But she had been made welcome by the president's sister, Maryam Khalili.

The two women conversed with compassion and hope, heart to heart. Maryam spoke of her deep religious faith. Mom praised her and her family for their public service. They explored world affairs, public health, housing for the poor, young boys lost in the Iran-Iraq War and Khatami's call for international dialogue.

My mother asked her questions about raising her children. Her older son worked for the university and headed a commission to create unity between Shiite and Sunni in Iran. Her oldest daughter was the principal of a high school in town; her other son was the principal of a secondary school in London. The youngest daughter was sixteen years old and still in high school. The room where my mother and Mrs. Khalili spoke was spare and spotless.

They sat on a carpet, and the whitewashed walls were dominated by a large photograph of her third son, who was killed in the war.

"He was only seventeen," Mom said. "She is still overcome by grief. I assured her that the death of a son was the greatest sacrifice a mother could give. She mentioned a German film crew that came to film her home during that time. 'They were given much hospitality,' she said, 'but then they betrayed our trust and misused the material.'

"Then her granddaughter came out, looking very pretty, and served us cardamom biscuits and tangerines."

As we drove off, my mother spoke about her plans for when we visited the Vatican of the Shia. "In Qom, I'll wear my full chador."

"No, Mom," countered the ever-fearful Chris. "*I'll* wear your chador in Qom."

I looked across the street as we made our U-turn. Still no police. Khatami's family chose to live modestly, a refreshing change from patriarchs in the clergy who flaunted their exalted status and newly gained wealth. As Nasrollah pulled away, I felt a flush of pride for my mother. Rarely do men summon up the courage to bridge barriers. We prefer to fight or accuse. Poison seeps into souls and hardens like cement. It's so much easier to refuse to budge than to reach out.

Once again, Mom was teaching us in her powerful way. Hope and reconciliation fill the human heart. No gift can be greater than the burial of fear. The Reverend Cecil Williams of Glide Memorial Church in San Francisco called it by another name: radical love. If we ever find Hassan, *insha'allah*, we'll be ready.

Ironically, many of the revolutionary figures who stormed the U.S. embassy that night of November 4, 1979, including Khatami's younger brother Reza, now called for normalizing relations with America. The twentieth anniversary of the occupation was approaching. Reformers treaded very softly indeed, sensing that change would come. On the other hand, one of the hostages, Barry Rosen, a diplomat who had been held for all 444 days, had publicly met in Paris with his former captor Abbas Abdi, and together they spoke of reconciliation between Iran and the United States. Any diplomatic opening would be a boon to the sick economy.

Yet such a breakthrough would gravely threaten the legitimacy of hard-liners as protectors of the faithful. What they risked losing was their raison d'être for leadership. For almost two decades, they had been guarding the Iranian people against the Great Satan, who once controlled the evil Yazid, incarnated as the Shah. What would happen if they shook hands with Evil? If the great divide was bridged, they might well have to quit politics and return to the mosques.

We drove north of Ardakan in the direction of Nain, still a long way from Hassan's village. A battery of ominous peaks tracked us along our western flank, jagged and sharp as razors. Collectively their pointed armor looked like a migrating herd of stegosaurs. To our right, along the eastern horizon, stretched a bleak salt desert, Dasht-e Khavir. "The desert between Yazd and Isfahan seemed broader, blacker and bleaker than any other," Robert Byron wrote.

We spotted a caravansary — *caravan-sahra*, "resting place for caravans" — off the road, and we pulled over. Constructed during the Safavid dynasty in the seventeenth century to provide shelter and protection from bandits for those plying the desert trade routes, it had seen better days. It included a four-hundred-year-old inn that could house and feed dozens of travelers, a storage building, and a huge fortified pen for horses and camels that also held a green grazing area. But now it all seemed haunted. Black crows hovered above two crumbling turrets. There was no sign of human life. A portal led to a courtyard where two mangy camels were tethered amid discarded truck tires.

Hassan used to tell us stories of caravans leaving his village. For years, his father had embarked in camel trains, lugging goods along the arduous north-south route. From the Persian Gulf port of Bandar Abbas, he had ferried over the Zagros passes north across the country. In Tabriz, he would pick up loads of wheat for his trip back. During his lifetime, he had witnessed the Soviet Union squeeze the last drops of overland east-west trade out of the central Asian republics.

Then, in 1941, a British invasion ended the caravans forever. From their Gulf staging base, Churchill's troops roared over the Zagros in huge, bulky trucks. Iranians called them *camions*. In Tehran, "Uncle Napoleon" shuddered; his greatest nightmare had come true. The British were coming! And come they did. Over the Persian highlands the tommys and Indian sepoys hauled war supplies north to besieged Russian allies dug in at Stalingrad, blocking Hitler's desperate dash for the Baku oilfields. Reza Shah was shipped off to Mauritius, and his son was propped up on the throne. Four years later, with Germany's surrender, the British troops withdrew, Hassan told us, leaving their trucks behind.

Hassan's father, who had once said that he would rather kill his own young son than one of his precious camels, now did the next best thing: he became a truck driver. The caravansaries along the trade routes became relics of the petroleum age.

We explored the artifacts: Chris whistled his way into the fortifications with his sketch pad, Kev fed the camels some dry hay left behind by an unknown benefactor, Mom and Dad crossed under the deteriorating archway hand in hand, and Rich scaled the walls above for a better view. How many people had slept here? I wondered. I leapt up on the bricks too. The footing was treacherous, but the vista was incredible. Climbing mud-brick walls had been a mad passion of mine in childhood.

After school, with Ahmad Khamsi, my Bahai friend, we would romp through abandoned construction sites with mountains of bricks and skeletal unfinished walls and roofs. Atop the walls, we slid along the crumbling mud like careful tightrope walkers. The bird's-eye views were exhilarating. How many hours had we passed like this? Hundreds. Each step was a gamble, a balance between a vicious bone-breaking fall and silent Zen-like poetry.

After the Revolution, Ahmad's family and other Bahais were labeled stooges of Zionist conspirators, Westernized apostates. The mullahs had always condemned as heresy this Iranian faith, founded in 1844 by Mirza-Ali Mohammad, who proclaimed himself the long-awaited twelfth imam. Accusers claimed that British imperialists, bent on weakening Iran, had promoted Bahais into key positions of power. Bahais were rumored to be a fifth column, doing the bidding of foreigners — the British and, later, the Israelis.

During the Pahlavi era, some Bahais amassed fortunes, causing great envy and thrusting them into the uneasy spotlight with another wealthy minority, Iranian Jews. The urbane, orchid-obsessed prime minister Amir Abbas Hoveyda, who ran the Pahlavi government in its final thirteen years, fueled the deep-seated belief that the Shah was controlled by Bahais and, consequently, foreign interests. Arrested after the Revolution and then dragged from his prison cell, Hoveyda was shot by a firing squad before his trial.

My friend Ahmad's family surely must have fled Iran, escaping for their lives. His father had no doubt been labeled an agent of the West. After all, he owned a Pepsi bottling plant and Iran's first television station. And his wife was an American.

Perhaps Ahmad's tightrope walking on decaying walls and dilapidated roofs had unknowingly prepared him for the years to come. Like Hassan, he too seemed to have disappeared in the shadows, fallen through the cracks.

Nasrollah inspected one of the caravansary's turrets, perilously weakened by the wind. Weathering had turned the outer walls to clay, from which grass grew.

"Not a good idea for brother Rich to climb up there," he said.

He showed me a gaping breach in the arch just below where Richard walked. A large dirt clod fell from the hole. Nasrollah picked it up. Then he looked over his shoulder and back at me, making sure no one could hear us.

"What if Hassan doesn't want to see you?"

Avo had obviously told him. I did not respond.

Nasrollah gestured like an actor, stroking a make-believe beard. "Maybe he became a mullah."

A knot gripped my stomach. "Don't make jokes," I said.

Nasrollah chuckled. *"Hameh Irani-ha khuband.* All Iranians are good."

When we returned to the van, Avo was snoring, stretched out in the back. Nasrollah checked the radiator, then got behind the wheel and drove through the dust to begin our final leg to Tudeshk.

"Well, lads," my father said, "let's hope someone's waiting on the other side."

With each passing mile, my parents and brothers became more excited and edgy. With six headstrong travelers, we needed a leader. Yet only anarchy prevailed. We finally resorted to an odd form of consensus decision-making. It went like this. Let's say someone made a suggestion. First everyone would make fun of it. Then we'd make fun of the person who made the suggestion. And then one of us would come up with a different idea, which often had no logic whatsoever besides being the opposite of the original suggestion. After that, whoever remained focused enough to keep yelling usually prevailed.

On the map, Tudeshk appeared to be just fifty miles away. Arguments broke out without prompting. The hostile landscape bucked back into the sky. The road promised to lead us over another jagged collection of rumpled mountains. High-altitude climbing strained every fiber of Nasrollah's poor van. He stroked the dashboard with pity and anxiety. Each grinding whine from the engine brought a wince of pain to his graying temples. It was as if we were beating and abusing his favorite horse. I grimaced in sympathy with him. He appreciated knowing that a fellow sufferer was on board. And we kept climbing.

Sharp switchbacks slowed our progress to a high-pitched crawl. Suddenly, hurtling around a particularly steep blind curve, an oncoming truck roared toward us in our lane. Nasrollah cut the wheel sharply, pitching us out of our seats. The truck whisked past us downhill. Avo woke up and looked at my mother in a panic. The whites of his eyes betrayed his flustered words: "Don't worry." Gathering his breath after our near miss, he launched into yelling at Nasrollah.

"What are you doing!"

"Shut up!" Nasrollah snarled back. He fixed his eyes on the road.

"Yeah, shut up, Avo," Richard yelled from behind.

"Why? He's crazy. We almost got killed." Avo's sharp voice sounded shrill, hysterical. No one was in the mood to listen. Especially to him.

"Calm down or I'm going to be upset," Rich's voice boomed over the clatter of the engine.

"It's my custom to yell if he makes mistake!"

"Listen. Shut up and don't speak to the driver." Rich's eyes flared.

Another hairpin turn. The sound of a horn somewhere. Nasrollah cursed, twitching his eyes, pulling at the wheel.

Avo turned to unleash another round of bellowing, but Rich cut him off.

"Aaaaggghh!" Avo screamed as Rich shook him by his ear.

"Richard!" cried Mom.

This time a bus hurtled around yet another blind curve. His blaring horn drowned out all sound. We gripped the seats, bracing ourselves. I prayed. It was over in seconds. Blazing past us in a suicide maneuver, the bus driver missed us with only centimeters to spare. A hat flew out the window and tumbled on the asphalt in the tailwind before curling over the cliff.

"Definitely a believer in fate," muttered Kev, turning to watch the speed racer blaze down the mountainside.

We descended very slowly into a sparse plain, still a bit shaken and subdued. Seeing another barren village of mud-brick houses, I looked at my map. Where was it? I measured distances and made calculations. The map promised signs of life. I scanned the horizon. To our right, in the distance, lay a small air force base. To our left, nothing, empty dry terrain. A line of *qanat* holes. Then, like a vision, a bright green road sign glowed with the magic words: *Tudeshk 20 kms.*

Our minds swam in disbelief. It all came crashing back: our casual jokes about my mother's memory over the years, our deep suspicions about ever finding the village, our ridicule about this mad idea. And yet now we were close. In this godforsaken desert, could it actually be Hassan's Tudeshk? After all these miles, after all these years?

"Mom, you were right," Chris said, hugging her. We cheered.

"My God, boys," she said. "I can't believe it."

Nervous excitement filled the van. Like chattering magpies during spring mating, our uncontrollable emotions bubbled over. We strained to spy the road ahead. And after twenty long minutes, where earth meets sky, we finally saw it.

A few mud huts lined the left side of the road. I struggled to recognize the village through Hassan's stories: silhouettes of walls, shapes of doors, contours of *qanats* and wells. Grim, dry land ringed the town's outline. Where was the farmland that Hassan spoke of? The orchards? The fortified town walls that protected the inhabitants from raiding Qashqai? Just a collection of rambling huts straddled the road. Not a shred of grass. No sign of life. Richard broke the silence.

"Let's ask someone."

Full of excitement and dread, we pulled over. The first storefront featured the worn-out sign of a bakery. A young lad, cloaked in a white film of flour dust, walked out the door to light a cigarette.

"*Lotfan*, please, Hassan and Fatimeh Ghasemi, do you know them?" Rich asked.

"Ghasemi?"

"Yes."

"*Hameh ye Tudeshk Ghasemiand.*"

"What did he say?" asked my father.

"Everyone in Tudeshk is Ghasemi," Avo translated.

"Everyone?"

"The whole village has that name. It's a common name, according to him."

My mother stuck her head out the window. "Hassan and Fatimeh," she pleaded.

"Hassan," the boy repeated.

"Yes, yes. Hassan. Fatimeh Ghasemi," she repeated loudly.

"*Mordan*," he said slowly.

"What?"

"They . . . they're dead, Mrs. Ward," Avo said.

I saw the anguish lace my mother's eyes. My father dropped his face into his hands. Richard didn't move.

"*Bebakhsheed, khanoum*, excuse me, lady." The boy walked away in his floury shroud.


He was right, nearly everyone in the village was named Ghasemi. And nearly everyone appeared to be under twenty years of age. Our inquiries about Hassan were met with vacant stares, shrugged shoulders and blank faces.

Two other young fellows coldly confirmed in unison, "Hassan and Fatimeh *mordan*, dead."

"Listen," Avo said. "There's nothing we can do now. Let's go."

"Maybe he's right," said Chris. "We just came too late."

"Mr. Ward," Avo said, "we can get to Isfahan before dark. We still have a big program ahead. There's the Chehel Setoun Palace . . ."

We began debating with my father whether to leave or stay.

"We should go," Chris said.

"I don't know. What do the rest of you boys think?" Dad asked.

I couldn't speak. Kevin mumbled something.

My mother opened the door and stepped out of the van. She began to walk away from us. While we debated our next move, I glanced out my window at her. That slow, determined pace I had seen before. Her gait was resolute. Nothing would stop her.

She walked along the roadside through the dust-stricken village on her sore ankle. I could see she was carrying the black-and-white photo from 1963. Stopping passersby, she showed it to one and all.

Chris stuck his head out and called to her, but she ignored him and kept walking. I got out and followed. Panting as I caught up with her, I studied her profile. Her eyes were set straight ahead, focused.

"Terry, they're here," she said with a look of polished steel.

"But . . ."

"Don't ask me why, I just know it."

I nodded.

"Now go and tell Chris I'm not getting back in that van until I find them."

So I turned back. When I told everyone what she said, the debating stopped. We all looked out the windshield at her. Nasrollah inched the van along in her wake, keeping at a safe distance, not interfering.

"*Khanoum* is strong," he said.

"I know," I replied.

Ten minutes later, in a greasy garage, she stood between oil-black motorcycle parts and in front of a heavyset, bearded bear of a hulk.

"Great," said Chris. "Now she's talking to Brutus, village chief of Hezbollah."

"We really should go," said Avo.

"We'll never get out of here," Chris whimpered.

I could hear her voice faintly: ". . . Hassan with Fatimeh . . . here's baby Ali . . . grandmother Khorshid . . . thirty-six years ago. Do you know them?"

"Hey, look," Kev said. "Brutus is really interested."

"Of course," said Dad. "This is the most excitement he's had in years."

Brutus looked over at our van. Chris was right — his stubbly beard carried an ominous tinge of thuggery. This was someone I wouldn't want to meet on a dark street. I waved sheepishly. He ignored my gesture and stared at Mom's picture again, his forehead crinkled in thought. Suddenly his face lit up. He pointed to a figure. Clearly, he recognized someone. I listened in. "Khorshid!" Fatimeh's mother! With boisterous excitement, he trundled off down a maze of back alleys with Mom right behind.

"Ke-Chri-Ter-Rich!" she called out in one word as she disappeared around a corner. We piled out of the van in hot pursuit. I caught a glimpse of Brutus dashing down another alley, waving his arms. Tudeshki children started emerging from nowhere. Soon a flood of villagers poured out of alleys as if on cue. In seconds, our small group grew into a herd.

I saw my mother totter to the right and vanish again. A break in the wall. We followed en masse, sliding through a narrow gate. Stumbling into a small compound, we found an emaciated pomegranate tree and an unassuming pale green house behind it. Across from the tiny courtyard, a bright blue door opened. An old woman stared out timidly. She looked sleepy. A flowered scarf covered her head and part of her face. Instantly, all eyes connected.

Then she threw up her arms, almost fainting. My mother moved forward and said her name. "Khorshid?" My father's jaw dropped. Kev couldn't believe it. Brutus held the photo, waving it for others to see. Khorshid took Mom's hand and told everyone who we were. Our throng of curious villagers — fathers and sons, daughters and sisters — broke out in loud cheers. Rich and Chris joined in. *Kheli sholoogh*, total confusion!

"Fatimeh, Hassan, are they well?" Mom asked. "And Ali? Mahdi? Where are they?"

"*Baleh, baleh, baleh,*" Khorshid answered. Then she spun on her heel and went inside her house. Then, just as quickly, she burst out her door again, holding up a box filled with familiar home-made cookies and sweets.

"Isfahan," she said breathlessly.

"Hassan and Fatimeh?" Mom asked.

"*Hameh dar Isfahan-and.* They're all in Isfahan." Above the din, she shouted out a phone number.

Scribbling it down, I asked a thin, wiry kid if there was a telephone nearby. He tugged on the arm of proud Brutus, whose scruffy beard turned in my direction.

He said to me, "Let's go."

Squeezing out the gate, Rich and I ran to a neighbor's house, which happened to belong to Brutus. I had now decided that his fearsome mug was only a front; inside, he was a complete sweetheart. In the house, women were busily working at their looms while he showed me the phone. Dialing the number, I waited nervously for the ring.

"*Boushy.*"

It was Fatimeh who answered. I recognized her voice instantly.

"Hello, Fatimeh," I said. "Terry *hastam.*"

"Ter-ry?"

"*Aareh.* Yes!"

A voice cried out, then an explosion rushed into my ear. Her receiver had fallen to the floor. Then her soft voice began again.

"Terry? Terry!"

"Fatimeh. Yes, it's me."

"No . . . Terr-ry, where are you?"

"In Tudeshk."

"What are you doing there?"

"We came looking for you and Hassan. My *maman* and *baba* are here too."

"No!"

"And also Ra-chort and Chris-tofer and Kevin."

"I don't believe!"

"And your Ali?"

"*Baleh.* All, Mahdi, Maryam, Ahmad, Majid, everyone is well. Come to Isfahan!"

"Yes, of course!"

"We wait for you. Come quickly!"

Reeling with emotion, Rich and I returned with the good news. More cheers. We embraced Khorshid — her name means sun in Farsi — and walked back through the village labyrinth. Boarding the van, Pat shook Brutus's hand mightily and waved goodbye to the throng of Tudeshkis.

"Divine Irish luck," said Kevin.

"I never thought we'd find them," Dad confessed.

"I always knew we would." Mom smiled. "But I was just worried sick."

My father slipped his arm around her shoulder.

Rich and I traded high-fives. "Hip hip hooray," Kev began, and we took up the chant. Even Avo beamed a big grin.

"Unbelievable," Chris told him. "You know, I think you'll have good luck now. Maybe things have changed for you. It's because you went to Cyrus's tomb, I'm sure of that."

"You may be right," Avo said.

Our long-lost Ghasemi family was only three hours away in Isfahan, the turquoise-domed capital of Shah Abbas the Great. Under a darkening sky, in great excitement, we headed west toward the dying sun.

10

# Isfahan Feasts, Bicycle Girlfriend

Last night I saw angels knock on the tavern door.
They kneaded the clay of Adam and molded it into a cup.
Those who live in the veiled and chaste sanctuary of Heaven
Drank strong wine with me, the wandering beggar.

— Hafez

IN ISFAHAN'S Abbasi Hotel, the desk clerk called up to our room. "Excuse me. The Ghasemi family is waiting for you."

Rich knocked loudly on my parents' door. "They're here!"

"Donna, let's go," said Pat behind the door.

"Quick, guys, I'm heading down," Rich bellowed from the corridor.

In that moment, our doors flung open like a Marx Brothers fire drill. We all burst out, bumping into each other, with ebullient Richard in front. Hearts pounding, we followed his lead, rushing down the stairs. Crossing the garden courtyard, we raced past a floodlit arcing fountain and strolling couples.

In the crowded marble lobby, Rich cried out, "Hassan!"

A mustachioed face looked up. Rich stretched his arms wide and the man responded by opening his own.

"*Al-hamdulillah!*" Rich bellowed. "At last."

Amazed, time melting inside me, I watched as these long-lost friends wrapped each other in a bear hug. "C'mon Ter. Over here!" Rich waved me closer.

The barrel-chested man laughed, opened his arms and turned

to face me. And then, over to my right, a pair of magnetic eyes seized me. I became slightly dizzy. My feet spun to the right. Before I realized what was happening, I found myself in a pair of waiting arms.

"Hassan?" I asked.

A grin flooded his cheeks. His eyes sparkled. I couldn't believe it: his lustrous black hair, the bold mustache, his height — all were gone. Instead, I looked into a weathered face, etched with smoky lines of age, that spoke of hard years. I stood taller, but his grip was stronger. All had gone except those radiant eyes. They still had that electricity. I was speechless.

Behind me, Kev said, "That's not Hassan."

"Oh, my God," Rich moaned. "I just hugged the doorman!"

Quickly Hassan broke away, straightening himself just in time to receive my exuberant father's outstretched arms.

"Mr. Ward!"

"Yeessss!" Dad burst out triumphantly. "Ah-hah!"

Chris, Kev and Rich circled in to give Hassan their heartfelt hugs. Then our crowd parted like the Red Sea for my mother. A deft hand reached out with a huge bouquet of red roses. As the bounty of flowers settled in Mom's arms, her mouth opened wide.

"Ohhhh!"

"*Khosh amadid*, great joy to see you, Mrs. Ward."

A small woman with a light complexion in a jet-black chador uttered those words. Fatimeh! I recognized her doe-like eyes, magnified behind black-framed glasses, the soft purr of her voice so familiar, so inviting.

"Thank you, Fatimeh! Oh, thank you," Mom said, shaking her hand.

Surprised hotel staff turned their heads. A few tourists gazed at us, bewildered. A small crowd pressed forward, all smartly dressed in their best chadors and suits, and into Mom's arms fell another bouquet, yellow and pink gladioli and white baby's breath.

Our meeting was contained delirium, with exchanges of hugs,

kisses and shouts of joy. While everyone talked at once, tears rolled down Hassan's cheeks.

"So happy to see you! Really, I never forget!"

We sat on the lobby's large leather sofas under Safavid scenes of wine-pouring unveiled damsels and dancers, painted in the decadent days when this lavish caravansary was reputedly the finest hotel in the Middle East. Polite introductions were made while a brood of small children with wonder-filled eyes peered up at us foreigners.

Maryam and Mahdi, once babies in our house, were fully grown, as were their two younger brothers, Ahmad and Majid, born well after we left. Ahmad bore a striking resemblance to his father, a carbon copy of young Hassan, dashing and virile-looking with a full head of hair. Like her mother, Maryam wore glasses that magnified her energetic eyes. Perhaps the most charismatic of the family, she schmoozed brilliantly. Her spontaneous smile was infectious. Only Ali was not there.

Maryam's watery-eyed husband, Rasool, cuddled their two precocious boys, Saeed and Masoud, who respectfully shook our hands. All these new faces! Lightly bearded, heavy-chested Mahdi softly introduced his shy wife, Mahnaz, and his two little tigers, Ali and Ahmad. The large Ghasemi clan rivaled our own.

Hassan clapped his powerful hands as if all had been settled.

"Mrs. Ward, how are you? Are you happy with your boys?"

"Yes, Hassan, they're all healthy, nobody's in jail," my mother joked.

"Hassan," my father said, "I'm so glad we found you."

"All these years . . . I was so worried thinking about you and the family," my mother said.

"Your family I never forget, really," repeated Hassan, shaking his head.

"Actually," my mother went on, "I wrote a letter for you and sent it to Mr. Gross of the Bank of America, but he did not mail it. He said there was no village of Tudeshk. All his people said it didn't exist. What could we do? Those fools!"

"In my parents' house, your picture is on the wall," Rich said. "Mom always looked at it and asked, 'Where is Hassan?'"

Fatimeh laughed. "I too. Where is the Wards? I asked God."

"How did you come here, in a bus?" Hassan asked.

We told him about our journey.

"And we found you because of Khorshid," said Rich.

"She looks just the same," said Kevin.

"Yes, my mommy doesn't change." Fatimeh nodded. "Not like Hassan."

She rubbed his balding head, and we all laughed.

"In Tudeshk, we showed this picture." My mother pulled out the black-and-white photograph of the Ghasemis. Hassan and Fatimeh looked at it.

"Ahh, that was before I lost my hair," Hassan said.

"Me too!" Rich rubbed his own head. He began singing a nursery rhyme, *"Katchal, katchal, kalache . . . ,"* that ridiculed a young army recruit whose head was shaved bare as a walnut. Maryam's little boys tittered as Rich pranced through the song, waving his arms. The doorman glowered at us.

"You're very good," Maryam said.

"Your *baba* taught me that song," Rich said, bowing.

"It's very silly."

"Don't forget, Richie, if hair were so important," Hassan pronounced, "it would grow inside our heads, not outside."

"Silly, you two," Maryam said.

"Did you know that Donna went to see President Khatami's sister?" Pat asked.

"Oh, really?" Clearly, Maryam was impressed.

"When the president's sister asked Donna, 'Why did you come to Iran?' Donna said" — Pat paused for dramatic effect — " 'To search for Hassan, of course.' "

Everyone laughed.

Any government informants who were in the Abbasi Hotel must have been as shocked as we were. The piped-in violin music — a traditional minor-key melody probing emotions of loss —

didn't stand a chance. It was all washed away by our spirited cacophony.

"Honey?" Mom tapped my shoulder. "Why don't you order some tea?"

Hassan put up his hands. "Thank you, but please, Mrs. Ward, we don't need any tea. Tomorrow for lunch, my son Ahmad will come and bring you to my house."

"Then tomorrow," Rich said, "you come to our hotel for dinner."

"No, no. If we come to your country, then yes. But in my country, no." He raised his hand to his heart. "You are my guests in Isfahan."

Compact and stocky, Hassan still looked healthy and strong, thanks no doubt to his daily workouts. His expressive face shifted fluidly from surprise to playful impishness to solemnity. All his cylinders were clicking. He and Fatimeh conversed amazingly well in English, a language they hadn't spoken for almost thirty years. And, as both had worked since the age of six, it was a language they had never studied.

"So you live here in Isfahan?" Pat asked.

"Yes," Hassan said. "We left Tudeshk, I bought a small piece of land here, and then we built a house."

"But when you were with us," my mother said, "you worked very hard, and you always told me that one day you would go back to Tudeshk to raise your children. I remember you said to me, 'Even if my village is dry, it's still the best village because it's *my* village.'"

Over the years, Mom had repeated this often at our gatherings. It had become part of our family lore, illustrating Iran's defiant pride and Hassan's strong roots.

"Well, I had land and also a small house. But it didn't work out."

"Because you wanted to be in Isfahan?"

"No, but I was offered a good job in the Kowsar Hotel. I was chef, with sixteen helpers in the kitchen."

"*Baba* even won the award for best cook in Iran," Maryam said proudly.

"Of course, you are the best," Mom said.

"Well, now I've retired after twenty years. They ask me to come back, but I say no. I'm finished with the hotel."

"Coffee? Tea?" Rich asked. "Should we go to the café to have something to eat?"

"No, no!" Hassan waved his hands. "I've worked in hotels all my life. I will never eat their food!"

On the other side of the table, Kev chattered away with animated Maryam, who also spoke English well, as did Mahdi. Joking with Chris, Mahdi introduced his cherubic little son Ali. Chris pulled out a photo of his own two small boys. Kev was amazed to hear from Maryam about Hassan's pilgrimages to Mecca, normally a once-in-a-lifetime event.

"Hassan went on *haj* six times?" Kev asked in disbelief.

"Yes, now he is a true *haji*." Maryam looked at her father with deference.

"I tell people, don't call me Haj Hassan, I don't want that. Just Hassan."

"OK, Haj Hassan, tell us how you went," I said.

He laughed. "There was a big group of Isfahanis going to Mecca," he said. "And my boss told me I had to go and cook for them."

"I'll bet it was the first time they ate baked Alaska," Kev quipped.

"In baking Arabia?" Hassan raised his eyebrows. "Kevin, you're still a crazy boy! Everyone was happy, so my boss sent me again and again. Six times! I asked to God, Please, not again. And God agreed."

"Where did you go when you left Tehran?" Fatimeh asked Mom.

"We moved like Bakhtiaris for seven years, from one place to another, always in California," Mom replied. "Then we settled in Berkeley, the boys went off to college, got married, had children."

"How many children?"

"Two boys for me," Rich said, "two for Chris, Kev has two girls, and Terry no."

"A bit like us," Fatimeh said. "Seven years passed before we built our house in Isfahan. Then Mahdi went to university. Now he's an engineer. And look at all the grandchildren."

"Hassan," Mom asked, "did you have problems because you'd worked with an American family?"

"No. No problem."

"And when the Shah left?"

"That was the happiest day of my life! Well, not the happiest. First was when Ali was born, my first son. Then, when the Shah went, no one could believe it. We were cheering. They told us, Iran will become like heaven. But then the war comes. We have to fight crazy Saddam. And so many must die." He shook his head.

"Fatimeh, it must have been terrible, all your boys fighting." Mom touched her arm.

"Hassan was the first to go to the war," she said. "Then Ali, then Mahdi. I stayed at home, crying and worrying all night. Saddam sent his rockets to Isfahan. Many people died and many went back to their villages. But I stayed here. If I was to be killed, it didn't matter. I never want to leave my home."

She revealed her personal torments quietly, with a wounded smile. Her eyes wavered as she revisited the nightly bombings on the city while her men were on the frontlines.

"You didn't want to go back to Tudeshk?" my mother asked.

"No! Not even for one night. I suffered so much there."

While for Hassan his ancestral village still had a special allure, even a romantic pull, for Fatimeh it was the contrary: Tudeshk was like a curse.

"For five years after we left your house, Donna, I stayed trapped in Tudeshk. We had only a mud house, no water, no electricity. It was so hard."

"Where was Hassan?"

"At first he tried to have a small shop selling fruit and vegetables, going back and forth to Isfahan to buy them. But people would take our goods and ask to pay later. Some never paid us, and what could we do? We lost everything except my loom. So Hassan agreed to leave for Isfahan and found work in a hotel. I stayed behind in Tudeshk with the children, because in the city we didn't have a home. All we had was a piece of land that we had bought with your money. So every day and night I made carpets, so I could sell them and build my house. Mahdi helped me, and Ali helped all my children. It was so hard, so hard." She rubbed her cracked hands that bore years of labor, and sighed. "That's why I look old."

"No, you don't. Fatimeh, look at me." My mother drew her finger across her forehead.

"Thank you. Now I have a house, a car, everything. In the summer Ali comes to visit, Mahdi has his own house, and Maryam has a nice house too."

"And where's baby Ali?" I asked about our favorite child, their firstborn.

"In Bandar Abbas."

"He's well?"

"Yes, yes. He's captain in the navy."

"With children?"

"Yes, one boy and one girl. *Al-hamdulillah.*"

"My heart really missed you." Hassan looked at us all. "Now you're here."

Fatimeh looked tenderly at my mother and caressed her arm. "You must be tired now, Donna. Such a long trip from Yazd across the desert. Please, you sleep. Tomorrow we see you. *Insha'allah.*"

"Yes, Patrick, Donna, you come for lunch tomorrow!" Hassan announced again, beaming with a newfound smile that washed away the war years.

That was the sign. Hassan stood up, and his whole clan began to rise. Once the women got up, we all began saying goodbye. Another long bout of men kissing men and, in respectful Islamic fashion, avoiding any shaking of women's hands.

As the entire family called out good night and piled into their canary-yellow Paykan to drive off, a warmth surged over us as we watched their waving hands out of the open windows.

"We found them!" my mother said, holding her bouquets of flowers.

"Incredible. And everyone's alive," echoed my father.

Intoxicated and giddy, we turned away from the balmy palm-lined street and meandered back into the marble lobby. Inlaid woodwork bespoke painstaking restoration. The lights dazzled off the magnificent centerpiece, an intricately carved silver goblet four feet high. I looked at this, then fixed my gaze on the distant teahouse in the garden courtyard. At that moment, an arm reached out and grabbed Rich. A familiar bear hug swooped him up, catching him unawares. "Ha-a-ssa-an!" the doorman crooned.

We had to calm down. It all seemed unbelievable. We sat out under the stars in the hotel's open-air café. Enveloped by sprinkling fountains, trees and budding flowers, bronze tea trays, bulbous domes of Isfahani fantasy, we silently tried to gather our emotions, which had been flung in ecstatic disarray.

"And they all survived the war," Dad suddenly said.

"There must be a God," Chris asserted.

"His mustache is identical," Rich said, still perplexed by the eager doorman.

Kev agreed. "Actually, I think he looks more like Hassan than Hassan himself."

Basking in the moment, we sipped our tea. Leaning back on his carpeted divan, Dad sighed, looking over the beauty of the falling water, the garden's flowers that filled our eyes. My mother's hand rested on his.

"Well boys," he told us, "just remember what Oscar Wilde said: 'The book of life begins with a man and a woman in a garden, and it ends with revelations.'"

My mother held her bouquets on her lap and stared out at the blue-tiled onion-shaped dome that rose above the hotel wall. Two turquoise-tipped minarets stood at attention.

That night, I watched my mother's face lose thirty years.

\*       \*       \*

*Taarof,* the Persian ritual of hospitality, is overwhelming: compli-cated, subtle, self-effacing and richly layered. *Taarof* elevates the guest to semidivine status. The host, by contrast, dons a humble cloak. One common *taarofi* expression is *ghorban-e shoma,* which means "may I be sacrificed for you," or "at your service." In short, the host is willing to give his life for you. Generosity in the West pales in comparison. Against this refined graciousness, we are but paupers next to princes.

At the heart of this hospitality is food. Each guest begins a culi-nary odyssey that seems to have no end. The journey is governed by timelessness. Lavish banquet portions are prepared, enough to feed a passing nomadic tribe. The host's hands are everywhere, serving food and drink, refilling plates and glasses. "You haven't eaten enough, *baba* . . . just a little more." Second helpings are of-fered, then thirds . . .

Needless to say, the feasting carries on for hours. The doubled-edge sword is this: as one can never eat enough to please the host, one also cannot refuse. Operating with the three times rule, one can decline food, but it will be offered again and again. Not to be rude, the stomach must comply, even if critically overfed and on the verge of explosion.

Certain rules of decorum and courtesy obtain: the host never sits when the guest is standing, never turns his or her back to the guest, never eats before the guest and, of course, continually apologizes for not having enough food while the table, or *sofreh* — a dining cloth laid out over the carpets — simply groans with a bountiful cornucopia.

At noon, we arrived at Hassan's home, on Bi-sim Street in the Bozorg Mehr neighborhood. Drops of water on the freshly washed yellow Paykan car dripped onto the gray tiles that cov-ered the bulk of the patio. A strip of soil adjacent to the house's walls grew two fledgling cypresses, a climbing grapevine, care-fully planted pink geraniums, violet pansies and blossoming fuch-sia snapdragons. Like my father, Hassan was obsessive about his flowers.

He welcomed us in a white shirt after a morning surely spent in the kitchen. His flat-roofed, cream-colored brick house had a 1950s southern California feel, with its central wooden door and two sliding glass doors to either side.

"What a beautiful house," Mom said. She had a lifelong devotion to family renovation projects.

"And your flowers?" My father asked. "Tell me." Comparing notes, the two elderly gardeners studied the small patch of land that held a scraggly apple, a quince and a young pomegranate tree. Neat, narrow rows of greens sprouted from the soil.

We slipped off our shoes on the white-tiled raised porch. The warm sun cast fresh light. In her long pistachio-green dress and modest ivory-colored scarf, Fatimeh greeted us. Once a woman is indoors, her chador is put away.

Helping my mother at the front door, she led us through a narrow hall that opened into a large, cool living room. Richly colored carpets in classic reds and indigos covered the entire floor. My mother admired the inside doors, which were decorated with diamonds, hexagons and octagons of stained glass in emerald and blue. We sat down in the living room. A sliding glass door overlooked the apple tree and the two fathers, who were still outside on Hassan's patch of land.

This day marked the beginning of our gatherings, where we reminisced about the long years apart. We wept, laughed and ate while listening to their stories of joys and sorrows, the tragic tales of war, and also the great news that all the children were alive and well. Equally unforgettable, Hassan created the Iranian version of Babette's feast.

The fragrant odor of saffron filled the kitchen and drifted through the house. A blue plastic *sofreh* was spread on the carpeted living room floor and we knelt around it. Zam Zam orange sodas stood in front of us. Plates of *sabze*, the mouth-freshening mixture of greens — mint, tarragon, basil, cilantro and scallions — colored the tablecloth along with crisp red radishes and moist white sheep's milk cheese. These were the colors of the Iranian flag.

While Kev chatted with Maryam about her profession —
counseling women — Chris and Rich played games of tic-tac-toe
with her sons, Masoud and Saeed. Curious about what was brewing in the kitchen, I got up to watch Hassan's steam and fire, and
to catch old scents.

Poking my head in, I saw his back, a towel slung over his shoulder. In a deft move, juggling two pots, he set down a tray of
freshly sizzled chicken kebab. He turned down the flame under
the steaming rice and pierced a piece of chicken with a fork, testing its tenderness.

"Taste it, Red."

He used my old nickname. My mouth watered as I bit into a
morsel that hurtled me back to earlier days.

"Saffron is the secret. The yellow one is good for laughing," he
said with a mischievous giggle. "You see, I mix lemon with garlic,
onion, sumac and saffron. Then I grill out there."

Outside the kitchen, in the back, a metal charcoal grill sizzled
away.

"Fatimeh doesn't want the smoke in the house, so I made that."

"I want to write down your recipe."

"Yes, but later." He scooped the steaming rice into a bowl.
"Now you must go."

"Mmmm." I snatched another piece while he wasn't looking.
"C'mon, let me help."

"No, no, you must go sit down." He shooed me out.

This was another rule of *taarof.* As a guest, you must remain
idle and offer no help. Don't even try. Your role is circumscribed:
you must be served, and your only duty is to consume your host's
embarrassment of riches.

The aromas from the kitchen triggered a reaction. Anticipa-
tion filled the air. Finally, heaping trays of white fluffed basmati-
style rice arrived with Hassan's memorable saffron chicken.
Oooohhh! Fried aubergine and lamb, *mosamma bademjan* — a
dish that always pays a high compliment to the guest — was
passed to my father. Bah, bah, bah! Fresh *barbari* bread, oval-

shaped with a crispy crust, and bowls of thick creamy yogurt descended onto the tablecloth. The Ward brothers dug in.

Hassan's clan had grown. Three generations filled the house, but we missed one. The eldest son I remembered so vividly, little Ali with the smiling face, was not with us. So, with little prompting, Fatimeh showed us color photos of him. Now a dashing captain, dressed in spanking navy whites against the blue Gulf skies, his brass buttons shone, his cap brim shaded his aquiline nose and confident eyes.

"So handsome," Mom said. "Like Hassan when he was young."

"I hope the damn American fleet in Bahrain leaves him alone," Kev muttered.

The second son, Mahdi, we had known only as a baby. His fate had always been in question. Numerous times, my mother had rushed him to the hospital with Fatimeh. Hassan told us that after we left, an English family offered to adopt him and take him away to Britain. But Hassan refused. Mahdi's compressed forehead, which once gave him the look of an ancient Mayan, had leveled out. A graduate of prestigious Tehran University, he was now an accomplished telecom engineer, running PBX and digital relay systems for the Isfahan Steel Company.

Maryam, on the other hand, had graduated with high honors from theology school and was a committed teacher. Her eyes had Hassan's spark, full of life and illumination. She told me proudly that women outnumbered men at Tehran University. She made a point of speaking about the deplorable life of women in Saudi Arabia.

"Can you believe, in Arabistan women cannot vote, work or even drive," Maryam said. "That is not Islam."

She spoke about the Saudi Wahhabi fanatics who were known to finance Osama bin Laden and the Taliban of Afghanistan, who imprisoned women, put them in purdah, even cut their throats. She was disgusted, calling them terrorists.

Abruptly she turned to Chris. "Tell me about your family."

"I'm like Hassan. I am the cook of the house. I do the cooking even for my parents-in-law, who live with us."

"*Mash'allah*, may God praise it. This is good." She nodded. "We know that blessed Ali helped the Prophet's daughter in the house. So husbands must help their wives."

"I do not agree," squealed her husband, Rasool Iskander, in mocking defiance.

Out of earshot of Maryam, Hassan laughed. "Of my five children, imagine, it is she who has become a mullah."

Rasool chatted quietly with me, and I could tell he was not very aggrieved by his wife's feminist talk. With his best friend, Maryam's brother Mahdi, Rasool had joined the army. In the war, he told me, the Iraqis captured and imprisoned him for five years. During a perilous night raid on the Iraqi front, Rasool had been one of the many wounded, and he had been left behind, unconscious, on the battlefield. He still carried a steel plate, from brain surgery performed gratis by the Iraqis.

Rasool turned to me rolling his puppy-dog eyes. "My good friend Saddam!"

"Don't be silly!" Maryam pushed his drooping shoulder. She played Hardy to his Stan Laurel.

"Yes, my friend Saddam!"

Maryam and Rasool had been engaged before he went off to fight, and she had waited patiently for five years before her love returned.

"The Red Cross saved him," she said.

"How?"

"They mispronounced his name. They called him Russell Alexander."

"That's right, I am Rus-sell," Rasool Iskander said with his ironic smile.

His Euro-friendly name, given to him by a Swiss relief worker, helped him stand out in a crowd of two hundred thousand emaciated prisoners of war. Saddam Hussein's mistreatment of captives was brutal. Fed seven teaspoons of rice a day and five teaspoons of soup, Rasool weighed about 110 pounds when he finally hobbled down onto the airfield tarmac and kissed his home soil. The Iraqis still held thousands of prisoners from a war that ended in 1986.

Mahdi also fell in battle but managed to crawl back through mud and barbed wire to his trench. Thankfully he was not captured. Shrapnel ripped into his skull, leg and hand, where it remains. He lost his hearing in one ear and has only partial hearing in the other.

"Every family lost someone," Mahdi said sadly. "I was lucky."

A photo of Hassan's nephew Daoud was brought out. He was only sixteen when he died. He had been a sprinter, very fast, and had a baby face.

Unexpectedly, Fatimeh emerged with some old photos of us, four little brothers in our long-lost Arcadia in north Tehran. In one picture, four grubby rascals are holding dachshund puppies up for the camera, with tiny Ali wrapped in a burgundy sweater by their side. In another, young Fatimeh rests her arm on Kevin's shoulder under pine trees, next to a trickling turquoise fountain.

My brothers and I, moved and dumbfounded, stared at the images. Fatimeh touched my head, calling us her sons.

"Your hair is not so red now, Terry."

"But they still call you Red," Rasool said.

"Maryam also has pictures of Kevin, Chris, Terry and Richie," Fatimeh said. "All my children have one."

"Wasn't it dangerous to keep these photos after the Revolution?" I asked.

"No, not really. They are in my drawer. Now tell me about all your children," she said to my brothers. Small photos eagerly appeared from wallets, and a new generation entered the room.

The Ghasemis' long journey back to Tudeshk, Fatimeh told us, began a month after we left Tehran. Hassan could not bear the thought of working for another family, so he moved back to the village. But Fatimeh hated living in Tudeshk, where she had suffered as a child. Since we had just been there, it wasn't too difficult for us to understand why.

"I had to carry the water for drinking, for washing. So bad for me, all the time I had to carry heavy water. I never want to see Tudeshk again."

Hassan tried to put a positive spin on the situation. "I like my village. I could live there, no problem. I don't care if I wash every day," he said. "I don't need much water, only a little to drink. I helped Fatimeh with her rugs, the cooking, buying things, even doing the washing. At night I took everything down to the *qanat*. The men would say, 'Hey, look at the crazy man who comes to wash his children's clothes and the dishes.' No men did any cleaning. Only the women. One man even said, 'If I were Hassan, I would throw myself off the mosque roof.' "

"Now all the men are washing dishes," Fatimeh said.

"Yeah, I started a revolution in Tudeshk," said Hassan.

"You became a hero for the women," my mother said.

"And enemy for men," Rasool whined.

"Good *baba*," Maryam said.

When Hassan first came to Isfahan to work, in the five-star Kowsar Hotel, a favorite of the ayatollahs, he was alone, without his family.

"I never forgot your mother's recipes, and I put them on the menu." He smiled.

Meanwhile, Fatimeh slaved away on her loom seven days a week.

"Mrs. Ward," she said, "I never knew what time it was, whether it was summer or winter. In the morning I woke up in the dark and began working by a kerosene lamp. After one hour, I woke up my children, gave them breakfast and sent them off to school. Then I worked until noon, cooked something fast for their lunch, then back to work. When it was dark I would go to the *qanat* to get water and do the washing, then again feed the children. I worked late each night and fell asleep in my clothes."

Her woven threads had paid for the sacks of concrete and truckloads of brick that built this lovely home where now we all had gathered.

\*      \*      \*

Fatimeh recounted again the dark days when Hassan and her sons were far away at the front. She remained in the house, praying day and night. Twenty-three thousand boys from Isfahan alone died in the war. Every mosque was now festooned with photographs of the martyrs. Fatimeh was one of the few blessed women whose men had returned.

Hassan shared his memories of the frontlines, the poison gas attacks, the slaughter of young volunteers. As a cook, he was commandeered to feed the troops, hundreds upon hundreds of them.

After dinner, tea, dessert and tangerines were served. As Mom and Fatimeh chatted away on the couch, Dad did the same with Hassan, huddled in the corner, leaning on pillows. We boys spoke with our contemporaries. Maryam, a dynamo with unbridled energy, also revealed she was an avid reader. Her favorites were *Dr. Zhivago*, *Jane Eyre*, the novels of Virginia Woolf, Daphne du Maurier, Pearl S. Buck and Balzac, and Maupassant's stories. She adored *Gone with the Wind*. Her brother Mahdi spoke about digital technology and wireless communications, and asked if we'd like to meet a fellow engineer who studied in America.

Sitting before me was the new Iran. The Revolution had opened doors to an entire class that would never have stood the remotest chance in the Shah's "Great Civilization." Hassan's children now served their country as professionals. An engineer, a naval officer and a teacher. It would have been unimaginable thirty years ago.

The night before, my dad had reminded us once again of the poverty.

"It was criminal," he said. "Never in my life had I seen conditions as grim. To be fair, none of us really knows how much the country's infrastructure — services to the desperate underclass — had improved during the ten years from when we left until the Revolution. But one thing's certain. Whatever changes took place, it was too little, too late. Those forlorn dust heaps of villages, cut off from the world, with no medical facilities, no school, no decent roads to get goods to market. There seemed to be no hope at all." And now a whole generation had grown up far beyond that, with a normal childhood and education, and many going on to university. "Quite a miracle," Dad concluded. "Whatever corruption there is now, they can't have stolen as much as the Shah's entourage."

This Revolution had embodied a paradox. Populist and socialist themes had been woven into a conservative theocratic agenda. What was billed as a religious revolution actually championed a radical social transformation. The revolt against the Westernized Iranians blasted open gates for the vast underclass. Gardeners, cooks, laborers and truck drivers saw their chance to break through unassailable boundaries. And they took advantage of it.

The vacuum left by the exodus of technocrats and the wealthy elite, who had managed the economy and occupied positions of power, was quickly filled by the mullahs and a peculiar coalition of religious nationalists, traditional bazaaris and Islamic socialists. They confiscated the Shah's wealth and the elite's private property, starting foundations in the name of *mostazafeen*, the oppressed. Those marginalized under the Shah's regime were promised work. The government launched an intensive "affirmative action program," with plum jobs going to the clergy, their faithful followers, and war veterans. Housing, welfare and education projects took shape. The foundations, known as *bonyads*, quickly amassed fortunes and were run like fiefdoms by the clergy.

Twenty years had passed. Many confiscated factories continued to run at a loss, draining the country of revenue. The *bonyads'* staggering wealth and economic power, which suffocated competition, were now a sore subject of criticism. But it was clear that schools, medical facilities and electricity had spread throughout the land. Universities flourished, with women students brazenly outnumbering their male counterparts.

Meanwhile, on Bi-sim Street there was a flurry of festivities and daily gift sharing. The following evening, the Ghasemi cousins came to the house. One remembered me vividly. Zahra was her name. Now a mother of three striking daughters, she fondly recalled her visit to our home thirty-five years earlier. She had stayed only three days, but it had left her with an indelible impression. By night she slept with baby Ali. By day I taught her to ride my red bike. Around the overgrown garden paths she rode, with me running behind, desperately holding her in balance. I was only nine then, and she a coy six-year-old.

Zahra's cheeks flushed when she gave me her present. Her teenage daughters were thrilled.

I slowly unwrapped the paper. Under glass and in a frame lay a hand-woven pattern in red and green, glistening with a gold thread border. It was the symbol of the paisley, the famous cypress tree, bent but never broken. Her daughters motioned that I should turn it over. On the back, I read what Zahra had painstakingly written: *Your bicycl girl-freind. Isfahan 1998, Iran.*

"*Kheli mamnoun, moteshakerram*, thank you very much," I said.

"*Basheh*, let it be," she replied.

I noticed that her husband, Ahmad, was sulking in a corner. Few men like to be reminded of their wives' earlier love stories. No matter what age. Ahmad was no exception.

I bowed in self-effacing *taarof* style.

We gratefully used the Farsi word for family, *fameel*. In fact, during our stay in Isfahan, the Farsi words describing family — *madar, pedar, barodar* and *fameel* — strangely began to sound like words of an English dialect, one spoken, say, in Savannah, Georgia. "That's right, y'all," Rich said to me while driving back to the hotel one evening, our stomachs full to bursting. "We are fa-meel-y."

In my hotel room before I fell asleep, my mother showed me a letter she had been writing. It was to President Khatami's sister:

Dear Madame Khalili,

I shall write to you later from my home in California. However, I wanted to send this note to you now to thank you for your gracious hospitality when I visited your home. As I mentioned, I lived in Iran for ten years (1960–1969), and my family's life here was filled with experiences of such joy and beauty that we longed to return to visit the people and the country we love. Your brother has done much to ease the tensions between our two countries and we thank him for creating an atmosphere that has made us feel welcome.

We grieve with you for the death of your precious son and for all of Iran's martyrs killed in the terrible war. We pray that with leaders like your brother, there will be more peaceful solutions to all future problems. We will do our best to speak of Iran's good intentions toward all people we meet in the world.

I greatly admire you and your family for the good work you are doing for the community. You have accomplished much in your life and have given a fine example for all children to follow.

We will leave Iran in a few days, but I know my four sons will return again. We found the dear family who worked for us many years ago in Tehran, and we will keep in touch with them, with their children and grandchildren.

We join you in praying that all nations and people follow God's will and work for peace and understanding. Your family's good works give us hope for a bright future for our children.

With fondest regards,
Donna Ward

11

# On the Banks of the Zayandeh River

> The Persian love for the ornaments of life pierces through
> religion in the domes of Shah Abbas: mistily lost in their
> blue patterns they melt above our heads like flights of
> birds into an atmosphere part heaven and part of the pale
> Iranian spring.
>
> — Freya Stark, *The Valleys of the Assassins*

IN THE CENTER of Isfahan's grand square, called Naqsh-e
Jahan — Mirror of the World — we had agreed to meet
Hassan at the immense fountain. Then we would plunge into
the bazaar. I was standing next to the splashing jets of water when
a young, muscular hunk with a dimple on his right cheek, abun-
dantly endowed with testosterone, began to quiz me. Like sports
fans around the world, he simply wanted to know one thing.

"Please, who's number one in America? Hulk Hogan or
Eleeminator?"

"It's difficult to say." Not terribly familiar with the WWF's
bionic heroes, I threw my lot in with the Eliminator, preferring
any masked man to America's blond poster boy.

"Ah-ha! Gre-eat!" he exclaimed, pleased with my choice. I
sensed this was the local favorite. "My friends watch every week,"
he said. "You must come. We have satellite dish."

"Isn't it against the law?"

"Oh, no. My father is very powerful in *Pasrdan*," he said. Hearing the word for Revolutionary Guards, I smiled nervously.

"Next match is tomorrow, from Los Angeles." He grinned, offering his forbidden fruit.

"Well . . ." He did not expect my lack of enthusiasm, but he gave me his address anyway.

"You will enjoy. Please come to my house."

Meanwhile, gliding airily by the fountain, two attractive young women approached my mother, whose eyes were fixed on a carriage clip-clopping around the square. Speaking first in German, then in English, they voiced their anguish over Princess Diana's recent death in a car accident.

"Poor Diana," one said, shaking her head.

"Charles never really loved her, did he?" her friend asked, as if my mother might know the answer.

The fountain acted like a magnet, with its opulent jets of water opening wide like the petals of a lily in full blossom. While Kevin eavesdropped on the conversation, a chic young mother approached him with her baby and a friend.

*"Pardon, monsieur."*

In French, the demure woman — Parvin was her name — bemoaned that her second language was no longer a lingua franca to the world. However, Kevin and she agreed that it still exuded "elegance and civility." Kev then inquired if her shy friend, a doe-eyed beauty, also understood French.

*"Oui, bien sûr, monsieur,"* she replied with a triumphant smile.

Deliciously cosmopolitan and curious, this young generation seemed connected to the wide world beyond their closed borders — still cultivated, urbane and suave. A bonus was the clear distinction they made between American politicians and ordinary Americans like us. So far, everyone we had met had proved unfailingly kind and polite.

Parvin's trilingual, well-groomed husband, Firuz, joined us. He had spent five years in Paris.

"Excuse me, I want to tell you how embarrassed we are about what happened," he said.

"But reforms are coming," Kev replied.

"We really hope so! Last night, did you hear on BBC? The mayor of Tehran, Karbaschi, was released from prison?"

"Great. That's a good sign."

"Our president speaks of human rights and *liberté*."

"Yes, he seems to be a very intelligent man," I offered.

"We all voted for him. Some students call him Ayatollah Gorbachev."

A band of giggling kids swarmed around us. The Parisian Persian stopped them with his hand.

"*Insha'allah*, we hope he does not become our JFK. Why can't the mullahs go back to the mosque and teach religion? They should stop being politicians and businessmen."

"They love money too much," Parvin said, shaking her head. "All prices are going up. There is too much unemployment. Our young people cannot find jobs. We have no freedoms."

"The mullahs sit on their thrones and make promises," Firuz said. "And their families get richer. Do you know the Iranian theory of relativity? It is special. All must go to relatives." Then he leaned over us, speaking *sotto voce*. "You know why the mullahs dream in green?"

"It's the color of paradise," I replied. "The color of the Prophet."

"No, no, no, *baba*." He laughed, grabbing my arm. "They love the dollar."

For all the talk of a "hard-line pariah state," something had indeed softened in Iran. Both the Pahlavi and Islamic regimes had earned grisly reputations for their ferocious security apparatus — the secret police who spirit adversaries away to feared Evin Prison — yet now people on the street spoke openly and unafraid, with typical Iranian humor. This stood in sharp contrast with the Arab world, where self-censorship had gripped tongues for decades.

At the fountain we answered more questions. Do you like Iran? And Isfahan, are you enjoying my city? Is it the first time? Are my people treating you well? Yes, yes, yes. Their civic pride was evident.

Isfahanis still earnestly boast, *Esfahan nesf-e jahan*, "Isfahan is half the world." Although the English prefer to imagine it as Iran's Oxford, Idanna disagrees. "Just call it the Florence of Asia," she says. "Not long ago, Florence officially proclaimed Isfahan its sister city."

Fourteen bridges span the city's Zayandeh River. The Khaju Bridge, with its two pavilions, one on each side, and its two stories of arcades and stone steps, rivals the Ponte Vecchio. As Florentine merchants built their city's fortunes on textiles and silk, Isfahani merchants' golden purse was silk as well. And just like Florence with its Guelphs and Ghibellines, Isfahan had its two antagonistic factions: the Haidari and the Ni'matillahi. All credit for Isfahan's renown falls to Shah Abbas of the Safavid dynasty, who in 1598 moved his royal court here from Qazvin in the north. Naming sleepy Isfahan as Persia's new capital, Shah Abbas, like Lorenzo de Medici, jolted awake the city with his ambitious plans, which spawned architectural wonders. The great square, the *maidan*, where we sat waiting for Hassan, has no rival in the entire world.

Begun in 1611, it is a majestic rectangle, seven times the size of Piazza San Marco in Venice, where polo matches were played before foreign ambassadors seated comfortably on the grand terrace of Shah Abbas's palace. In 1620, an Italian diplomat, Pietro della Valle, reported, "Every evening the Shah lights fifty thousand lamps for illumination." This much-loved king often left his palace alone at night to wander incognito through the bazaars and coffeehouses, conversing freely with his people. He listened to criticism and was slow to anger, except when he heard of corruption by an official. For such an offense, justice was swift.

In the seventeenth century, a visiting Englishman, Sir Thomas Herbert, looked upon Shah Abbas's creation in Isfahan: "In my mind, it is, undoubtedly, the most beautiful square in the world . . . the most spacious, pleasant and aromatic . . . in the Universe."

*          *          *

From our strategic viewing place at the central fountain, the four points of the compass offered up ravishing landmarks. To the west towered the royal palace, Ali Qapu, the Lofty Gateway. There, on the grand second-floor covered balcony, Shah Abbas entertained guests with fifty-course banquets that ended with tangerine sherbet, made with ice transported from snow-capped mountains many miles away. Legend has it that the clever king fooled foreign dignitaries about his military strength by parading the same soldiers in the square over and over again. Circling the drilling troops into the arcade below allowed for swift costume changes. Diplomats watched from the terrace, drinking generous servings of Shiraz wine, as four thousand soldiers multiplied into forty thousand. Reports of an invincible civilization galloped back to European capitals.

Opposite the palace, to the east, stood the Sheik Lutfullah Mosque under its delicate café au lait dome. Upon viewing its luminous interior, the highly critical Robert Byron gushed, "I have never encountered splendor of this kind before." He compared it to "Versailles, the porcelain rooms at Schonbrunn, or the Doge's palace or St. Peter's. All are rich, but none so rich." Vita Sackville-West wrote in *Passenger to Teheran:* "In the 16th century Isfahan Persians were building out of light itself, taking the turquoise from their sky, the green of the spring trees, the yellow of the sun, the brown of the earth, the black of their sheep and turning these into solid light." During the Iran-Iraq War, Saddam Hussein tried to bomb these treasures, knowing he would strike at the Iranian heart.

To the north of the square, the royal bazaar opened its beguiling portal onto a world of dark shadows and merchants' desires. The vast square symbolically balanced the secular on one side with the spiritual on the other. Directly opposite the bazaar's huge gate, fifteen hundred feet across the square to the south, a sublime mosque soared, designed for the unsettled spirit. Yin and yang.

Once known as Shah Mosque and renamed the Imam Khomeini Mosque in 1980, the building arches into a glistening sky-blue dome. Its minarets reach 150 feet into the air. The bulb-shaped dome, with its eighteen million bricks and nearly half a million aquamarine and canary-yellow tiles, is so daring a design that perhaps its only earthly rival is Brunelleschi's terra-cotta Duomo in Florence. A zenith of Islamic architecture, the Imam Mosque, the very symbol of Isfahan's seventeenth-century renaissance, simply staggers with its grandeur and proportion.

Crossing the dramatic arched portal of hanging sky-blue stalactites, we passed from the profane to the sacred. Inside, scores of artisans quietly pieced together new tiles, delicately crafting the mosaic work in a never-ending project. Two inner cloisters glowed Mediterranean warm with glazed azure, lemon and emerald tiles, here before the Neapolitans splashed their Santa Chiara *chiostro* with majolica. Subtle ceramic vegetation grew all around, myriad budding flowers and intertwining branches of trees of life. Swirling calligraphy breathed Koranic verse over the praying faithful, onto gusts of wind, into the heavens.

Historically, the dome is indigenous to Iran, born during the third-century Sassanian dynasty. Originally, classical domes like the Pantheon of Rome could rise only from circular walls. But Persian architects conceived of a dome supported by four square walls. With their ingenious breakthrough, a square evolved into a dome through honeycomb arches sprouting across the angle of the meeting point of the two walls at each corner. Domes of all shapes and sizes then became possible. This elevated form was central to Byzantine, Islamic and European Renaissance sanctuaries. Constantinople's Saint Sophia, Agra's Taj Mahal and, of course, the Duomo in Florence trace their origin back to early Iran.

Hassan arrived on foot wearing his usual white shirt and black pants, sweat glistening on his forehead. He apologized for being late.

"I had to go with Fatimeh again to the market."

"It's our fault. We take you away."

"No, it's my fault. All the shopping for tonight's dinner."

"*Baba*, it's mine," said Kev, patting his stomach. "I eat enough for ten people." Hassan laughed and stood straight, wiping his forehead with a handkerchief as he began his introduction to his adopted city.

"Isfahan is the city of three D's," he began. "*Derakht* for trees — never have you seen so many trees. *Docharkheh*, bicycles — you see them everywhere. And *derayat* — oh yes, Isfahanis are cunning. In the bazaar, they'll lure you with their sweet words. But they joke only to make a sale. When you think you got the best price, they give you a compliment. Of course you feel good. But you don't know what happened. *You* are the loser. There is one rule here: you cannot win against an Isfahani bazaari."

"Sounds tough," Chris said.

"You don't have to buy," Mom counseled.

"After coming all the way here?"

"Then grin and bear it," my father added.

"Yeah, it'll hurt so good," said Kevin, who had targeted the bazaar for days.

Before we had left the hotel, Avo had warned us. Nursing his upset tummy, he had chosen to stay behind, but his advice was unmistakably clear. "Watch out. Isfahani bazaaris are so cheap they'll put cheese inside a bottle and rub bread on the outside to give it taste. With them it's simple," he said. "Either you lose or you get a knife in your back. Good luck."

At breakfast, Rich had read aloud from Freya Stark's *Beyond the Euphrates:* "A merchant was doing very well in the bazaar. When his son grew up, he took him into partnership. The son cheated the father till he reduced him to bankruptcy." The story ended when the old man realized what his own son had done. Instead of condemning him, he burst with pride.

Eagerly, we crossed the square, following Hassan into a long, vaulted arcade echoing with syncopated hammers ringing out like xylophones. Down one alley, I spied men sitting atop ladders, beating into shape giant copper bowls the size of hippos.

"For wedding feasts," Hassan explained.

"Those cauldrons can hold enough rice for a tribe," Kev commented.

Sensing an endless walk ahead, my parents eyed a café. We climbed a stairway and settled them on reclining pillows on an outdoor patio perched over the bustling bazaar's arched gateway that dominated the vast panorama. They both preferred the big picture of the "Mirror of the World" to the merchants' maze.

We scrambled back down and spun left along a corridor, following in Hassan's footsteps just like our childhood days. With his four boys in tow, Hassan deftly maneuvered through streaming crowds, plunging inside the medieval portal. From this entry point, the covered bazaar, cast in semidarkness, stretched four miles under sun-bleached arched roofs like an invisible spider web. Sealed off, the light did not spill down in luminous pools as it did in Yazd. Shadowy labyrinthine paths were lit only by gold and fluorescent lights flickering above storefronts filled with treasures. Antique silver tea sets; miniature polo scenes painted on camel bone; vegetable-dyed tribal carpets; inlaid boxes of walnut, ebony and bone; carpets in classic crimson and midnight blue; hand painted and glazed mosaics of Aegean azure and sunflower yellow with curling ivory calligraphy — all were displayed as bait, waiting for the catch. Hanging bronze lamps shed intimate glows through their lacy cutout patterns.

Chris and Rich strolled past the notorious carpet merchants. Polite voices called out to them. "Pleeeze, come, look."

It was a challenge to remain aloof, and Hassan understood.

"Aren't these carpets the most splendid things you've ever seen?" Chris whispered to me.

With their images of paradise, those magic woven gardens had grown out of glowing colors. Medallions swirled with climbing vines and entwined leaves, nature and poetry in motion. Arabesques, garlands and palmettes: their lustrous, sensuous surfaces were delightful to touch.

Carpet making originated with pastoral nomads four thousand years ago, when women first spun their sheep's wool. Wooden looms that could be strapped onto the backs of mules limited a carpet's size, and thick yarns limited the design choices. Once the craft migrated down from the hills and into the cities, artisans' workshops created more refined products. Three innovations liberated the art form. First, with larger, stationary looms and small hands of child weavers — mostly girls — laboring on the same enormous carpet, entire palace floors could be covered. Second, fine wool and luxurious silks allowed for smaller knots. Curved lines and fine details became possible. Clear representations of budding flowers, blooming trees, leaping gazelles, galloping hunters, virtually any image could be woven. Instead of working from memory while weaving, and singing age-old tunes to call out the patterns, artisans designed elaborate compositions on paper to guide the weavers.

Persian carpets even included poetic script, as this one from four hundred years ago:

This rug which I have made for her to tread on . . .
I have made the warp and weft of this rug from the thread of my soul.
For the eye which weeps pearls here, I have transformed on a rug the dust with paint on the path of my beloved.
Under her steps I have decorated her carpet with flowers with the blood of my eyes, in the hope of penetrating behind the enclosure of her pink cheeks.

Words woven into the border of another, royal carpet spoke of even greater sentiments:

. . . This is not a rug, but a wild white rose, a veil for the houris with large black eyes.
It is a garden full of tulips and a thousand flowers where the nightingale sings as in his kingdom . . . but one where the autumn wind cannot linger.
When one has contemplated the gold of its roses, one can look no longer at the sun or the moon . . .
O Phoenix, lift up your hands that the work will be completed.

Into Europe the carpets flooded, thanks to Venetian merchants. They were placed on palazzo floors and used as props in paintings by Mantegna, Carpaccio, Brueghel and Velázquez. Tintoretto painted a nude resting on an Isfahani rug.

I watched Chris turn over a carpet to inspect the knots. The shopkeeper smiled, knowing that a fish was nibbling on his bait.

"You have good taste, Mister."

"Thank you. Just looking. I don't want it."

"Of course not."

"How much?"

"Tabrizi is one of the best. But for you, my brother —"

"No, *he's* my brother." Chris pointed at me.

I took a bow. "I must protect him."

Laughs and bluffing. For Chris, it was the game he loved. A strange breed, no doubt, these carpet dealers, who always claimed to be your long-lost *baradar*, who think nothing of swearing on the Koran or their departed mother's soul. Otherwise, a trustworthy bunch of cultivated pirates. Hearing that my wife was from Italy, the shopkeeper introduced himself as Reza and slid into fluent Italian.

"*Come va la vita in Italia?*" Soon we were speaking about the expatriate Iranians working in the San Lorenzo market in Florence. Did I know them?

"*Certo*, sure, I pass them each day," I replied.

Chris bargained, and I sat down while carpet after carpet unrolled before us. The ceremonial tea arrived. Looking at the curled balls of wool dangling from a miniature loom in the shop, I remembered the bobbles that used to hang from Fatimeh's loom like ripe fruit drooping from branches: peach, lemon and plum. Her quiet hands plucking away.

In one of Italo Calvino's mythic cities there lay an extraordinary carpet:

It is easy to get lost in Eudoxia: but when you concentrate and stare at the carpet, you recognize the street you were seeking in a crimson or indigo or magenta thread which, in a wide loop, brings you to the purple enclosure that is your real destination. Every inhabitant of Eudoxia compares the carpet's immobile order with his own image of the city, an anguish of his own, and each can find, concealed among the arabesques, an answer, the story of his life, the twists of fate.

In the end, we didn't buy. Chris complimented Reza.

"A real charmer," he whispered to me.

Next time, we explained. He understood, of course. It simply wasn't ethical. No, we couldn't buy. At least not yet. It was only our first pass. Plus, we had to rescue Kevin, Rich and Hassan, who were caught in other fishing nets across the passageway.

As we moved deeper into the bazaar, arched doorways with crumbling mosaics split by cracks of time opened onto secret courtyards, dried-up water pools and ancient warehouses. Hassan entered a strangely empty court and then stopped next to a fountain that hadn't seen water for decades.

"Come sit," he said.

"It's so amazing to be here with you, Hassan," Kev said. "It's like a dream."

"For me too. I don't come to bazaar often, I'm too busy, but this is a quiet place." Hassan rubbed his finger along the fountain's edge. "It reminds me of a story. Would you like to hear?"

"Yes, *baba*," Rich said. "But before that, tell us one from Mullah Nasruddin."

"Okay, Richie. But then I tell you this one."

He leaned back, drew a deep breath, paused with theatrical silence and then looked at us with his glistening eyes. Rich slumped down next to me. Hassan took another breath and began.

"Once Mullah Nasruddin was going to town with his donkey, and he also had his son, who was a young boy only six years old. So he let the boy ride the donkey and he walked behind. People along the way called out, 'Hey, old man, are you stupid? Why don't you ride the donkey and let the boy walk?' So to make them happy, he said, 'Okay.' He put his son down and got on the donkey. But soon people were saying, 'You selfish man. That little boy should not be walking.' So both of them got on the donkey. They went a little farther. Then they heard, 'What are you doing? That poor donkey will die carrying both of you!'"

Rich slapped his knee, laughing.

Hassan nodded. "Imam Ali said making fun of people is not good, but joking is good. You remember? It's called *tanz*. Even if it makes you happy for no reason."

"*Tanz* . . . of course," Rich repeated.

Like Charlie Chaplin's little tramp, the Iranian folkloric character Mullah Nasruddin was wise in his stupidity. A proverbial mix of clever foolishness and absent-mindedness.

Hassan straightened his back and wiped his forehead. "Here's another silly one for you. One night, Mullah Nasruddin wakes up. He hears something outside his house, goes to the window, takes his gun and shoots at this thing moving in the dark. Next morning, he looks out at his pajamas hanging in the wind to dry, and he sees there's a big hole in them. 'Hey, hey, hey!' he says. 'Thank God I wasn't wearing them last night.'"

We all chuckled. Chris's existential fears were dissolving.

"*Allah-al-Akbar, Allah-al-Akbar* . . ." The call of the muezzin, amplified over loudspeakers from the mosque, rolled in undulating waves toward us, rising higher and higher in pitch before cresting and spilling into a placid baritone tide pool.

"Ahhhh!" the audience in the mosque echoed in unison. This sent Kev tumbling back to his youth. I saw his eyes glaze.

"*Ashahadu ana la illaha il-Allah* . . . I testify there is no deity but God . . ." Anticipating the muezzin's vocal dexterity, the faithful hung on each note while the aria peaked. On the final unexpected note they released again: "Ahhhh!"

A good muezzin can stop you in your tracks. Indeed, that is his purpose, to shake you and urge you to pray. When done well, the hypnotic cadence is inescapable. The *azan*, the call to prayer, is one of the sublime religious vocal expressions.

"One more, Hassan?" I asked once the voices settled.

During the *azan*, I could see that Hassan had plumbed his memory for another tale.

"I remember once there was a *tar* player," he began, "a man who had played for years as court musician for the king. When old age took him and his notes were not as sweet as in his youth, he was dismissed and ordered to leave the palace. The musician didn't know what to do. He had no money, no food, only his *tar*. So he went into the mountains, where he found shelter in an empty room in a village. He took off his red coat and hung it on the wall. And then looked up to God and said, 'Now I'm going to play for you. All my life I've played for food and coins. I'm tired, and I want to play only for you. This is my gift.'" Hassan turned his eyes upward as he spoke.

"So, all alone in his room, he began to play. And how sweet he played! All from the heart. So sweet, like honey, that his notes reached God. And so God visited the king in a dream and told him to take a bag of gold and go to this village, to a room with a red coat hanging on the wall. The king obeyed and went to the village, looking for the sign. He found the red coat and heard music, but he could see no player, and he left a bag of gold. The old man was facing the wall, in the dark, playing purely from the heart, and he did not see the king.

"Later, when the musician turned around and found the gold, he was overwhelmed. 'For seventy years,' he thought, 'I spent my life playing for people's pleasure and, at the end, had nothing. But the one time I make music for God, just once, look at what happens!'"

I recognized Hassan's tale. It was a version of the classic *"Pir Changee,"* "The Old Man" by the poet Rumi, known to all Iranians as *Maulana*, the Master.

"You have to let go of things," Hassan explained. "If you live from the heart, then rewards will come to you in ways you can't even imagine."

"This we all feel, *baba*, by seeing you again," I said. My brothers nodded in agreement.

"*Baba*, just one more?" Rich pleaded.

"Well, I told you that this fountain reminded me of a story." He opened his palms to the sky. "Once there was a man in Isfahan and he had a dream. A voice told him, 'You must go to Cairo. You will find a treasure there waiting.' So he went by caravan across the desert and over the mountains. When he arrived, he was so tired that he fell asleep in the mosque. What he didn't know was that three men also sleeping in the mosque were thieves. In the middle of the night, the police came and arrested the thieves, taking the Isfahani away too.

"When they took him in front of the court, the judge asked him why he had come to Cairo. So the man told him about his dream and the treasure.

"The judge began to laugh. 'You foolish man. I have dreamed of a house in Isfahan three times. There is a garden. In the garden there is a sundial, a fig tree and a fountain. And under the fountain there is a treasure. Did I believe this? No!' the judge shouted. 'You shouldn't either. Go back to your city, and never set foot in Cairo again. Here, take this money and go!'

"Well, when the man got back to Isfahan, he saw his own garden. Amazing! It was exactly the garden the judge had described, with a sundial, a fig tree and a fountain. So he grabbed his shovel and started digging . . ."

"And?" we all cried out. Wiping his forehead, Hassan looked at each of us.

"Soon you will leave Isfahan. When you get home, don't forget to look under the fountain in your father's garden. There you'll find the treasure!"

"Hassan, how did you know that Dad's garden has a fountain?"

Hassan's eyes sparkled. "It's my secret. Come on, let's go back and find your mom and dad."

As we rose to leave the quiet courtyard, Hassan said one more thing. "It's like the old poem. If you open the eye of your heart, then you can see things that cannot be seen."

In his exhaustive work *The Arabian Nights: A Companion*, Robert Irwin uncovered the epic's numerous incarnations and tracked its footprints back to the source. These tales were in fact originally Persian, not Arabian. They were called *A Thousand Tales*, from the Farsi title *Hazar Afsaneh*. Translated into Arabic between the eighth and ninth centuries, they were renamed first *Alf Khurafa* and then *Alf Layla*, or *A Thousand Nights*.

Irwin traced the historic link back to Ibn al-Nadim, a ninth-century bookseller and compiler of an extraordinary annotated bibliography called *Kitab al-Fihirst*, which listed all the books known to have been written until that time. Al-Nadim wrote that these stories were first told in pre-Islamic Sassanian Persia, and reported that the collection was originally composed for Humai, the daughter of Shah Bahram of Persia.

The background of these tales is a glamorous royal betrayal, when King Shahryar has his faithless wife executed. From then on, he marries a new damsel each day and puts her to death the following morning, before she has time to betray him. A gruesome cycle begins. A heroine is needed to break the chain. Enter Scheherazade, who will do just that. Armed with her feminine charm and the genius of a storyteller, she begins on her wedding night, fueling it with a never-ending story.

By daybreak, she has artfully built up suspense, captivating her husband without revealing the ending. When she pauses, the king balks. Her execution is postponed. The following night, the story continues. Narrate or die. Spellbound, the king keeps reprieving her. A thousand and one nights pass, in which time she gives birth to three male heirs. Finally, the king abandons his plan. And her tales become immortal.

Europe's first translation was in French, by Antoine Galland in 1717. Soon Ali Baba and his forty thieves, Aladdin and his lamp, the fisherman and the genie, Sinbad the sailor and the magic horse stormed into Western literature with fabulous adventures, aristocratic and bawdy, romantic and satiric, even supernatural. The exotica of the mysterious Islamic East, with camel trains, desert riders and calls to prayer, filled the outward senses, while inside each fantasy lay a moral core: the unseen hand of fate mapped out each human path.

Inspiring writers' pens and imaginations, the unseen hand touched all the great literary masters: Joyce, Proust, Borges,

Calvino, Poe, Melville, Goethe, Pushkin and Tolstoy. And of course it inspired Rimsky-Korsakov, who composed the unforgettably bewitching *Scheherazade.*

The art of storytelling that flourished in medieval Persia is ingrained in the Persian character. *Naqqals,* or storytellers, were endowed with prodigious memory and knew how to work the crowd, reciting their repertoire from Ferdowsi's *Book of Kings* on request. Sir Richard Burton, the Nile explorer, wrote, "The two main characters in the *Nights* are Pathos and Humor, carefully calculated to provoke tears and smiles in the coffee-house audience."

For us four wide-eyed boys, Hassan, in his own way, had a narrative gift richer than Scheherazade's. Our Persian father had told us tales on summer nights that still live on. Today, my small nephews and nieces listen to the same suspenseful stories. When Hassan unrolled his flying carpet, it was big enough for us all. Tapping into his own tradition, he had flown us across many seas.

We escaped the daunting caverns of the grand bazaar and its fraternity of scrupulous merchants with only slight damage: two small Bakhtiari carpets that Kev could not resist. Stepping out into the blinding light behind Hassan, we were momentarily dazed. Hassan was climbing a flight of narrow stairs. We found Mom and Dad happily seated right where we had left them. Kev showed off his trophies.

"And then Hassan told us stories," Rich said.

"Only one or two," Hassan said. "With my boys, I'm feeling young again."

"I feel I've come to Tír na nÓg," my dad said with a wink to me, referring to that enchanted Celtic land of youth.

"Well, let's go back to my house for lunch," Hassan said.

Catching two cabs beneath the gateway, we flew back to Bi-sim Street.

Bap-te-bap. "Hey, hey!" Hassan clapped his hands. Cooking class was in session. He spun toward me in the steamy kitchen.

"Terry the Red! Look over here. The *ghormeh sabzee*, stew with vegetables, this one is special. You take leeks, parsley, fenugreek, dill and a little spinach. You wash and cut, then you put in a big pan with water. Now, in another pan you put a little oil and fry onions until you see them brown. Then you mix lamb, beans, onions and dried lemon from Oman in with the vegetables."

Lifting a spoon, he showed me the cooking herbs.

"Ah, but you know, most important is the rice."

"I still can't make it like you used to."

"Because you have to soak it in salt water for four hours."

"Salt?"

"That's right. You boil it for seven minutes, ten if the rice is good quality, then you pour it out and run warm water over the grains. Place it back into pan with little water boiling on bottom. But keep the flame low! Then you add a bit of oil and put a cloth over the top for steaming. Wait an hour, the rice will be ready, and on the bottom you will find the crispy crust of *tadig*."

Scrumptious *tadig* — crunchy golden rice, broken into tempting wafers — I had craved for years. Until now, it had been an elusive mystery. Hassan was decoding a culinary Rosetta Stone for me.

"If you want to make *sabzee pulou*, then put chopped dill into boiling water one minute before the rice. For *sabzee shorkh-kardeh*, sauté the beans and vegetables, then add dry lime. And remember, you must have pepper, turmeric, ginger, curry. And of course" — he held up the golden stems in a tiny glass bottle — "don't forget the saffron from Khorassan. It's the best for laughing!"

After lunch, I peeked into the room of Majid, Hassan's fifteen-year-old son. Next to the far wall stood Fatimeh's wooden loom. How many hours had we spent in her small brick house in our garden, where a kerosene heater with its blue flame hissed warmly through the winter months? Whenever we dropped by to play with baby Ali, Fatimeh would offer us cups of tea and we'd sit quietly watching her mesmerizing fingers at work. Newly born

Mahdi, in the arms of his grandmother Khorshid, rocked back and forth. Weaving along the horizontal weft, her hands moved around the ivory, burgundy, ebony and lapis threads.

Her design rested on the left side of the loom. Pasted onto thin brown fiberboard, the paper with hand-colored geometric shapes showed a blown-up section that indicated the color of the knots. Following the design, running across the weft, she slipped in the thread and with a twist swiftly knotted it. After she tied each knot, her knife cut the thread. Ever so slowly, her fingers traversed the width of the loom's white woolen strings. Silently, hypnotically, she drew us into her interlocking world, defined by the borders of her loom.

I felt a hand touching my shoulder. "You remember?" It was Fatimeh.

"How many knots is this one?"

"Oh Terry, as many as stars in the sky, sand in the desert, raindrops in the Caspian. Thousands and thousands."

Jorge Luis Borges once wrote that the "thousand" of *The Thousand and One Nights* implied "endless nights, countless nights." So a thousand and one, he concluded, "is adding one to infinity."

What then of Fatimeh and her carpets? I wondered. Were her fingers weaving anything less than infinity? I had watched her create gardens of paradise with plump roses, budding leaves, running deer and water vases. From the first winter frost through the melting of snows and the sudden burst of spring, each day she wove. She knew that sooner or later her carpet would warm someone's feet, brighten a room and transport viewers to an imaginary world. Once the carpet reached its final destination, the lucky owner would sit in Fatimeh's eternal garden where no leaf ever fell, where no fountain ran dry, where no songbird ever died, where winter had no name.

Desert rivers bestow outlandish generosity upon their cities. Isfahan is no exception. In Africa, the White Nile and the Blue Nile merge in Khartoum and crash down past Aswan, Luxor and Cairo. Flowing across a Sahara that sees no rain, each mile of waterway defies nature. No wonder the Isfahanis call their river Zayandeh, the Life Giver. The river is fed by countless rivulets and tributaries. Acting as arteries and heart, the Zayandeh pumps the very lifeblood of the city. And at night, there is no more pleasant place to be than on its banks.

We walked down Isfahan's Champs-Élysées, a wide promenade called Chahar-Bagh, or Four Gardens, with its abundant *chenars* — Persian plane trees — casting shade and incomparable beauty. The Eight Heavens pavilion and garden sprouted a small merry-go-round with its plinking music and flashing orange and green lights. An equally small ferris wheel rotated in the sky.

Drinking in the cool air, we joined the Isfahani *passeggiata*, crossing the Khaju Bridge, where hundreds gather each evening. On wide stone steps beneath the glorious arches, families congregated in a pleasing ritual. Lost in thought amid the waterway's gushing roar that drowned out the noise of traffic, people gazed for hours at churning white waves surging down open chutes. Infinite liquid spirals danced before flattening out into the green, tranquil, slow-moving current.

"We come here many times, Fatimeh and I. We sit there." Hassan pointed to his favorite spot.

Couples strolled, students gabbed in groups, cotton candy vendors spiked sugar cravings of little kids while pink and orange balloons tempted mothers. Along the riverbanks families picnicked on broad grass lawns or took brightly painted rowboats out for a paddle. We walked along the river to a Safavid footbridge, named for its thirty-three graceful arches.

Hassan slipped into the teahouse tucked under the arches. We followed him, and as twilight lingered, we puffed on water pipes in the middle of the life-giving river. Three open bay windows overlooked the lights bouncing off the darkening water. Curling up in one of these niches, my brothers and I rested against rust- and saffron-colored kilim cushions, Hassan facing us. Warm and inviting, the vaulted ceiling shimmered in amber light, goldfish swam in an aquarium, dangling lanterns lit antique photos of musicians and portraits of Imam Hussein, and red plastic hibiscus

flowers leaned lazily out of pink porcelain vases on wooden tables. Worn carpets covered the floor.

"I love it here. It's like Ali Baba's cave," said Kev.

"No, much better." Rich toyed with the burning coals on his
*ghalyan*'s cone of tobacco, then took a long, soulful drag, releasing
smoke in a dignified exhalation. He coiled the long red tube and
handed the wooden nozzle to me, and I sucked on the pipe. It
burbled peacefully.

A blue-vested tea boy arrived with our first round: a brass tray
of cylindrical glass cups, a rose-hued steaming pot. From hidden
speakers a *tar* rang out, its plucked strings bending tones, sending
notes soaring. A flute soon joined in.

Hassan's eyes lit up. "Ah. This is *Maulana*."

"Rumi?"

"That's right. The story of the shepherd and Moses." His eyes
accompanied the sound. "Listen! No, I will tell you." An undulating voice curled around the sound of the flute. Excitedly, he began. "The shepherd is saying, 'O God, come here. I will prepare
your bed. I will fix your shoes, comb your hair,' he's telling God.
Then Moses comes to him and says, 'Hey, what are you saying?
God is not like you or me, needing someone to make his bed,
comb his hair. He's not like that.' The shepherd gets very sad and
begins to cry in the middle of Sahara."

Hassan provided his translation as the warbling singer repeated
the refrain under the flute. 'I will kiss your hand, sweep the floor.'
And Moses says, 'Hey, shepherd, what're you talking about? This
isn't you and I who have shoes. This is God you're talking to.
Why are you saying this nonsense? A big fire will come down
from the sky and burn us all up. What the heck are you talking
about?'"

The flute spiraled again, then the singer, and Hassan repeated
right behind.

"So the shepherd walks away. And God speaks to Moses: 'Hey,
you made him go away from me. You are here to put things together, to bring people closer to me, not to separate them from
me. What did you tell this guy? You should know better. I don't

care what people say. I look only inside their hearts. That's what I listen to, not their words.'"

Hassan's eyes glistened in the lantern light. The voice rolled over and over. Even the tea boy looked up at the ceiling, as if in a momentary trance. Again the flute and the voice.

"So Moses runs after the shepherd and says, 'The word has come from above. You can worship God in any form and shape you want. You got it right. I got it wrong.'" The voice modulated in rolling waves. Hassan repeated, "Moses runs after the shepherd and finds him and says, 'I bring you the best news. Whatever is your heart's desire, say it!'"

The music crescendoed with the drumming of a *daf* rising to an ecstatic peak. And as suddenly as it began, it ended. The whole teahouse seemed to exhale.

"Incredible," murmured Kevin.

"So you see," Hassan said. "Maulana says, through the love of the shepherd, the prophet Moses learns big lesson."

I looked at Hassan and at my three brothers. Scents of burning tobacco wafted out our window. Lights twinkled off rippling water. A sudden warmth came over me. I made a mental engraving of this scene, carving it deep into memory, to hold close when we would be far apart.

"Remember," he said. "'If you open the eye of your heart, then you can see things that cannot be seen.'"

Out into the inky fresh night we walked. Hassan led us in silence. The river's moist breath washed over us.

"Come sit, I must tell you something," he said quietly. Kev and Rich sat on the fresh-cut grass. Chris stretched out on his side, looking at the passing river.

"I remember," he began, "many years ago, when your mother would go out to the airport with bottles of fresh lemonade to greet the *hajis* coming back from Mecca and the hot desert. I told my friends about it. They were surprised that a foreign woman was doing something even Iranians didn't do for the *hajis*."

Raising his eyes to the stone-white moon, he leaned toward us.

"Your mother and father do their acts spontaneously, from the heart. Every time Ali or Mahdi was sick, your mother would say to Fatimeh, 'Put the children in the car and let's go to the hospital.' Just by looking at the eyes, she understood. Fatimeh was so young. Khorshid, her mother, didn't know. Your mother did, and she was always there for us. I never can forget that. Ali's and Mahdi's clothes were better than Prince Reza's. She ordered them from a catalogue. Why did she do that?"

Hassan looked out to the river, then into our eyes again. "When Moses went to the mountain, God said to him, 'I'm going to send down diseases to kill everyone. Tell your people to hide under the ground.' So Moses told the people to dig tunnels. And all the people, rich and poor, worked together to build everything. But then nothing happened. Moses went to God and said, 'Hey! Why didn't you send down the plague?' God told Moses, 'I saw the people together, helping each other. It made me very happy.'"

"*Baleh,*" Kev said.

"Hafez tells us it's not the prayer beads, fancy robes or prayer rugs. The best prayer is when you help others. Each morning I wake up at three. It's the best time for praying. This is when I speak with God, and He speaks with me. He always listens."

Hassan looked at each of us and said, "I know why God brings you here."

There was a long moment of silence. None of us could say a word.

"We are old. Soon we will die. The only thing that stays is what we do in life. Some people have a lot of money but a black heart. They don't care, they don't know how to give. God is aware of this. If people don't want God in their hearts, then he just leaves them alone. And many times bad things happen to them. But God loves most of all the people with a heart, who help others. This is how he chose the three prophets, Moses, Jesus and Mohammad."

A passing car hummed by.

"You know, the day you left Tehran, we cried. In all the time we spent in your house, your mother and father never got mad at us. They never acted like they were higher than us. With the people they were always polite. They looked at us like family. And I never forget."

"But Hassan, we also never forget," Rich said. Hassan waved his hand so Rich would stop.

"At night, I pray for my teacher, Ustad Ardabil, who taught me Koran in Tudeshk when I was small. I also always remember a woman who helped me when I was seven years old. I used to work as a shepherd in Tajrish. This woman saw me passing one day with the sheep. I was very dirty, with my clothes torn. She called me inside her house and washed me in her pool. She washed my hair, my clothes. I never knew who she was, her name. And I never saw her again. Why does she do such a thing? Maybe she's dead now, but I always pray for her.

"I'm nobody, just a simple man. I ask why does God do this for me? You see, I know why you come." He paused and looked up at the moon. "Not even brothers do what you did. I told this story to one of my friends, and he began to cry. I say that thirty years ago I worked for your mother and father and they left far away. Then they came back, over the ocean and across the desert. I told him it's very hot, the desert's very hot, and they came. He said, 'Oh, I can't believe this.'"

He plucked at a blade of grass, searching for the word in English to explain.

"*Mojezeh*, Fatimeh told me yesterday."

"What's that?" I asked.

"Like when the man is dead and Jesus makes him come back, this is *mojezeh*."

"Back from the dead?"

"Yes."

A shiver went down my back. He looked each of us in the eye. "*Delam barayeh shoma tang meshavad*, my heart likes to have you here."

# 12

## Video Nights in Imam Khomeini's Tomb

> This time either Islam triumphs or it disappears.
>
> — Ayatollah Khomeini

> Drink until the turbans are all unbound
> Drink until the house like the world turns around.
>
> — Hafez

OUR SUSPICIONS that Avo was a spy were laid to rest. Not only had he spent the past three days in his room with a stomach flu, but we concluded that the only skullduggery that he could ever hope to master was his Inspector Clouseau buffoonery. Kevin, feeling a tinge of remorse, brought Avo some apples from Hassan's house. Perhaps it was Kev's lingering certainty that he had passed on his New York bug to him. In a Florence Nightingale moment, Kev asked him the secret to living in Iran.

"Beating the system is easy," Avo explained. "You just have to know how to do it. I know many people who can. For them it's easy."

He reached for an apple, then sat back to take a bite.

"Not for me, unfortunately," he confessed. "But for them it's easy."

Over the past week, I had taken note of some of his sayings, under the heading *The World According to Avo.*

On trust, he advised: "Sometimes you have to lie to build trust, like when a girl asks, 'How do I look?' " On working for the secret police: "Sometimes you work for them and you don't even know it and they don't even pay you." On being a guide: "I only use the *baba* system. I don't bother with names, guidebooks or dates. I talk to the *babas*, you know, the old men who hang out at the sites. I just ask them and translate. What more do you want?" On his conversation strategy: "I always disagree. It makes things more interesting, don't you think?" Describing my father: "He's the strong, silent type, more or less." When a waiter in a café asked him to tell my mother to put on her headscarf, he shot back: "Why? Do you think I'm with them?" On girl watching: "You only get to look at the face to satisfy yourself, but sometimes its enough." His favorite quote about the Shah: "A lie is halfway around the world before you've got your boots on." And his quote from Khomeini: "This time either Islam triumphs or it disappears."

In the neighborhood of Julfa, long renowned for its vibrant Armenian-Christian community and its red wine, we found the magnificent cathedral of Vank. Its chandelier-lit interior revealed a Safavid-inspired star-studded dome and Italianate frescoes depicting the Last Judgment.

A disoriented Avo, who had been roused out of bed for the visit, stood silently to one side. As an Armenian Christian, he embodied the character of a religious minority by blocking out any unsavory questions of persecution. Did he use humor, like the foolishly clever Mullah Nasruddin, to deflect conversation until he had made up his mind what to reply and how much to reveal?

Staring up at the gold stars, he repeated, looking perplexed, "Terry, I still don't know if Armenia is a country, a culture, a language or a religion."

Armenia, in fact, was all of those. A people whose ancient nation was the first to embrace Christianity, in the third century, Armenians were among the most talented and cultured citizens of the Middle East. Their tragic geography — wedged in the southern Caucasus Mountains between Ottoman, Persian and Russian empires — had subjected them to centuries of suffering and dispersal.

Julfa dates from the early seventeenth century, when Shah Abbas brought as captives two thousand Armenian families from a town that straddled the northern border of Persia. He entrusted the Armenians, known for their business acumen, with building commercial links for his all-important silk trade. He also rewarded them religious rights.

In only fifty years, these merchants established a network stretching from the English Channel to the South China Sea, placing Isfahan at the center, with entrepôts all over Asia. These Christian traders from Persia had been crucial to the early British penetration of India.

The portly, charismatic and Oxford-educated Right Reverend Goriun Babian, wearing his black robe, kindly invited me into his residence and offered me fresh coffee from Lebanon.

"Technically, this diocese extends much farther east," he explained. "It comes from the halcyon days. Actually my title is Bishop of Isfahan and India. Ahh, India."

"Meanwhile, back here at the ranch," the bishop unexpectedly said with a smile, "you should know that the Armenian Church remains stronger under the minarets of Islam than in the melting pot of the West, where our values are vanishing, not simply because of social assimilation. In 2005 we will celebrate our four hundredth anniversary in Isfahan. But who knows what the future has in store?"

He sat pensive for a moment, then spoke of Madonna, appearing onstage practically naked, wearing a cross. "A sacrilegious act and she becomes an icon of the masses," he said. "I don't understand where Western culture is going. After seventy years of communism and capitalism, we've reached the same exact point: God is dead."

Another cup of coffee arrived. "And as Nietzsche said, if God doesn't exist, then everything is possible. When values of basic dignity are lost, and the exception becomes the rule . . . well, you get my point."

Looking at America through his prism of piety, I could only agree: there was much backsliding to answer for.

It was evening. In Hassan's living room, my mother and father sat at opposite ends of the dining table with their four sons, in their prescribed places like the old days. In the kitchen, Hassan was working his alchemy again for our last dinner. And in supreme *taarof* style, our hosts would not eat with us.

"Yet another delicious meal from Hassan!" my mother saluted. "Twenty-nine years, and here we are where we left off."

"All my lads in place," Dad concurred. "Now, Kev's got a toast."

Kev stood. "Here's to Richard, long may he reign. He brought us great joy, he brought us great pain. He enhanced our tourist lives again and again. Whether heaven or hell, low or high, Rich will make sure that you tour or die!"

"I suffered so," Rich confessed melodramatically. "From one five-star meal to another. My pants no longer fit. I'm dying."

"I can't eat anymore," Chris wailed. "Wooooah!"

"Get ready. Our new motto? Eat or die!"

"A warning for any American tourist traveling to Iran."

I offered another warning: "Expect to suffer from excessive hospitality."

"It's hard," Kev agreed. "You come back looking like Orson Welles."

"So," Chris asked, "where are the terrorists?"

My father said, "I've searched everywhere for one of those guys, but not a bit of luck."

Donna looked up to share news. "Hassan has made a huge picnic basket for our trip tomorrow."

"Thank God!" Kev exclaimed.

Fatimeh entered with serving plates. "Have more, please!"

"I can't say no!" Rich cried in mock pain.

"Delicious fish, delicious sauce," I said.

"What kind of fish is it?" Kev asked.

"Whitefish, very tasty, from the Gulf. Here, have one."

My father playfully placed two fingers above his head, Great Satan style. "So, I've got to put my horns up like this."

"Pat, don't do that," my mother pleaded. "You're too old to be acting this way."

"Nah!" chaffed Fatimeh. "Not American people, but government is bad!"

"Pat, stop it!" My mother pulled his hands down as he grinned at us all.

"Things will be better, Fatimeh," my father said. "I'm going to fix it all when I get back to Berkeley."

"Dear Fatimeh, all our children are healthy, that's all that matters," my mother said, changing the subject just as Hassan entered with a tray of pomegranate duck.

"The rice is to die for, Hassan," I said.

"Here's the *fesenjan!*" he announced.

"Oh, my God," Rich cried again. "I just can't say no!"

"We love Isfahan, Hassan," I said, spooning his pomegranate sauce onto my rice.

"Then you should stay with us," he said. "We don't have a bed, but we have mattresses."

"You should see what we have in the van," my mother said. "Foam pads ready for any floor."

"You can all sleep here," Hassan said. "Last summer we had Ali's and Maryam's families staying here at the same time." He smiled heartily.

"Iran's like that," Fatimeh explained. "When the family comes, we stay together all night."

With all the serving plates emptied, Fatimeh left the room, then reappeared.

"Oh, we got lemon meringue pie!" Rich cheered.

Kevin's eyes brightened.

"When we go to look for our old house in Tehran," Dad said, "we'll close our eyes and remember these tastes."

Hassan spoke about his old job at the Kowsar Hotel. "Sometimes five groups of fifty people or parties would come, and I cooked ten lambs and twenty fish."

"So your pots were this big?" Rich opened his arms wide.

"Yes, very big," Hassan exclaimed. "Like the ones we saw in the bazaar. If I fell in it, I couldn't get out!"

We all laughed.

"I'm very happy I'm not there now," he went on. "One more day in that kitchen and I would be dead."

"So our coming here was good timing?" I asked.

"Yes, yes. If you had come one year ago, I would not be free. Each *Nowruz* the hotel had a big buffet. It was the busiest time."

"So you could never leave?" Mom asked.

"No, we worked twenty hours a day. For twenty-five years, I spent every *Nowruz* working."

"This is the first year you spent New Year's with your family?"

"Yes!"

"And then we arrived a week later?"

"That's right."

"So, after thirty years, it *was* perfect timing." Mom smiled.

"But you've never stopped cooking," Dad said.

"I like to cook for family!" Hassan laughed as Fatimeh entered with a rosewater rice pudding. "You know, years ago Fatimeh told some friends if they wanted to find a husband for their daughter, don't even think of a cook, because she'll never see her husband."

"That's right," Fatimeh said. "Every night after his work, Hassan came home so late. But when I cook, he always says, 'Oh, that's not good.' "

"He did win the award as best chef in Isfahan," my father said in his defense. Dad pointed at Hassan's framed award, which hung next to a color photograph of the holy mosque in Mecca, bathed in early morning light. We toasted Hassan with our Zam Zams.

"You see, Fatimeh," my mother diplomatically said, "in the end it all worked out."

"Yes, Donna." She sighed with her warm smile. "Yes."

\*　　　\*　　　\*

The next morning, I woke with the sun and headed alone for Hassan's house.

"Allo!" Hassan opened the gate with a shovel in his hand. Dirt covered his shoes. He had been digging in his patch of earth.

"Looking for the treasure?"

He smiled. "I have it here." He reached down and pulled off the bud of a magenta snapdragon for me.

I studied his tiny garden while he worked. Violet and saffron pansies and his prized snapdragons lined both walls. All of it was hard-fought land won in battles with Fatimeh, who objected to dirt and mud being tramped into her immaculate house.

"If she could," he said, "she'd pave over the whole yard."

I watched him turn the precious soil. He told me that he had removed one row of tiles to plant his flowers and greens, to bring forth color and life.

"People say I'm crazy because water is so expensive, and it costs me twice as much to grow vegetables than to buy them in the market. Fatimeh says, 'These are my gifts to Hassan.' She doesn't understand why I care so much. Women only think of the house, of practical things."

He took the hose and motioned for me to turn on the tap. He had dug little trenches to trap water for the sprouting greens. Twelve rows, to be precise. Apple blossoms burst from the branches of an ancient trunk, whose bark peeled and cracked during tortuously hot summers. He sprinkled the vibrant snapdragons.

"You remember these at the old house?" I asked.

"Of course! Flowers I must also water. These I cannot eat. But I enjoy them so much. They are my prayer to God," he said, handing me a snapdragon. " 'If you turn your heart to the continent of love,' our poet Saadi says, 'then you will see that the whole world is full of flowers and beauty.' "

"But now that you've retired, what will you do?"

"I would like to get some sheep and just be a shepherd. Anywhere, even in Tudeshk. But that's not possible. Fatimeh doesn't want to hear that. I'm a simple man. I don't need anything, just to walk in nature with my sheep. That's all."

"A shepherd?"

"That's right."

"What about a small farm?"

"Here in Isfahan, land is too expensive. Sheep are best for me. But Fatimeh won't let me do it. She wants to stay here on Bi-sim Street."

All Hassan dreamed of was to go back to a simple life. Working in a garden with his beloved flowers or wandering as a shepherd with his flock, as he used to do in his first job as a boy of seven. Either would be enough for him.

I heard my name, a faint voice calling.

"It's Fatimeh. She wants you."

Leaping onto the porch, I slipped off my shoes and padded through the spotless hallway and then into the sun-drenched living room, but saw no one.

"Come, Terry, I want to show you something." Fatimeh was calling from under the kitchen. I followed her voice down the stairs and into her spacious, orderly basement. I found her, pointing to an ironing board and a chest of drawers. "This your mommy gave us." The legs of the board were strapped into wooden blocks, repaired carefully over the years. I recognized the pale yellow chest Dad had crafted by himself.

"And also this fridge." In a country that ingeniously repairs and recycles the simplest possessions, the thirty-year-old refrigerator was still running.

"You see, Terry, we have everything we need."

She led me upstairs and guided me through the precious objects on the finely carved wooden shelves that lined one wall of the living room. Each shelf was protected by a delicate strip of white lace. There sat our old coffee pot with its plastic filter, now very fashionable in its fifties design; two decorated glass bowls and a small red flower vase; and two identical jade-green porcelain teapots that I vaguely remembered.

Fatimeh pointed to a tall cobalt-blue mug and laughed. "That," she said, "was your daddy's beer glass."

Mementos of our shared life together. I studied each one as if they were windows onto a regained childhood.

Still now, I realized, each evening as my parents sat in their Berkeley home to watch the news, their feet resting on Fatimeh's ivory and indigo carpet, ten thousand miles away in Isfahan at dawn, Fatimeh began her day by opening our old fridge that held Hassan's breakfast cheese.

Even though Hassan and Fatimeh's life, like that of many other Iranians, had improved greatly, their demeanor had not changed. I felt like a youngster looking now at Hassan tending his flowers. His weathered, cracked hands could not conceal the years of toil.

His face, unlike Fatimeh's, had lost the looks of the handsome Persian I remembered. Now his skin was darkened and worn from two decades of exposure to steaming cauldrons of fire and heat. Grueling times on the frontlines, caring for and feeding young boys in battle, had also taken their toll.

We had been divided by opposite worlds, a political divide that cast two peoples as enemies. Our life apart had to be threaded back together. Our bond could be sealed only by weaving our disparate experiences into a common prayer.

To hear Hassan say "my son," to hear Fatimeh echo those same words, poured rain on parched soil. The edges of cliffs folded over, the harsh precipice eroded, and earth filled the chasm that for so long had split my heart. What was once a gaping divide disappeared.

Leaving the Abbasi Hotel, our van resembled a Bakhtiari encampment made ready for migration. Hussein, a former ambulance driver during the Iran-Iraq War, was our new driver; patient Nasrollah had already headed back to Shiraz, his hometown. We had grown accustomed to his taste in music and his road warrior spirit. Reluctantly, we had waved him off. Hussein's van was less roomy and much noisier. Everything, including my mother's wheelchair and our bazaar booty, had to be squeezed into the back, behind the seats, and lashed on top, along with Fatimeh's two carpets, destined for Richard's young sons.

"We've left the spiritual and plunged into the material," I moaned, loading the van.

"Yes, but the prices were so low, Ter, it was spiritual," Kev pointed out.

Heavily burdened, we drove back to Bi-sim Street for our final farewell. I rang the bell and, as the small metal door opened, Mom presented blushing Fatimeh with a bright bouquet of yellow roses.

"*Shoma gol hastid?*" Fatimeh said. "You are a flower yourself. Why did you bring flowers?"

We all sat on the porch for a family portrait, and Hassan pulled out his gift: a light blue Styrofoam picnic basket packed with fried chicken, rice, fresh tomatoes, tangerines and yogurt.

"Promise you won't stop in any place to eat until you get to Tehran." He wagged his finger in warning, proud purveyor of home cooking that he was.

We promised.

"Inside, you have enough for the whole family, even for Avo."

"Whenever I tell my friends Mrs. Ward went to my village to find me, after *so* many years, they don't believe," Fatimeh gushed. "But I tell them it's true." She took my mother's hand in hers.

"Well," Mom replied, "in the end, we hoped and prayed. And here we are together at last. *Insha'allah*, we'll return soon."

"We'll be here waiting for you."

"We'll be back, Fatimeh, we will." Her voice breaking, Mom spoke for all of us.

Hassan threw his arms around us. "We never forget you. Never. We wait and think, and never forget."

In a flurry of waves, our heavily laden van coughed into gear. Lurching down the street past the neighborhood mosque, we turned back to look for the last time. They had vanished, slipping back inside their walls.

\*       \*       \*

Isfahan — its rivers and bridges, gardens and mosques, bazaars and boulevards and sprawling suburbs — quickly faded behind us. Tehran lay 240 miles north. Our track crossed a rugged range with its snowy peak, Kuh-e Karkas, or Mount Vulture, staring fiercely down at us.

Millennia of high winds and flash floods had gashed and riddled the copper-gold land. These high steppes bore their ancient scars artistically, each finely carved by snaking river traces: ornate fractals, veins of a leaf, pointed tridents. Cracked-open plateaus floated by, all barren except for a dusting of green where a spring burst through the arid crust. These were the solitary signs of man's humble addition to nature's complex geometry. Somewhere to our left, hidden in the ocher folds of rising hills, lay the pomegranate-stained village of Abiyaneh.

We turned off the main highway, left the wasteland and came upon a narrow river valley. The weaving road climbed along a gorge, curling left and right past groves of poplar and mud huts. We met a shepherd tending his flock.

"Where is your town of Abiyaneh?" Avo asked.

With his walking stick he pointed up the mountain.

"What's up there to see?" Avo asked.

We didn't hear the shepherd's answer.

"What did he say?" my father asked.

"Mr. Ward, he said he hasn't been there in eight days, so he's not sure."

"What the hell, Avo, did you think there might be an arts festival?" Dad looked exasperated.

We drove on for another twenty minutes until, tucked away from the world, we found it, between arid peaks and lush groves of apricot, cherry and plums well watered by melting snows. Two fortresses guarded the entrance to a mountain river valley. Tall plane trees triggered memories of rushing streams and patches of meadow.

"I've had dreams about a place like this," Kev said.

Radiating a burnt siena hue, the adobe village of Abiyaneh clung to the cliffs, one house stacked atop another, each growing out of the roof below like the ancient pueblo dwellings in Chaco Canyon. And what of Abiyaneh's rare sunset glow? The skin of pomegranates, we were told, mixed with earth before building, gave the adobe walls their reddish stain.

At the end of the road, a shaded meadow welcomed us. Hassan's picnic lunch was soon devoured, and then an elderly forest nymph appeared in a white headscarf. Here, apparently, black scarves were traded in for white ones with red roses. Curiously, she told me her name was Fereshteh, which means angel. Fereshteh slowly opened her stash of fresh pressed apricot and cherry rolls, called *lavoshak*, wrapped in a flowery cloth.

Chris couldn't resist. "May I buy some?"

"Of course," she slyly said.

"All of it?" Immediately, Chris bargained for the entire supply.

"Oh, no," Fereshteh whispered. "Here he comes. Don't speak to him. He's really crazy."

She pointed at a gangly, big-footed man walking in our direction, then quickly collected her money and fled back into the grove.

When the man arrived, he asked where Fereshteh was. We gave no answer. He scratched his head, rubbed his shoe in the grass.

"She's crazy, you know," he said. "You shouldn't talk to her."

We felt we had somehow stumbled upon a scene from *Waiting for Godot*. Two people stop and talk to strangers, each calling the other mad. Yet at the end only they remain on the stage. "Maybe," Rich suggested, "they're both hopelessly in love, just too shy."

In that idyllic place we felt lifted, light as a feather, under the trees by a rushing stream. "What more could we want?" my father asked. Our reunion with Hassan had filled us with a giddiness, a warm certainty, a bold confidence. Humanity and grace were very much alive. We felt newly born.

Every country has its Newark. Between bare, scruffy hills by the great Salt Lake sat Qom. It was a gloomy, polluted place. We visited Qom because it held the gold-domed shrine of Masumeh, sister of Reza, the eighth imam. Qom was Iran's Vatican, the heart of the Shia clergy and the *axis mundi* of the Islamic Republic. It was here that Ayatollah Khomeini spoke out against the Shah in 1963, provoking his own arrest and inflaming rioting crowds in Tehran. It was here that, a year later, he spoke against the shameful bill approved by the Majlis that gave American military personnel blanket immunity from the courts. And it was here, in January 1978, that the first shots were fired on seminary students protesting a newspaper article slandering Khomeini. Qom was the epicenter. It was here that the spark of revolution was lit.

The city sprawled like a massive low-budget stage set. Women were covered completely — no mere scarves here. It felt tense, full of hectic confusion, no lightness like the cities we had left behind. Every passing police or army officer stared at us. No smiles. No waving. I lowered my camera. Two minarets rose above the bazaar, and we followed the signs of Allah.

True to form, our driver Hussein — who, as Avo said, "loved danger" — stopped right in front of the mosque and beckoned us to go inside. Mom remained on board, apprehensive about the unwelcoming vibes coming from the holy place.

"More ayatollahs here than any place on earth," Avo warned. "Now, for God's sake, don't get me into trouble."

This time he was right. Clerics, in their black or white turbans, streamed out the doors. When we tried to enter the mosque's courtyard, guards stopped us. Were we Muslims? We said no. The call to prayer echoed in rich, piercing cadence. We could go no further.

In his penetrating and sympathetic book *The Mantle of the Prophet*, Roy Mottahedeh explores the world of Qom through the life of a young mullah, Ali Hashemi, who comes of age during the Islamic Revolution. Mottahedeh, a professor of Middle Eastern history at Harvard, maps out the unique theological education of Iran's seminaries. The Islamic colleges he describes focus on grammar, rhetoric, Arabic and logic; on the philosophers Aristotle and Avicenna; and, most importantly, on the Koran.

Like the Catholic clergy, the Shia have their hierarchy as well. *Talebehs* are students or "seekers" who come to Qom's colleges. After years of study, a student hopes to become a *mujtahid*, a "jurist" with the right to interpret Islamic law. A higher level is *hojjat al-Islam*, "proof of Islam." At the top, *ayatollahs* are the "light of God."

Calling these mullahs "the last true scholastics alive on earth," Mottahedeh greatly admires the intellectual rigor required by the students who master the ancient texts and intricate interpretations of Islamic law. However, he has little sympathy for those scholars who betray their traditional vocation of teaching to enter politics. At the end of *The Mantle of the Prophet*, Ali Hashemi abandons the political arena and returns to Qom, where he will teach once more. This is Mottahedeh's strong plea, that other mullahs will do the same. And he is not alone.

"Back to the mosques" was a constant refrain during our journey. Iranian society and the clergy were torn by that debate. In the ongoing struggles between the clergy and secularists, traditionalists and modernists, Mottahedeh appealed for reconciliation. But this was Iran's political quandary: those in power had too much to lose.

The Islamic Republic's constitution, passed in a 1979 referendum, enshrined the concept of *valeyat-e faqih*, governance by an Islamic jurist. This cemented the clerics' hold on the Islamic Republic. Yes, the president and parliament would be elected in voting far freer and more democratic than that of any regime in the Arab world. But at the top, the Supreme Leader — first Ayatollah Khomeini and now his appointed successor, Ayatollah Khamenei — had the final say on all matters.

Appointed for life, the Supreme Leader represented God's voice on earth. In Khamenei, along with the Council of Guardians — which made judgments on key issues, such as approving candidates for election and laws passed by parliament — there existed an institutional check on any attempts to reform the system through democratic means. The Supreme Leader maintained control of the state-run radio and television, the police, the military, the courts and the prisons.

After two decades, the Islamic Republic had reached a crossroads with the election of the new president, Khatami. Foreign diplomatic visits would attract promises of investment and technology, the benefits of the global economy that the country so desperately needed. But internally, the president had only limited influence. He could, for example, give permission to publish a newspaper. And he did. An explosion of dailies flooded the newsstands during our visit. A new, powerful voice of open questioning, critical analysis and investigative journalism was taking the country by storm. The Islamic Republic was reshaping its identity.

Avo tried admirably to bluff our way into the luminous gold-domed shrine of Masumeh. The gap-toothed guard simply told us to leave at once. We had come to the one religious site in Iran where nonbelievers were not admitted. The courtyard was filled with mullahs and theological students, strolling and speaking in hushed tones. We backed away and silently boarded the van, feeling thoroughly unwelcome. Hussein drove on.

My mother broke the silence by reminding us about our previous visit to Qom many years ago. "Probably only Kevin was old enough to remember, but last time we were here, we —"

"Were stoned," Kev said with a grin.

"This was before Hassan came to work for us. Otherwise, it would never have happened. It was our fault. We didn't realize it was Moharram."

She described our ordeal. Our blue Opel was packed to the brim for a camping trip in the south. When we reached the outskirts of dusty Qom, we saw black bunting and flags fluttering in the wind, signaling the period of mourning. Then the streets narrowed and traffic slowed to a crawl. Limping along a boulevard, we came to a red light. As we stopped, we heard a loud thump on the car, then another. Rocks were flying. One came through the window. Dad panicked. He flipped the car in a U-turn and sped out of town.

"The choice of Moharram for a family outing was not a bright idea," Mom said. "Had Hassan been with us, he would never have let us go."

"What did we know? We'd only just arrived," Dad said defensively. "How could we know that religious fervor, resentment of foreigners and kids' joy of target practice all peaked during Moharram?"

"The blind leading the blind." Kev sighed.

"And so," my mother continued, "we drove west into the hills." She recounted how we left the car parked on the road and hiked up, carrying a food basket and water with us. We found a lovely place to picnic. "There was this beautiful tree," she remembered. "But as soon as we had sat down to eat, Daddy realized we weren't alone." In the distance he saw five figures in dark clothes walking in our direction. He looked through binoculars and said they might be trouble. "Then he told me, 'They've cut off our path to the car. It's too far to run. Wait here with the boys.' Before I could say anything, he was running down the hill toward the road."

"Oh great!" Chris said. "Dad abandoned us."

"My only hope was to stop a passing car for help," Dad said.

"A mile away?" Rich needled.

"While we're up on the hill like sitting ducks," Chris added.

"And once Dad disappeared from sight . . ." Mom was about to continue when my father felt he had to explain.

"Look guys, we were alone in the desert. The threat was clear. We had no protection. But I was lucky, a truck pulled over. I was frantic and don't remember what I said, but the driver gave me his tire iron."

Armed with the weapon, my father told us that he ran back to Mom and prepared for a confrontation. One against five. As the minutes ticked away, the squinting eyes and beaded sweat on the approaching black-shirted thugs signaled ill intent. My father held the tire iron firmly at his side.

"And then loud bleating erupted behind us," Mom said. "We all turned around, and there was a huge flock of scruffy sheep surrounding us in a sea of glorious, stinking dirty wool. And they began munching away at our picnic!"

"Thank God for those hungry mutton mouths," said Dad.

"Their shepherd kept pushing and thwacking them, but his sheep just wouldn't budge."

"Of course not. There was more food in our picnic basket than in all the burnt scrub for the next three miles. It was feeding time!"

With his red cheeks shining, Dad went on, "So when the thugs arrived, they saw us engulfed in this herd that wouldn't move. You should've seen their faces. All of a sudden they burst into gales of laughter. They loved seeing the sheep trampling our picnic blanket. Mom held baby Rich above the flock while you all were hugging those smelly sheep." His eyes were brimming, my mother was laughing.

"We quickly thanked the shepherd," Mom said, "and headed back down to the car as fast as we could. Daddy made a U-turn and drove back half a mile to the waiting truck driver who had helped us. As he handed back the tire iron, the man told him, 'Very lucky. Dangerous for you, so easy to disappear and be thrown down a *qanat.*' From then on, we always stayed at home during Moharram."

Qom's eeriness lingered as we nibbled on *sohan*, that holy city's severely addictive pistachio brittle that Pat had bought outside the Masumeh shrine. At sunset, we enjoyed one last view of the magnificent gold dome, gleaming in the fading light. Under the shrine's walls children played on seesaws in a park built along a dry riverbed. We watched as prayers ended and mothers, daughters, mullahs, ayatollahs and students streamed out of the mosque to begin their evening walk home for their waiting supper.

An hour later, Hussein's van was hurtling along a six-lane highway toward Tehran, city of our memories. Rich lay down in the back, Kev stared to the west at the last glimpses of light on the gray horizon, my parents dozed with their heads resting on each other while Chris pored over an enormous map of Tehran with his flashlight.

We all remained quiet. A dreadful storm brewed before us, sweeping down from the northern mountains, blackening our route ahead. Lightning split the sky. Thunder followed. Dark rain started to fall in broad sheets as we drove into the brooding monsoon.

After passing through the deluge, magically the clouds lifted and an ocean of lights flickered in the distance. Tehran! Before us blazed four Disney-like spires of shimmering light.

"An oil refinery?" Rich asked.

"No," Avo answered solemnly. "Imam Khomeini's tomb."

A debate immediately broke out over whether to stop or drive on. Rich and I were adamant about pulling over. It was late, Chris said, and he was exhausted. My father nodded. After a vote of four to two, we arrived at a large parking lot that held a few buses, a handful of cars and an all-night convenience store. Starkly immense, flooded with light, the memorial shrine with its four airy minarets stood with no rival structure in sight. Next to a vast cemetery of the war dead, this ground held magnetic power. It was near the slums of south Tehran, where the regime drew its greatest support for mass rallies and demonstrations. Pilgrims flocked to pay their respects to the founder of the Islamic Republic. A busload of turbaned Afghanis with Mongolian features joined us as we entered the mosque. Avo and my father had finally agreed on something: they both remained in the van.

Removing our shoes at the door, we padded in. As we passed through a metal detector, a guard told us not to take pictures. Green marble with cream streaks appeared here and there between the carpets covering the vast floor. Tiny pieces of mirror, like mosaic, lined the dome. Stained-glass red tulips, a symbol of martyrdom, circled the rim. Erected hastily after the ayatollah's death, the structure in its immensity reminded me of New York's Javits Center with its acres of interconnected aluminum roofing. Two children scooted past holding their soccer ball. Families sat on the carpets, nibbling snacks. Others napped soundly wrapped in blankets.

Under the monumental dome rested the sarcophagus, surrounded by a silver protective enclosure. A massive crystal chandelier, suspended from the dome, dangled over it. I approached with Kevin. Worshipers huddled close and prayed. One woman was sleeping with her fingers gripping the bars of the enclosure. A white-haired grandfather spoke softly to a child in quiet reverence. A middle-aged man in a gray suit came toward us.

"May I kindly ask you where are you from?"

"Ireland," Kev replied, disguising his American accent.

"Welcome, brother."

"Thank you."

We shook hands. "Ah, Irish. You know, we changed the name of Churchill Boulevard," he told us as if it were something we should know.

"Yes? Well, we've just arrived in Tehran."

"It's now called Bobby Sands Boulevard."

"Oh, thank you, sir." Kev bowed as if accepting a gift. The regime had obviously chosen the name of an Irish hunger striker to tweak the nose of the British lion. Martyrdom bonding their friendship, Kevin and the man walked together.

"Are you Muslim or Catholic?"

"There is only one God," Kevin answered obliquely. His new friend smiled, taking his words as a yes for Islam.

"Yes, only one God."

Gliding toward us like an apparition came a figure covered head to toe in a chador. It was my mother. Her beaming face protruded from her pitch-black wraparound like a Cheshire cat's. What grace she had, with her soft smile and heartwarming eyes. Silently, I took her arm in mine and slowly we circumambulated the hall. After a peaceful ten minutes, we walked out of the shrine behind Kevin and his philo-Celtic buddy.

Still inside, Chris underwent an altogether different experience. He was accosted by a soldier.

"Is there film in your video?" the soldier snapped, his rifle slung on his shoulder.

"Y-yes," Chris replied nervously.

"Did you take pictures?"

"No, of course not."

"Nothing?"

"Nothing."

The soldier studied his worried face.

"No, I swear," Chris insisted.

The guard exploded, "But why not, *baba?*" His expression turned into a pained look. "Everyone else finds it so beautiful. You don't like it? *Baba*, take some film now or you'll miss it."

Before Chris could say anything, the soldier had handed him the rifle, taken the video camera and turned it on. While we stood waiting in the semidarkness outside, I saw two silhouettes walking out of the mosque. I was sure that my brother was in trouble.

"Oh God, Terry, has he been arrested?" my mother asked.

"Don't know, Mom. It looks like a soldier. He's got a rifle."

Then we heard a voice cry out, "Mom, come meet Ahmad!" Soon Chris was introducing us to his new best friend, who was very pleased to hear that we had made Ayatollah Khomeini's tomb our first stop in Tehran. We all shook hands. I suggested they pose for a photo.

"Ready?" I lined them up with all four golden minarets streaking skyward in the background.

Ahmad straightened his green fatigues, his face gripped in a rigid pose. "Ready," he said.

"I'm dreaming," Chris said.

In 1926, Vita Sackville-West, after a grueling overland drive, described her entry into Tehran: "The air at this altitude of nearly four thousand feet is as pure as the note of a violin. There is everywhere a sense of oneness and of being at a great height; that sense of grime and over-population, never wholly absent in European countries, is wholly absent here; it is like being lifted up and set above the world on a great wide roof."

Now, twelve million people called Tehran home. It seemed overly immense, gargantuan, beyond any proportions of memory. We recognized nothing except the familiar Elburz peaks, soaring thick and rugged, snow-streaked and lit with fairy lights fluttering on the upper slopes. The roads seemed strangely new. I felt lost. Chris was unfazed; he'd turned altogether sappy after his trial by fire in the mosque. "After that, nothing can scare me now," he told us. It was late at night. A light sprinkle of rain was falling. The streets were empty and endless. Then a brightly lit pavilion, a white marble beacon, pierced the darkness.

"Rudaki Hall! Remember?" my father burst out. "The Vienna Boys' Choir, the L.A. Philharmonic, Nureyev and Fonteyn?"

Ground zero for the cultural elite under the Shah's "Great Civilization," Rudaki Hall had entertained Tehran sophisticates with musical and dance performances of world-class caliber. And now?

"Not much," said Avo. "I never go. The performing arts aren't on my social calendar, if you know what I mean."

Our hotel, the Laleh, was a welcoming sight at midnight. Once called the Intercontinental — the enduring home of the world's journalists during the hostage crisis — it now had a revolutionary name: *laleh* means tulip, the flower of martyrs. Disgorging all our belongings from the van proved embarrassing, as it took three sleepy porters to help us haul everything inside the brightly lit lobby. A sympathetic sigh was cast my mother's way when her wheelchair appeared. Checking in at the front desk, I felt the hotel waking up to sudden action.

Eager autograph seekers circled a pair of close-cropped men wearing warmup jerseys that read across the back: IRAN. Squeals of delight sounded from the young boys who had emerged from nowhere, half asleep, to greet regal and handsome soccer players who had just stepped in from the night.

"Is this the national team?" Dad asked the concierge.

The concierge nodded. "Tomorrow is big match against Hungary."

Not missing a beat, my father leaned over the desk. "*Agha*, sir, I need six tickets. Can you get them?"

"It's not so easy, sir."

"I'm sure, my dear friend, if anyone can find them, you can."

"I will try, sir."

The concierge turned to whisper in a colleague's ear. A flurry of movement began behind the front desk while my father and I surveyed Iran's young soccer hopefuls. The concierge and Dad traded knowing nods until a small envelope was slipped over the counter along with our electronic room cards.

Dad picked up the envelope and held it triumphantly aloft. Winking at me, he turned back to the concierge and said, "Better than opening-night tickets to a Broadway show, *agha!*"

And he meant it.

13

# Valleys of the Assassins, Black Five Millionaires

Every homeland constitutes a sacred geography. For those who have left it, the city of their childhood and adolescence always becomes a mythical city.

— Mircea Eliade, *Ordeal by Labyrinth*

RACING NORTH like homing pigeons, we drove past a long lime-green curtain of plane trees that still hugged Vali Asr Boulevard, once called Pahlavi. New highways and overpasses crisscrossed the megalopolis in confusing patterns. Tall residential towers and huge apartment complexes flashed by. All this was new to us. I began to understand Rip van Winkle's disorientation after his long sleep.

In the northern suburbs, behind high walls topped with broken glass, we had spent our days in elegant gardens dressed with fruit trees: cherry, mulberry and pomegranate. Weeping willows hung their long tresses over a welcoming pond, like Narcissus hypnotized by his reflected beauty. We expected now to wander again through those footpaths of memory, but the new landscape resisted easy nostalgia.

Up Pesyan Street in Velenjak we went, searching for our home. Closer to the mountains, all our senses came alive. The street turned past the old *barbari* bakery, hemmed in by a suffocating chain of walls. Burgundy marble and gaudy structures suggested visions far from Islamic taste. But in the northern hills it was always so. Cosmopolitan influences abounded behind the walls: French Empire, Russian dacha, neoclassical columns and Italian statuary.

We soon found ourselves driving in circles. Apartment buildings had replaced open green spaces, orchards and gardens. The entire landscape was transformed. We drove past elephantine construction sites, our emotions trampled. The land was now full. Empty fields walled in. Blindly lost, we parked the car and started walking to an open space on our left. Suddenly the view opened up in front of us. Here was the gorge of our childhood!

But nothing around it made sense, only the riverbed below and the hint of caves in the eroded chasm where we used to play and hide. We peered west across the ravine to a plateau that once served as a resting stop for migrating nomads, who pitched their tents for the night and lit flickering fires under the stars. It was now concrete.

"This gully used to be like the Grand Canyon." Forlorn, Kevin picked up a stone and tossed it down the cliff.

"And over there it was all barren," my father said, pointing west to the sprawl of new buildings.

"That hill we used to climb and plant our flag — Rich, remember?" Chris stared up at the rising foothills. Rich nodded.

At least the rugged mountain flanks above us were still untouched. The craggy outcrops had proved too steep for land-hungry developers. We strolled slowly along a dirt path looking at our wild playground below. Then Kev scaled the stone wall that bordered the ravine to peer on its other side.

"I found it!" he yelled to us.

"You're sure?" Mom asked excitedly.

"Yes, but . . ." Kev paused, staring over the top.

I climbed up the wall to look. Chris and Rich scrambled up too.

"There's a fifty-foot hole in the ground," Kev said.

"What do you mean?" my mother asked.

"Not even a tree was spared."

I clung to the wall. Our mythical garden! Someone had destroyed every trace of it. A colossal hole had been dug, ready to receive the foundation of another mammoth high-rise. The villa, the verandah, the rose bushes, the pool, rows of slim-lined poplars, the weeping willow, the cherry orchard, Hassan's rooms, all gone.

Chris mournfully began singing: "Memories are so beau-ti-ful and yet . . ."

Rich told him to stop. Chris's off-key voice only added to our collective anguish.

We had to get inside. The old wall looked impenetrable; the back door was bolted shut. We continued alongside, traversing the compound. Mom and Dad followed in silence. But then we saw our red gate. It was unscathed. And open. We entered.

Before us lay our old place. Yes, the cherry orchard, along with Hassan's four-room brick house, had been swallowed by the crater. And our villa — was it in the rubble under a cement high-rise under construction? Impossible to know for sure. Only three slender pines remained. Where was the statue of Venus? And the Neapolitan grotto where a shepherd seduced his nymph with a magic flute? Where was our swimming pool the size of a small lake?

We did not hesitate, and moved as if regaining possession of some familiar territory. Frantically, Chris called out to us as we stumbled punch-drunk around some rubble.

"Guys, aren't we glad we found Hassan and Fatimeh? Places don't matter, people do. Right?"

Dad scanned the property. "Thomas Wolfe was right," he said. "You can't go home again."

"Say goodbye to the old homestead," Rich said.

"They paved paradise," Kev said, "to put up a condo."

Steeling ourselves for a dignified exit, we chatted calmly with a man who had appeared beside us. He said that the land had been sold six years before.

Then Kevin shouted to us. In a small shed at the far end of the garden, he had found two sculpted figures. I walked over and was stunned. There they were, the two Hellenic lovers who once sat transfixed in our grotto staring deep into each other's eyes. Broken, arms missing. These lonesome stone relics brought back memories of when we fell asleep under the summer stars listening to Hassan's voice. Discarded in this new puritanical epoch, the lovers were symbols of a decadent bygone time.

"Let's take them with us," Kev said, holding the pieces of stone.

"Can you imagine the questions at customs?" protested Chris. "Do you want to be locked up? Besides, we gotta think about getting our carpets out."

"Kev, just leave them," Dad said, touching his shoulder.

"We can't let them lie here," Kev pleaded.

But we did. We turned our backs on the construction site and left.

Mom vowed to return for the statues.

Drooping wisteria climbed the walls. Weeping willows hid behind the tall gates. We drove past copper roofs atop cream-colored brick houses. Some parts of our neighborhood, it seemed, were still intact. Soon we wended our way back to the main boulevard, Vali Asr. In bumper-to-bumper traffic, we moved at a snail's pace under the familiar canopy of leafy plane trees. We advanced as we had so many years before.

"Tajrish Square! It's still here!" I cheered. The elegant square opened up dramatically just under the rising mountains.

"Where would it go?" Avo said, puzzled.

"Quick, let's check out the bazaar."

Scrambling out of the van, we all scampered toward the dark entrance bordering the crowded bus stop. Plentiful fruit stalls splashed welcome natural colors. Under bright lights, wooden carts held bounty arranged geometrically: pyramids of blood oranges, kiwis and glossy tangerines, strawberries and green watermelons, violet grapes and hanging bananas. Butchers' hooks dangled long flanks of lamb and freshly killed chickens. Fresh seafood and three-foot silver carp were handsomely displayed on chopped ice. Heads of lettuce, bunches of dill, long cucumbers, rich eggplants, towers of tomatoes, even string beans and red cabbage.

Rich marched straight into the market.

"The mosque is over there. I remember it so well," he said, leading us to the corner where we once bought baby chicks and ducks. Chirping in cardboard crates still lay an assortment of chicks, dyed in pink, orange and blue fluorescent colors, hoping to catch the eye of a child or his indulgent parents.

"At least here, nothing's changed," said Chris, petting a bright pink chick while I gazed out at the expanded courtyard with its turquoise-domed Imamzadeh Saleh, the mosque and shrine where Hassan used to pray.

The upscale gold bazaar was new, as was an overhead sign in English that read, *Believers are men who neither commerce nor sale diverts from the remembrance of God — Quran 24/37*. Wishful thinking for bazaaris, I thought as I fished through a small box of silkworms munching on green mulberry leaves. In a pharmacy, Kev found his favorite shampoo, honey and egg. He opened the cap and sniffed. In Proustian fashion, his eyes rolled shut.

"This smell puts me right back in the bathtub at our old house."

"And the bazaar?" Chris asked.

"It isn't as big as I remembered it, but infinitely cleaner."

"No donkeys, no flies. What do we navigate by?"

"In the old days, I used beams of sunlight."

Chris pointed out Levi's along with competing jean brand names: Cowboy and Cash. I caught a glimpse of Adidas sneakers, a poster of Dizzy Gillespie's silhouette, two Stars-and-Stripes T-shirts, purple-polished toenails and Revlon faces, Champion sweat suits and Swatch watches, Nissan auto parts and a poster of Dexter Gordon blowing his sax.

Back in the square, outside the bazaar, I spotted our driver animatedly exchanging words with a defiant police officer. Avo stood aloof.

"It will cost two thousand tomans," Avo muttered as I came

near him. "It's just between those two, not to write a ticket, you know."

Our ambulance driver discreetly handed over the money.

"He's not selling himself," Avo explained about the police officer. "He's just doing his business."

So much had changed that our memories were useless: the Tehran we once knew was now almost incomprehensible. Disoriented and confused, we drove on wide freeways dotted with huge, surreal hand-painted billboards of martyrs' faces and slowly trekked across the mushrooming city.

After seeing our disemboweled home in northern Tehran, we balked at revisiting the Community School. Far better to leave those images and sentiments intact, we all agreed. Cruising south to the Laleh Hotel, Hussein turned off the main street because of a traffic jam, swerved up a side alley and turned again. Then, in a hysterical voice, Dad called out from the back seat: "That's it! Stop! The old Iran-American Society."

The van screeched to a halt. Outside our right window rose the familiar concrete ornamented dome. We had to pay our respects at this holy site. After all, it was under that dome that all of my father's theatrical productions were nurtured, staged and celebrated: *Our Town*, *The Music Man* and *A Thousand Clowns*, to name a few.

The sight of six *khareji* seeking entry to the theater complex provoked confusion among the staff, until a pleasant but officious woman in blue arrived to ask us our purpose — and she spoke flawless English.

"Madam," my father said, "thirty-five years ago I directed a play that opened this theater to the public for the first time. Would you mind if my family and I could see it one last time?"

She pulled back, hesitant. With a nervous tremor in her voice, she began speaking defensively of written permission and cultural ministries. Then a silver-haired custodian in a green suit appeared and quickly started to explain to her about my father.

"He says that he remembers," she translated, "the drama plays then. He has been working here since that opening day."

Dad reached over and hugged the custodian.

"Please come in," she said. "He will show you." Then, after a moment's reflection, perhaps to protect the sanctuary from any historic claims, she added, "But you may only see the outside."

"Even so, we would be thankful," my father replied.

She nodded and our custodian guided us down the open staircase until we stood before the lofty glass pavilion framing the entrance doors. A poster of Jafar Panahi's film *The White Balloon* hung in the same place where I once remembered a Day-Glo orange and magenta poster of two surfers in *The Endless Summer.* The theater was used for movies and theatrical productions. Inside the doors lay the stage where Pat had directed Thornton Wilder's *Our Town* before packed houses for the inaugural of the Iran-American Society. He'd molded an amateur troupe into respectable players.

"*Our Town,*" mused my father. "Donna helping backstage and selling tickets, you kids racing about. Terry, you were onstage. It was a four-week run. Magical!"

"And Pat," my mother said, "it was so universal. Grover's Corners could just as easily have been Tudeshk."

"That's why I chose it," Dad said. "The final scene with Emily in the graveyard looking back at her family and calling out to them, 'Each moment of life is so precious! Can't they see it? Don't they know?' But of course none of them can hear her." He whispered, "It all passes by too fast."

Wanting to say one last thing, he turned to us, opening his arms. He laughed, but with tears in his eyes. No words came.

Even if our Tehrani past had been paved over, America's pop culture was curiously alive in the streets. A reincarnation of Colonel Sanders, but with a curly black beard and a dark cloak, was posted in front of a fast-food joint advertising "Kabooky Fried Chicken." At the checkout counter of a supermarket, I thumbed through a magazine listing banned American films, such as George Lucas's *Return of the Jedi.* To my right, a girl in a chador had her magazine opened to a frightening bald Demi Moore as *G.I. Jane*. A passing car boomed out Madonna tunes.

There were music cassettes of my favorite Latin artists, Santana and Paco de Lucia. Another tape, called *Strains of Andalucia*, featured Spanish guitarists jamming with Persian *tar* players. Then I saw his face: the inexplicable New Age phenomenon Yanni in front of the blazing Acropolis. How did he get here? I turned and another mustachioed man stared at me, the Qajar dynasty ruler Nasr-e Din Shah in full regalia. He was everywhere, painted ubiquitously on pink porcelain teapots. Was pop monarchical imagery now chic?

Driving past the Samad building, one of the first luxury highrises built during the pre-Revolution boom, I saw spray-painted graffiti: Run-D.M.C., Mötley Crüe, NBA Techno and Jason Kevins. Who in the world, I wondered, was Jason Kevins?

Around the lively Tehran University campus, sipping a cold Coolack cola, I wandered past bookstores that were doing a booming business. I perused a few English-language titles: *Sons and Lovers, The Secret Agent, Animal Farm, The Adventures of Tom Sawyer* and *The Godfather.*

This country, I decided, was anything but bottled up.

For a fleeting glance, Hussein slowed down in front of the former American embassy. We stared out at the brick wall of the "Den of Spies." It now housed a computer training center for the Revolutionary Guards, Hussein told us. Chris recalled the fireworks that exploded in the night skies on the Fourth of July, and Kevin remembered our touch football games on the back lawn.

Hussein reminded us that half of Iran's population was born after the landmark date of 1979, the year of the hostages. "Many sons and daughters of the Revolution," he said, "watch bootleg videos and disco at home."

"And some," my father added, "are soccer fanatics."

In the balmy twilight of April 21, sixty thousand passionate fans swarmed into Azadi Stadium to cheer for Iran's national team.

Skydivers parachuted onto the field, red-hued smoke bombs burned in the stands. My father's nimble legs raced through the crowd, bobbing left, dashing right, into the midfield stands, where he found our seats. He felt at home here. We all straggled down the steps while he was already busily clapping, cheering and shaking hands with his neighbors.

"So, your dad's been here before," Avo observed.

"Go Iran!" my father howled, the consummate fan.

Iran's resurgence as a soccer power began in 1990 with the Asian Games victory. Most rabid fans, I was told, were divided between Tehran's two top clubs, one of which had a very non-Islamic name, Persepolis. Positioned for the World Cup in June 1998, Team Iran had only six months before miraculously squeezing by as the final qualifier in the thirty-two-nation tournament. In Europe, no embargo was in place for footballers. Three Iranian stars played in the German Bundesliga: Karim Baheri, Ali Daei and Khodadad Azizi.

Soccer passion terrified the authorities. On November 29, 1997, when Iran tied Australia with two late goals to qualify for the World Cup, excitement spilled into the streets. At midnight, millions joined in exuberant celebrations, teenagers danced on their cars, music blared from car stereos, police joined in cheering, some women took off their scarves. It was by far the biggest demonstration since the Revolution. The country quite simply spiraled into collective hysteria.

"It was spontaneous joy, like Carnival in Brazil," our new friend in the stands, a young man named Mahmoud, said. "We cried and laughed and danced all night long. Wheeew!"

"And the big game against America?" I asked.

"That will be even bigger if Iran wins. But America is very good."

"So is Iran," my father screamed. "Get ready, Mahmoud, baby. Put on your dancing shoes."

Young Mahmoud translated Dad's words for his friends, which spread through the stands. Within minutes, Dad was the most popular fan in Deck D. Hands reached down to shake his, students flashed thumbs-up signs, bearded hulks grinned childishly with flaring eyes. Our sports ambassador had scored big on this most delicate of diplomatic missions.

Like a fervid New York Mets fan who memorizes every conceivable statistic, Mahmoud methodically described each player on the field, finishing with his favorite: ". . . And our prize goalie is called the Eagle of Asia."

A minute later, the ball shot past the Eagle and into the net of Iran. The deafening, throbbing roar quieted to dead silence. A wounded look settled over Mahmoud's face.

By the end, the Eagle had laid a goose egg. Iran lost to Hungary, 2–0. Chris, himself a goalie, began mocking the easy goals and demoted the Eagle with a new name — the Turkey of Tabriz, he called him. Dad was enraged. Iran's Croatian coach was openly cursed for his conservative defensive style. "Bring back the Brazilian!" the fans cried.

"Outta here. Let's breeze," Dad said.

As we left, we saw angry fans burning their programs in protest. My father took off like a bolt of lightning. For him, there was a definite Darwinian survival chain among international soccer fans. Those who found great seats and then left the stadium quickest were clearly among the fittest. So, living up to his reputation, he made his way through the crowd, seeking out Hussein's van among dozens of blue buses in an endless jammed parking lot with policemen posted at the exits.

We found Hussein standing under a solitary tree. Unscathed by the home team's loss, he had an uncommonly wild look in his eyes. My father yelled to him as we jumped into the van: "Come on, let's go, quick!"

Hussein turned aggressor, weaving amid the cast of thousands, gunning through a narrow opening between columns of parked buses. Seeing two armed guards at the nearest exit, he accelerated. No choice, they jumped out of the way. We cheered as he screeched the tires and peeled off ahead of the madding crowd.

"Now we know why he drove ambulances during the war," Avo said. "He has to have his excitement."

To ski or not to ski, that was the question. To exorcise the collective sense of loss, we knew we had to do something drastic and fun. The morning after the match, we left Mom and Dad plotting the rescue of the two lamed statues in our former grotto, and Hussein drove us into the snowy Elburz Mountains along steep, razor-carved river valleys, climbing on switchback roads.

Dizin, the French-designed ski resort built by the Shah after we left, was empty on a sparkling day. The treeless mountain bowls were blanketed in brilliant spring snow. Strapping on our rented skis and wearing our lift tickets — total cost, $4 — we boarded the gondola and spotted our first wildlife: a snow bunny. Her long light brown hair flowed out of her cap as she slalomed gracefully down the slope sporting a flashy pink jumpsuit.

"So, do you have any last words?" I asked Kev.

"*Baba*," he said. "I haven't fallen in years."

It was a familiar refrain from our childhood days. Hans, our Austrian ski instructor in Tehran, repeated his sacred mantra until it was ingrained in Kevin's mind: "Lean back, skis always together." Kev always looked so elegant gliding over the moguls at top speed. But, from old ski haunts at Ab-e Ali and Shemshak in Iran to Heavenly Valley at Lake Tahoe, he had sometimes paid the price. Over the years, his obsession with style over common sense had led to frightening wipeouts.

"I have no plans of falling today," Kev proclaimed.

"Famous last words," Chris said.

In truth, my brothers skied better than I did. They had learned to schuss and wedel in that "winter of Hans" — whose father had been an Olympian ski jumper — while I stayed at home because of a ripped cartilage in my knee. It had happened the first week of skiing at the Noor Club, an exclusive ski resort, also built by the Shah, on a blinding glary afternoon. My Bahai friend Ahmad and I had raced all day without a break, and we had just started our last run. Flying down the slope, I remember the silver horizon and the sky melting together. The shimmering light left me sightless, with no contrast, no focus. I was going much too fast. And then I blacked out. Evidently, my left ski went into a hole created earlier by a hill-climbing woman in high heels chasing her son on his sled. My right ski flew over my left. And my bindings did not release.

When I came to in the lodge, Ahmad was leaning over me. "Terry," he said breathlessly, "the Shah was skiing behind you and saw the whole accident. He ordered people from the lodge to pull you out and carry you down here. You're so lucky. A helicopter is coming." I was never able to thank the Shah for his gesture. It was the closest I had ever came to meeting him. My brother Richard, on the other hand, had come much closer.

It was a year later when Rich, hurtling in his usual downhill-racer tuck position, lost control, then dug in the edges of his skis and veered sharply right, hoping to slow down. Chris and I watched from the Noor Club summit in horror. He was headed straight for his royal highness, who was wedeling slowly down the bowl flanked by his usual two skiing bodyguards. Missing full impact only by inches, miraculously Rich raced over the back of the Shah's skis. Instinctively, the bodyguards swerved off in tandem after the little cannonball. When they saw Rich vaporize in a snowbank in a glorious white puff, they gave up pursuit.

Now, at Dizin, the four brothers would push the alpine envelope one more time. And despite Kev's self-assurance, he did fall. It was an outstanding double twister on our second run that left him digging deep to find his skis. An ethereal halo of snow topped his head. We laughed uncontrollably.

Down at the lodge, we met some classic ski bums and three ski patrollers who spoke French, German and some English. Having the mountain to ourselves, we felt uncharacteristically relaxed. We decided to get in a few more runs. Later that afternoon, as we stepped off the highest gondola, the bundled-up lift operator pointed straight at me. "Telephone," he yelled.

Impossible, I thought. He yelled again as I slipped off my skis. Who the devil is it? I crunched through the snow toward him.

A bulky headset that belonged on a World War II aircraft carrier was handed to me.

"Hello, hello," I said. The earpiece was ice cold.

"Hullo." A crisp British accent. "Kasra Naji here, old boy. CNN."

"Yes, what can I do for you?"

"This morning at the Laleh I heard about four American brothers skiing up in Dizin. Then I met your father, and he confirmed it. So here I am. It's for a piece on the New Iran. What do you say?"

"Well, you better get up here soon. My brothers won't wait for anyone, especially when they're skiing."

"Camera and soundman will be up there in a jiffy. I'm staying down here where it's warm. See you back in Tehran. Dinner tonight, the Ali Qapu, eight o'clock. Bring the whole family."

"Let's go, Ter!" Kevin bellowed. His skis were on and he was furious.

"Yeah, quit wasting time," Richard yelled.

"I'm on the phone!" I shouted back.

"Phone? Who is it?"

"CNN."

"Really? CNN? Where?"

I was wrong. They could wait. My brothers' demeanor changed radically. They began sprucing up, combing their hair, eagerly scanning the arriving gondola cars. We were moments away from Warhol's fifteen minutes of fame.

Soon, a huffing two-man camera crew were seated on a platform with their equipment. Akbar, the soundman, stomped through the snow and immediately told us why he had come.

"Americans skiing. We heard about you at the Laleh Hotel." Akbar giggled, finding it all a little surreal.

The Elburz peaks stretched east to west, a panorama of white shark's teeth. Clouds steamed in the valley underneath us. A crisp wind blew. The sun and sky glinted off the ice and spray. We went down the slope in synchronized fashion for the camera, kicking up snow crystals as we slalomed back and forth. On what started out as a Jean-Claude Killy–type wedel run, Kevin shortly picked up speed, whirled artfully over moguls and wiped out one more time.

That evening, we all met at Ali Qapu restaurant, a high-priced Tehran dining spot decorated in traditional style. Our host, Kasra Naji, intrepid war reporter and TV producer, kept his camera rolling. The suave and handsome British-educated CNN correspondent wanted more footage for his special on the "New Iran," and we were a "story."

Grinning, Kasra faced our patriarch with his first pointed questions. He was uninterested in our story about Hassan. There were more important points to discuss, he said.

"Did you feel safe in Iran during your stay, Mr. Ward?"

"Are you kidding?" Dad said. "Kasra, old buddy, it's safer than the streets of New York."

"Really?"

"Tell me, Kasra," Dad asked. "Do *you* feel safe?"

"Well . . . yes."

"There, you see?"

The microphone turned to my mother. "And Mrs. Ward, will you come back to Iran again?"

"In a heartbeat," she said.

In retrospect, Kasra seemed a bit bored with our rosy picture. I think he, like most everyone, would have preferred to hear the usual horror stories: close calls and police raids. Born in Iran, he had spent many years in Britain before joining CNN as a freelancer. A courageous and rather sympathetic fellow, Kasra spoke to me about the "good old days" covering the ten-year Soviet-Afghan conflict and the Tajikistan civil war. He deplored the victory of the Taliban. Overnight, they had cut him off from his favorite post by banning decadent TV cameras from Kabul. Once every three months, he was able to visit his English wife, posted in Bangladesh with the BBC.

While he lamented to me how much he missed combat reporting, three musicians began playing and singing classical Persian music, which continued through the long meal. Then, at dessert time, we heard a familiar tune.

"My God, do you hear that?" Kasra asked me. "*O Sole Mio*" rose over the women's headscarfs and the hanging lanterns. "I don't believe it. This is so radical," he murmured. "Times are really changing."

As he stared in disbelief at the singer, a Mediterranean sunsplash from the Bay of Naples slowly filled our smoky cavern.

We should have known better. "New Iran" indeed. Some things do not change, especially CNN. "Go for the jugular" has always been their motto. And, back in London, the editors did just that. In typical fashion, they spliced our images — four brothers rollicking on the ski slopes, Kevin's spectacular wipeout, my father's blanket denial of any fears and my mother's fresh, reassuring humane words — between footage of rumbling tanks, screeching jet fighters and stomping heels of soldiers parading on Iranian Armed Forces Day. The parade's highlight this year, Kasra reported: "The American flag wasn't burned."

For the average viewer, snug at home in Europe or North America, the underlying message was loud and clear. Tourism in Iran? Fugeddaboudit! Those lunatics are outta their minds. Don't even think about it.

Friends called my wife, Idanna, from Athens, Jakarta and Oslo to tell her they were shocked to see her Terenzio on CNN, slaloming with his brothers in Iran's mountains. Their next question was "Are they okay?"

That evening, on the occasion of Avo's birthday, a friend of his offered him a gift, claiming Scotland as its source: a bottle of whiskey called Black Five Millionaires. "Extra Special," the label said. No doubt the local Tehran liquor cartel did a booming business, employing creative directors with a sense of humor. The bold ebony and gold label featured five tuxedoed men hamming it up on a stage. The silhouettes looked like the Las Vegas Rat Pack —

Frank Sinatra, Dean Martin, Joey Bishop, Peter Lawford and Sammy Davis, Jr. Close inspection revealed the bottling date: 1977, two years before the Islamic Revolution.

"Good Scotch, no?" Avo said. "It's from Scotland."

"Really?" I was dubious.

"It does say Scotland. Look, Black Five Millionaires, blended and bottled in Dundie."

"A clever name."

"Yes, *baba*."

"Tehrani chic."

"Don't say such things. You hurt me."

"I'm sorry."

"You know, my friend paid imported price for this bottle."

We raised our glasses to Avo. Kevin, in his usual style, made a toast thanking our Armenian friend for his unique insights and continuous wise use of the "*baba* system." His closing words were "Never has so much been done to so many by so few."

Avo looked ecstatic as my three brothers gulped down his Scotch. Then Rich coughed. Kev gagged. And Chris faked a mild seizure, falling on the carpet. Dad and I did not drink; we flicked ours into the flower vase on the table. "Happy birthday, Avo!" my Mom said, sipping her Zam Zam.

Black Five Millionaires: an odd name for a Scotch, perhaps, but an apt one for the five oil republics — Azerbaijan, Iran, Russia, Turkmenistan and Kazakhstan — poised to divide up the black gold beneath the Caspian Sea. Their treasure hunt rekindled the flames of the "Great Game," the nineteenth-century power struggle for central Asia. Just that week another headline about the Caspian republics asked, Where was the new pipeline going? An estimated two hundred billion barrels of oil were at stake. As the North Sea wells were running dry, the new oilfields acted like magnets for global corporate leaders and war strategists. Would this be the site of the twenty-first century's Desert Storm? Black Five Millionaires indeed.

In preparation for our children's future, American agents, Russian operatives and Chinese analysts were already mastering the obscure geography of central Asia with the same scrutiny as the Pentagon strategists who memorized every inlet and island, every oilfield and airstrip in the Persian Gulf.

For the moment, the Caspian coast was still a holiday desti-nation. There, in a seaside resort by Badar-e Anzali, Hassan, Fatimeh and their family spent four relaxing weeks. The children romped about, covered in sand. In their black chadors, the women entered the waves.

14

# The Color of God

> I want to beg you as much as I can . . . to be patient towards
> all that is unsolved in your heart and to try and love the
> questions themselves . . . Do not seek answers which cannot
> be given to you because you would not be able to live them.
> And the point is to live everything. Live the questions now.
> Perhaps you will then gradually, without noticing it, live
> along some distant day into the answer.
>
> — Rainer Maria Rilke

MY FRIEND Nezam's driving passion was a lifelong quest for the mystical places in Iran that for centuries had evoked the sublime in all pilgrims and seekers. So I could imagine his excitement when a British archaeologist sought his assistance for a BBC film about a search for the original Garden of Eden.

Challenging the foundations of Near Eastern history, this archaeologist had pored over topographical maps, using clues from Genesis and paleo-environmental imaging, and deduced that a certain lake was the one that fed the four rivers of Paradise. The lake was close to the city of Tabriz in northwest Iran. No stranger to controversy, he had challenged scholastic orthodoxy years before by arguing that the original Pharaohs migrated down from the Zagros Mountains to found their empire in the Nile Delta.

Nezam lived in northern Tehran with his wife, Nora, a painter, in a large red-brick house with unkempt hedges and climbing ivy. Over the years of widespread confiscations of private property,

Tehran's prosperous families understood the need for shabby exteriors. The logic was clear: if you fix it up, they may take it from you.

Inside, their home was an eclectic mix of Bakhtiari tribal carpets, low divans in front of the fireplace and Nora's oil paintings — enormous feminine Cycladic figures with encircling cuneiform script, hieroglyphics, Sanskrit and Chinese characters, like a unified Babel.

Raised in northern California, Nora had moved back to Iran during the time of the Iraqi War. "You know, Terry, once you leave your place of birth, you lose your center. Don't get me wrong," she said, nibbling on a sweet, "San Francisco and Marin, where my parents live, are beautiful, we all know that. But I always felt like something was missing, like I didn't quite belong. That's why we came back. I didn't want my children to go through that experience too. Now they speak Farsi and they know their culture. When they grow up, they can choose."

Fariba, another painter, had stopped by. She was Nora's close friend, a brunette with short hair bunched in trendy spikes and heavy kohl shadows on her lower eyelids. She lit a cigarette. "Do you know Lou Reed?" she asked, catching me by surprise.

"The musician? Sure."

"Great. Can you give me his address in New York?"

"What?"

"I need to let him know," she purred, "that all my new work is based on his latest album."

Nora explained. "She loves Lou's music. She's crazy about him. Her latest painting is called *American Flag*, after one of his songs."

Fariba handed me a photograph. I saw her figure dwarfed by an immense canvas splashed, Basquiat style, with yellow streaks and emerald green and electric blue geometric shapes. I offered to help her find Lou Reed. Her flag gave new meaning to President Khatami's call for a dialogue among civilizations.

And what about Nezam's scouting trip for the BBC? It had been quite different from what he had expected. He was bone-weary. They had driven eight hundred miles. The trip had been a travesty.

"The cameraman would get out of the van," Nezam said, "spend ten minutes setting up his tripod and sound equipment, and by the time he was ready, a cloud would block the sun. Instead of waiting, the archaeologist would yell, 'No, no, sorry chaps, no time. The hell with it.' And off we would go without the shot."

Their grand quest soon became grand folly, all frenzied energy and nothing to show for it.

"The whole time, we were searching for this one spot, mind you, the garden of Adam and Eve with the four rivers. Paradise. And all the time I was thinking, Just look, can't you see it? It's all around us. But they couldn't see it. If they had just looked, even just in the eyes of a simple villager, they would have seen it all!"

"But did you finally find the garden?" I asked.

"Yeah, in Urumiyeh. So they said."

"And what did it look like?"

"It was at the end of a backbreaking journey. Our van broke down twice that day. When we finally arrived, we all looked out on a valley."

"And?"

"Well . . . it's a bit industrial now. There's a huge cement factory."

"And the rivers?"

"No rivers. At least I didn't see any. There's a lake nearby, heavily salted. No fish, no life."

"So what about this film on Paradise?"

"Well, you know," Nezam said, smiling, "computer graphics can do wonders these days."

Behrouz had refused to serve in the army and was without a passport. He lived in a kind of limbo, waiting for the government's amnesty. Only then would he be allowed to leave the country, join his sister in New York and finish his university studies. His field was cognitive neuroscience, viewed from both Eastern and Western traditions.

In his basement flat near the British embassy, we listened to two jazz guitarists, Pat Metheny and Charlie Hayden. He sipped a liqueur made from raisins. Two posters hung on the wall: a wild-haired Einstein and Brueghel's Tower of Babel. We talked about Charlie Parker and movies. Then we shifted to other matters.

"Abdul Karim Soroush is the most powerful agent of change," Behrouz told me. The scholar Soroush was an ideologue and a spokesman for the reformers in Iran. He had introduced the student movement to modern ideas — democratic principles, freedom of speech, human rights, the rule of law — while stressing the absolute importance of keeping the Islamic Republic in place. Change and tolerance must come only from within, from the people, Soroush said, always mindful of the Islamic identity of Iran. Although he was attacked by the hard-liners, students flocked to his lectures.

I thought back on the journey that brought us to Tehran. In the historic cities of the south — romantic Shiraz, splendid Isfahan, remote Yazd — people lived traditional lifestyles in keeping with the culture, surrounded by artistic and poetic wonders. But here in thoroughly modern Tehran, a megalopolis with little history or charm, I felt a clinging sense of angst. While Isfahanis, Yazdis and Shirazis lived with one foot squarely in the past, Tehranis struggled daily with the future.

After leaving Behrouz, who kindly invited me to a party later that evening, I walked alone down Bobby Sands Boulevard past the British embassy. I thought of the delusional "Uncle Napoleon" and the conspiracy of all things British, and it seemed only natural that Churchill Boulevard would be renamed after the Revolution. I couldn't help but smile. After all, the British Unionists and the Irish nationalists were finally sitting down together at a peace table after four hundred years and speaking of sharing power. But could this peace last?

*       *       *

Every Friday in downtown Tehran, crowds gather at the flea market to sift through generations of relics. The Juma bazaar holds court in an underground parking garage.

Kev and I, determined not to miss it, hailed a cab. The driver, thrilled to hear we spoke some Farsi, began to chat. We had grown accustomed to free-ranging discussions.

"You know how the mullahs deal with reformers?"

"No."

The cabby pointed his finger like a gun. "They kill them all." He shot at an imaginary victim. I followed his finger's trajectory and spotted a passing car with an American flag decal on the bumper. Kev quickly tried to take a picture, but the car raced ahead in the river of traffic.

"They're hypocrites, liars, the mullahs. No one believes them anymore. At the beginning, yes, we all hoped. They promised free electricity, free gas. Heaven on earth. Hah!"

Kev and I did not interrupt his tirade.

"You know, now taxi drivers won't stop for clerics anymore. I heard one mullah complain that he waited two hours for a taxi, and they kept passing by. He had to go and change his robe before he could get a ride."

Loud beeping sounded behind us.

"Years ago, the Shah and his friends stole all the money. Now the mullahs and their families do the same. Poor Iran! Whoever has the power always takes from us."

He made a sharp turn.

"Bad Shah and his corrupt thieves. Bad mullahs, they abuse our God and bankrupt our nation. Poor Iranis!"

The cabby raised a finger to his mouth. *Saket*, silence. But it didn't last long.

"We wait. We've put up with the Greeks and the Arabs, the Mongols and the Turks, the British, the Shah, and now . . ." He paused as he ran a traffic light that was changing from orange to red. "Now we must wait again for our children to grow up, the new generation."

We screeched to a halt. I handed him the fare. But he refused my money with a sweep of his hand.

"No, please, you are my guests."

"Please."

"No."

"Please."

"A thousand times no."

Down two flights of stairs, in the underground parking lot, I gasped on the exhaust fumes lingering in the air. Kev used a hand-kerchief to cover his sensitive nose. Thick layers of pollution clung to gray concrete walls. There was no natural light, only flaring white gas burners. It was the opposite of the traditional se-ductive bazaar charm. And to top it off, it was frantically popular.

Each vendor displayed his wares on protective blankets or rugs spread on the floor. We passed antique pocket watches, a cuckoo clock, bronze Russian samovars, aged dolls, water pipes and used fluorescent yellow tennis balls. The Shah's portrait — ramrod arrogant, dripping with medals — covered old currency collec-tions. Kev spotted a miniature Model T Ford that was not for sale, a painting of the Last Supper on velvet and an Arthur Mur-ray *Let's Dance the Cha-Cha-Cha* record.

I studied two faded photos of the Wailing Wall and Washing-ton's Capitol and examined an African wooden mask, a pair of used boxing gloves, an accordion and a weathered libretto of Verdi's *La Traviata*, from its premiere at La Fenice in Venice, dated March 6, 1857. As I leafed through it, a high-pitched "Ex-cuse me" yelped behind me. A girl in her teens skated by on Rollerblades, narrowly missing me. "Sorry," she peeped.

A group of diplomats' wives took turns haggling with Afghan refugees over their tribal carpets. A young Iranian stood out in the dense crowd with his baseball cap and Stars-and-Stripes shirt. Another young man, surely a war veteran, hobbled by on crutches, one leg missing, sporting a T-shirt with a beach scene of Pattaya, Thailand.

We sifted through czarist coins, Buddha figures, and Prussian medallions. I was tempted by an azure tile with Moses holding the Ten Commandments, a painting of green-turbaned Saint Ali and a figurine of Christ hanging on a cross. But my only purchase from that day now hangs in my kitchen: an engraved copper plate crafted by an unknown artisan. Below a profile of John F. Kennedy are the dates 1917–1963. Around the edge an inscription reads, "And the glow from that fire can truly light the world."

Like most Persian musicians, Dr. Safvat combined sacred verse with rhythmic, hypnotic improvisation. Using only the ear and the heart — no written notation — he raised classical music to a religious dimension. A master of the *sitar* and *santur*, he also delved into the realm of the soul. Many superlative Persian musicians are mystics. Dr. Safvat was no exception. His white hair crowned a face that shone with boundless serenity. Educated in France, formal yet warmly welcoming, he invited me to his modest home.

Beside him, a Kurdish *ney* flute player sat in silence.

Dr. Safvat spoke of our human dualist nature, the physical and the spiritual.

"The body," he said, "needs food. So does the spirit. All the world's prophets speak about the need to nourish the spirit. They each say the same thing: we must try to connect with God. Love is everything, and art is the food of the soul. About one hundred and fifty years ago, the Industrial Age, with science as the new religion, brought disbelief in God, and now many wander in darkness."

We sipped our tea. The *ney* player twisted his dramatic handlebar mustache and offered to take me into the mountains of Kurdistan, a rugged region along the border with Iraq long known for its spiritual power.

Dr. Safvat spoke again about our bifurcated nature, but this time he called it "the carnal and the angelic." "Creative power in he who has only a carnal rapport with life," he explained, "provokes superficial excitement, which is transient art. But he who connects with God and finds the angel within will create art that will live on in the future."

I asked him about the present government. He paused, cleaning his glasses, and then said, "We must approach the mullahs with a defensive posture, retaining the holy gift of forgiveness. This is the path. Politics is bad for mental health, bad for the soul. Begin with humility, evolve yourself, and then you can help others. Remember that any system built on the wrong foundations has no future. In time, it will collapse under its own weight. No need to push."

An hour later, stepping into a cab, I immediately noticed the driver's grand drooping mustache, like that of the Kurdish *ney* player.

I dared to ask him, "Are you a mystic?"

He smiled and turned toward me. "Yes, of course."

"Me too," I offered.

"That's great," he said, amused, as he maneuvered effortlessly through traffic, curly hair flying in the wind.

Dr. Safvat's parting words still clung to me: "We must fight the darkness with *ishraq* illumination. Listen to Hafez, Rumi, all our great poets."

Who were now the keepers of the flame? Who, in this highly politicized climate, focused on the culture's enduring power?

When I met the filmmaker Majid Majidi, I was struck by his humility and depth. Under his wavy dark mane of hair, his eyes held a well of sensitivity. His words were thoughtful, measured, as if he wanted to impart a secret that clearly had transformed him. I asked him why he chose film to tell his stories.

"In film, I can speak to the world through a universal language," he said. "Many people are searching for God. They go to the mosque, to church, to the synagogue, and still they ask, 'Where is He?' My belief is that God is inside each of us."

Majid is a lion of Iranian cinema. Nominated in 1997 for an Academy Award for best foreign film, his *Children of Heaven* has touched film buffs around the world with its poignant story of the love between two children, brother and sister.

"As a child," he continued, "I always wanted to touch God. If someone wants to see God, just tell him to take a good look at nature. The hero of my latest film is Mohammad, a blind boy. One day during filming, he touched a small stone and uttered the word 'God.' I marked that stone and mixed it with other, similar ones and then asked him to choose one of the stones. He picked up the same stone and said, 'Mr. Majidi, the name of God is right here. I'm going to take this stone and translate for you.' Now," Majid said, "I'm conscious that maybe God is in the stone I'm about to step on.

"I'm having an unusual experience with Mohammad. I'm discovering that nature has its own language — one we can't read — but it's there all the time speaking to us. This new language is like Braille."

I did not know then that this film, known in the West as *The Color of Paradise*, would earn Majid his second Oscar nomination. In Iran it was called *The Color of God*.

I asked him about the filmmakers he admired.

"Intellectual films affect only intellectuals. Action films are in fashion but have no endurance. Instead, filmmakers who aim for the heart, like John Ford, Hitchcock, Rossellini, Pasolini, never lose their power."

Majid rarely uses professional actors; he gathers his players from real life. But Majid is not the only Iranian filmmaker who chooses to tell stories from the heart. Defying all politics and censorship, Abbas Kiarostami, winner of the 1997 Palme d'Or at Cannes, paved the way, unashamedly revealing his country's human face.

Following the Great Depression, several American moviemakers painted compassionate portraits of dignified Americans in the grips of economic hardship. Movies like *The Grapes of Wrath* and *It's a Wonderful Life* gave Henry Fonda and Jimmy Stewart arguably their noblest roles. These socially conscious American films and the later Iranian films shared a celebration of the common man. And it is this universal theme that still connects with audiences everywhere. Like his fellow storytellers, Majid penetrates the inner sanctum of simple homes and lives, endearing his

people to us. He is one of the unappointed ambassadors carrying
the message of humanism to the world. He is one of the keepers
of the flame.

I told Majid about our own journey, our search for Hassan
and how we found him at last. I spoke about Hassan's late-night
prayers, his love of nature, and Majid smiled. "You see, Hassan
knows," he said. "You must come back to Iran."

"*Insha'allah,*" I replied.

A pink Frisbee flew by my shoulder. Two buddies took turns
sending each other off in hot pursuit of this small plastic creature
with a mind of its own. It was our last night. My parents and
brothers were back in their rooms packing new purchases. In
Laleh Park, just behind the hotel, these spirited kids ran back
and forth in their makeshift game. Nearby, four older men huddled together, chatting under the warm lamplight, fondling their
prayer beads.

I strolled along the winding paths. An amorous young couple
sat beneath a protective weeping willow. The boy lay on his back
with his feet propped up on the tree. His head rested on her lap.
Beyond the park, the hum of the city was barely audible, drowned
in slumber. I heard the couple speaking softly. The sky showed
few stars.

Walking in the darkness, I wondered about this country's mag-
netism and beauty, its inner and outer faces, the duality of forces
with equal weight that push and pull. These people, so long cut
off from the world, possessed such acute insights. They offered
their humor in healthy doses and a profound friendship that will
conquer any who encounter it. I thought of Hassan watering his
tiny garden and wondered about his life — a simplicity of possessions, but a wealth of spirit. In the face of such civility and re-
finement, I felt overwhelming humility.

My father, Patrick, who grew up in the Depression and battled
as an activist for social justice, never dismissed the mark of hardship on people's lives. This social awareness had forged his compassion and respect for the common man. He shared a great deal,

I decided, with Majid Majidi. They viewed the world through the same lens.

In 1975, when I returned to Berkeley after a long winter working above the Arctic Circle on a wildcat oil rig, I naively asked my father why all his friends from Tehran days, expats and Iranians both, were wealthy and we were not.

"Didn't you ever have any chances to take kickbacks or bribes?" I asked.

"Of course," he replied.

"You did?"

"They would say, 'Name your price.'"

"And what was your answer?"

"I'd say five figures."

"And then?"

"When they offered five figures, I'd say six. Each time they were ready to pay, I'd add a zero. Pretty soon they understood I couldn't be bought — much to their dismay."

Around us was a house in chaos — bare wallboard and unfinished rooms. This was the first home we ever owned.

"Look, Terry, the most important thing in life is to wake up each morning and be able to look yourself in the mirror and know you're clean."

He smiled as his words burned into me.

Because of my parents' social conscience, I now knew why we had related with our hearts to Hassan and Fatimeh as a family — befriended, worked, played and grew with them. In the end, we had no choice but to try to find them. Perhaps this was the most precious gift that my parents had given us. With it, they had connected us to the world.

"Are you awake?" My mother knocked lightly on the door. It was still dark when we dragged our bags down to the lobby. On a bulletin board Chris read a last-minute note for an Italian tour group going back to Rome: "*E per l'ultima volta, anche oggi speriamo che Allah vi accompagni.* And for the last time today, we pray for Allah to accompany you."

At the front desk, a feisty blond journalist from Vienna wearing a cream scarf confronted me as I paid our bill. She too was leaving, and bursting with news. With great agitation she confided that President Khatami would soon resign. The hard-liners whom she had met with in Qom insisted upon the need to create "pure Islam" in Iran. Each had told her emphatically, "I own the truth."

She had railed, she said, at the ignorance of some university students who did not know of the "one-night-stand provision" in the Koran whereby a man could marry a woman in the evening and divorce her the next morning. She spoke about rampant prostitution and runaway girls. She informed me that heroin, cocaine, opium and liquor were all available in Tehran. She assured me that she knew where these things could be found.

"Interested?"

"No thanks."

At Mehrabad Airport, a queasiness seized my stomach. The last time we had been here, on July 4, 1969, was the day we had left Iran. But now our four carpets had to pass through customs. We needed time and we were late. Unlike the easygoing feel of the Shiraz airport, here a large illuminated yellow sign greeted sleepy arriving passengers at the baggage claim: "In Future Islam Will Destroy Satanic Sovereignty of the West."

Rich asked Avo what he intended to do now that the trip was over.

"I'll just go to my boss and say that's it."

"Good. Then you'll take five months off," I said.

"Before you commit to anything else," Rich added.

"Great idea," Avo said. "Yeah, I'll have a lot of free time, but I guess I've earned it. Maybe I'll go down to the bazaar and sell Pat's shirt."

My father rolled his eyes. "That's supposed to be a gift! You really give new meaning to 'taking the shirt off someone's back.'"

"Let's take him with us!" my mother joked. "Come on, Avo, get in my wheelchair. We'll sneak you onto the plane."

"It's too late, Mrs. Ward. If you wanted me to come with you, we should have started all this much earlier, like out by the parking lot. These guys have already seen me walking," he said with his deadpan delivery.

We loaded our bags onto the conveyor belt as Kevin spoke with a tall, gruff man at the Iran Air counter. Luckily, Kev uttered the magic word: Yazd. Thrilled to hear that we had passed through his hometown, the man began to tell us about his stay in America years before. In 1963, his army training took him to Dallas. "Yes," he said, "I arrived on November 22, the day John Kennedy was assassinated."

I leaned back in my seat, and the Iran Air 727 taxied down the runway. The overhead bins rattled. My mother squeezed my arm. Dawn was breaking with its first pale vermilion fire over Mount Demavand, the mythic volcano. The plane thrust us skyward over the sleeping city of flickering lights, above dark Laleh Park and its gardens. We circled over Ayatollah Khomeini's minarets shining above his tomb and then straightened out over open desert.

As the silver wings dipped once again, a beam of sunlight blinded me at that sacred moment of dawn. Now, looking out my window at thirty thousand feet, with my mother already snoozing in the seat next to me, I thought back to that midnight porch in Yazd where I had felt so humbled, lost and desperate. On that night, Akbar had told me, "Don't worry, my dear friend. Even if you don't find him, something else will happen. In the end, you will find many Hassans along the way."

I had no idea until this morning how prophetic he had been.

# Epilogue

"Journeys to relive your past?" was the Khan's question at this point, a question which could also have been formulated: "Journeys to recover your future?"

— Italo Calvino, *Invisible Cities*

M Y FRIEND Behnam called me excitedly on the summer solstice, June 21, 1998. It was two months after our return. The match between Iran and the United States was being shown live, he said, in the Coles Sports Center of New York University, with a satellite-link dialogue among students of both countries. I ran down to NYU to watch Iran's stunning World Cup victory over Team USA, 2–1, which capped a week of unprecedented American overtures, first by Secretary of State Madeleine Albright and then by President Bill Clinton, who expressed hope for "a genuine reconciliation" between the two nations.

Lighthearted cheers greeted TV images showing Iranian and American players posing together, arm in arm like old chums, for a group photo before kickoff. In *taarof* fashion, lilies and gladiolis were handed to the somewhat bewildered Yankee players. Surely, none of them had ever received flowers from opponents before a game.

Classy sportsmanship in the match was roundly applauded by the packed audience, and afterward I rushed home to Gramercy Park to phone Hassan. At three o'clock in the morning, Isfahan time, he was awake.

"My whole family is in the streets celebrating with friends and neighbors," he said. "No one can sleep. The whole city is up!"

My parents and brothers, I told him, had rooted for Iran. Before we hung up, he asked me, "Terry, when are you coming back?"

"Soon, I hope," I replied.

"*Insha'allah.* Next time, don't forget to bring *khanoum,* your sweet wife."

Hassan's daughter Maryam had promised to write, partly so she could practice her English. When her first letter arrived, I realized she had become the self-appointed scribe of the Ghasemi family.

Dear Terry,

We received your letter in July 4 and became very happy. July 12 was the birthday of our prophet Mohammad and that day was my brother Ahmad's wedding. We wished you were in Isfahan and had seen our ceremonies for wedding.

We became very happy for football match between Iran and America, not only for winning, but for nearness Iran's nation and America's nation. Chris telephoned our home and congratulated us on the winning.

Hassan is at home. He cooks, gardens, and repairs house hold furniture. He says: we miss for you very much and look to you pictures everyday. Hassan and Fatimeh and we say to people about you and your kindness, because you came to Iran after 29 years for seeing us. Pardon me if I wrote this letter with unskill. This was the first of my experience.

With highest regards and warmest friendship, your Iranian family,

Hassan, Fatimeh, Maryam, Rasool, Ahmad, Majid, Mahdi, Ali and all of us

At the end of February 1999, in Florence, I heard the BBC report that President Khatami's candidates had won another landslide victory in local elections. Three towns south of Tehran would be governed by women. As votes were still being counted, Khatami embarked on the first state visit to the West by an Iranian president in twenty years. In Rome, he was asked why he had chosen Italy as one of his stops. "Because here, Roman civilization and the Renaissance were born," he answered. "For us, this is important." His long-awaited dialogue among civilizations had begun in earnest. At the Vatican, the ailing white-robed pope greeted the charismatic black-robed cleric.

In Fiesole, just north of Florence, I sneaked into the European University, where Khatami delivered an address. He spoke of the need for dialogue with America, appealing for noninterference and respect. After his speech, I approached the podium. I wanted to tell the president that my mother had met with his sister in his ancestral town of Ardakan, and that theirs was the same message. But tight security surrounded him, and he was whisked off before I could reach him. That next morning, the Florentine edition of *La Repubblica* trumpeted, "The New Iran of Khatami."


On March 20, 1999, three days before *Nowruz*, thousands of youths in Tehran lit bonfires and set off firecrackers. I called Hassan to wish him Happy New Year. Then I asked about Fatimeh.

"She's out," he said, "with Maryam and the kids, jumping over the fires."

In north Tehran's middle-class districts, young people were also jumping over fires, dancing and singing. This time, officers looked on without intervening. The *Chaharshanbe Souri* fire festival, long attacked by hard-liners as a pagan relic, had been marred in the past by clashes. But now the authorities took a different tack. The moderate interior minister Abdolvahed Mousavi-Lari publicly praised the tradition. Liberal newspapers publicized the event and highlighted the country's pre-Islamic heritage. The racket of firecrackers was heard all over the capital.

Then, in a bold gesture that took the Ghasemi clan by surprise, a week later brother Rich arrived on Hassan's doorstep with his family. On Bi-sim Street they spent four days of the *Nowruz* holiday together. It was Rich's wife Ellen's first trip to Iran. All the brothers had vowed to take their wives to meet the Ghasemis. I was next. Another letter arrived from Maryam.

Dear Terry,
Richard and Ellen came to Isfahan with their lovely boys and stayed from 23–26 March. We spent the sweet hours together. But we were heavy hearted (homesick) for you. We are sorry because we are far away from you. We hope you visit Isfahan with Idanna soon. We will never forget you and your kindness. Ali was in Isfahan in Nowruz and wished to see you.

from your father, Hassan, your mother, Fatimeh, your sister, Maryam, your brothers, Ali, Mahdi, Ahmad and Majid

Unexpectedly, in July events in Iran burst onto the world's front pages. Student protests against the shutdown of a pro-reform newspaper had swept the Tehran University campus. Soon mass demonstrations shook the city. Undercover police and Revolutionary Guards struck back, viciously attacking dormitory rooms at night, leaving five students dead, hundreds wounded. Students watched helplessly as the hard-liners in the courts, police and the Council of Guardians worked in tandem to silence opposition.

Seven months later, on February 18, 2000, a broad coalition of reformers aligned with President Khatami won a resounding election victory in parliament with 80 percent of the vote. Christiane Amanpour, voicing the sentiments of many Iranians, explained in the *International Herald Tribune:*

These elections have not been about overturning Islamic law. Iranians are proud of their revolution — it really meant something, because for the first time in thousands of years, the country was standing on its own two feet, no longer a lackey of the US or any other country. That part of it they don't want to give up, and why should they? People just want a more livable life — that's what they voted for.

On March 29, on Shelter Island, New York, the Ward clan got together at Kevin's house to celebrate my parents' fiftieth wedding anniversary. The black-tie affair featured Broadway musical routines that retraced the route of their lifelong odyssey. Kev reminded us of my mother's prophetic words to Pat fifty years before: "There's only one way for us to fit in, if we move to someplace like Afghanistan." I then stood to read a note that had just arrived from the Ghasemis.

> Dearest Pat and Donna,
> Accept heartfelt congratulations for golden wedding anniversary that we send from far away. We hope all moment will be overflowing with love and happiness!
>
> "Beauty doesn't produce Love, but love produces beauty."
> — Leo Tolstoy
> All Ghasemi family, Isfahan

In April, I finally flew back to Iran, as I had promised Hassan, this time with Idanna. The U.S. embargo on caviar, carpets and pistachios had recently been lifted, and Idanna welcomed the prospect of spending three weeks in a manteau and *rusari*. "What bliss," she said, "not to have to worry about fashion."

In Isfahan, on Bi-sim Street, we embraced Ahmad Ghasemi's new bride, Rezvan. Maryam, we learned, had seriously considered running for parliament. "Who will serve me breakfast in bed if she wins?" Rasool Iskander asked with a whine in his voice. Idanna went off with Maryam on her teaching rounds, where scores of women gathered, in private homes, to hear her speak and answer their questions about family, work, daily problems and, of course, the Koran.

Fatimeh told me that when she passed through Tehran on her way to the Caspian for last year's summer holidays, she asked Ahmad to drive her to the site of the old house. Seeing the Ward family after such a long time had awoken old memories in her. She was curious to see it all again. When they arrived the gate was open. She looked out on the open pit that once was her home. "I almost cried," she said.

During our stay, I worked with Hassan in his garden, puttered around watering the flowers, took naps in the warm afternoons, watched him cook his delicious meals and listened to him recount story after story. On our last day in Isfahan, Fatimeh bade us farewell.

"I want to say goodbye to my friend and son, and my new daughter."

Misty-eyed Idanna hugged her new Iranian mother. Hassan made me promise again to come back soon.

When we arrived in Tehran, the Canadian political attaché invited us for dinner. A BBC reporter — who was flying down to Shiraz to cover the trial of thirteen Jews charged with treason — joined us. Over coffee, he confided to us his latest dream. "Last night," he said with a troubled face, "I dreamed I was nailed to a cross, surrounded by a mocking crowd."

International observers and diplomatic protests of the trial had little effect. Behind closed doors, with the help of confessions, the court found ten of the defendants guilty, but no death sentences were handed down. The cat-and-mouse game between the hardliners and the reformers was being played out yet again.

The night before we left Tehran, an explosive event took place on German soil. Iranian reformist leaders, flush with their election victory, attended a conference in Berlin to discuss their new agenda. It was a disaster. The ill-prepared conference sponsored by the Green Party was hijacked by Iranian protesters, many of whom had sought political asylum in Germany over the years, and who rejected the Islamic regime completely. Shouted insults and catcalls drowned out the reformist speakers onstage. Then, in a bit of shock theater out of the sixties, two audience members rose, stripped naked and danced on their chairs. And it was all caught on film. In the Laleh Hotel we watched the film clips, replayed endlessly on state-run TV, surely to embarrass and discredit reformers. The Berlin event burned across Iran's political landscape, fueling a crackdown on intellectuals, writers and journalists. Reformist leaders who attended the conference were arrested upon their return for insulting Islam.

Back in New York, one day in August, I met my friend Manijeh. Breathlessly, she grabbed my arm.

"Terry *jan*, did you hear? Googoosh is coming!"

I couldn't believe my ears. Stepping out from her seclusion in Tehran, the Persian singer did the unimaginable. She had flown to North America to perform her first concerts since the Revolution. After twenty years of silence, she was rising like a phoenix.

From Toronto all the way to Los Angeles, Googoosh's warbling voice unleashed ecstatic floods of nostalgia and emotion. Crowds wept, cheered and sang along. The thousands who flocked to Long Island's Nassau Coliseum spanned three generations.

In an elegant white gown, the mythic Googoosh moved on stage like a vision on the bridge of memory. In the soothing sounds of her music, the multitudes of exiles forgot the pain of separation from their land and loved ones.

By December, hard-liners in the Council of Guardians had closed down thirty-two newspapers. In just two years, the euphoric Tehran Spring we had witnessed had turned into a Siberian deep freeze.

To greet the new millennium, I sent a letter to Hassan, and a response arrived from Maryam in January 2001:

> Dearest Terry and Idanna,
> We received your affectionate letter from Florence and became very happy. Happy New Year! We hope New Year for you will be a year with happiness, blessedness and coming to Iran and Isfahan again and again! We are all good and we anxiously await you. Why don't you come? The weather in Isfahan is very good. It seems here is spring. We all wish to see you and all Ward family in Isfahan. By the way: Ahmad and his wife Rezvan will have a baby in July or August!

We saw a lunar eclipse 3 night ago and we wished we would see you on our side that moment. Come early, soon and quick and make us happy. Give our warm greetings to Donna and Pat and your brothers and their family.

With all our love,

sister Maryam and all Ghasemis

Her letter arrived on an important anniversary, which passed nearly unnoticed. Twenty years before, as Ronald Reagan was being sworn in as president, fifty-two American hostages walked out of the U.S. embassy, ending their 444 days of captivity.

Several days later, I read that a week-long fair devoted to women, the first since the Islamic Revolution, drew thousands of women in north Tehran. Fashion models strutted in red, bright green, khaki and blue dresses, freed from their long dark gowns and headscarfs. Unwieldy chadors were nowhere to be seen. Curiously, I also read a statement by Mohammad Javad Larijani, a political theorist of the hard-liners, in the daily *Aftab-e Yazd.* "Dialogue should not be considered a taboo. If our national interests require we should talk with Satan in hell. We should defend our national interest. We should hold dialogue even with our most hostile enemies if necessary."

I circled the key word: dialogue. This statement signaled the all-important green light.

The growing realization that, while preserving the Revolution, Iran must open up to the West had been agreed upon by all political camps in Tehran. The economic crisis was no longer blamed on enemy plots or the collapse in oil prices; *Kayhan,* the government newspaper, bluntly wrote, "The problem is mismanagement." The real question was, How much to open up? Inflation was soaring, eating away savings and retirement stipends. Many survived on ration coupons and rice and bread at subsidized prices. Massive subsidies and price controls were burdens on the state-run economy. Unemployment was as high as 30 percent among the educated youth. During all the years of economic hardship, it had been the ingenuity and resilience of the Iranian people that had kept the country afloat. Caught between the pull of tradition and the demands of globalization, a balance had to be struck. Iran had dramatic choices to make.

As 2001 began, I watched with surprise as a flood of Persian culture crested over established geopolitical barriers. Consider these examples. In March, Yo-Yo Ma premiered his "Silk Road Project" at Lincoln Center, honoring Persian classical music. Kurt Mazur conducted the New York Philharmonic in three concerts featuring *Blue as the Turquoise Night of Neyshabur* by the Iranian composer Kayhan Kalhor, *Through the Ancient Valley* by Richard Danielpour, an Iranian American, and Rimsky-Korsakov's *Scheherazade*. A week later, at Cooper Union, Shahram Nazeri, Iran's most popular singer and a master of the Sufi repertoire, mesmerized a packed house, with his son accompanying him on percussion. The event, entitled "Drunken Love," was a tribute to that best-selling Persian poet, Rumi.

Then a new wave of Iranian films crashed ashore. In New York a two-week festival, "Iran Through the Eyes of Children," opened. A month later, at the Museum of Modern Art, Marzieh Meshkini's *The Day I Became a Woman* premiered, as did Jafar Panahi's *The Circle*, a searing portrait of six single women in Tehran, which won the Golden Lion at the Venice film festival. An unheralded release from an unknown director, *Smell of Camphor, Fragrance of Jasmine*, earned high praise from New York reviewers, one of whom called Bahman Farmanara, who directed and starred in the film, "Iran's Woody Allen."

On the political front, the long-awaited presidential elections were held in June. Mohammad Khatami won his second four-year term, with 21.7 million votes and a majority of 76 percent, surpassing his previous victory margin of 1997. The beleaguered reform movement garnered enormous popular support.

My interest in Tehran's bitter power struggles, however, had been transformed. The words of Hassan and Akbar, Dr. Safvat and Majid Majidi compelled me to look beyond the predicament of politics — derived from a long history of hardship, exploitation and deception. I was now drawn to the timeless, immutable soul of Iran.

The great Atlantic waters that once separated me from high Elburz snows have shrunk to a trickling stream. In my dreams, I no longer chased after Hassan's vanishing heels. Instead, I woke feeling his gaze. And I obeyed my father's words: "If you listen carefully, my son, you will hear his heart beating on that far side of the world."

But the predicament of politics returned.

On a crystal-blue September morning, Idanna called out, "Terenzio, come quickly. A tower is missing." I found her peering out a window that overlooked the city's downtown rooftops. We stared in disbelief as a colossal black plume lifted high above New York's skyline. Then the second tower collapsed.

In the horrific days that followed, our stunned city reeled from the shock and fear of the terrorist attack on the World Trade Center. Manhattan's gaping wound cut deep into the nation's psyche. Phone calls came at odd hours from around the country, asking if we were all right. Then one day I heard a distant voice on the other end of the line.

"Allo, Ter-ry. How are you, your brothers, your mommy and daddy? Are they safe? We are so worried."

"Fatimeh!" I cried. "Yes, we all are OK."

"Thanks God! *Al-hamdulillah*. We are so sorry for the families of people who died."

Maryam then took the phone from her mother. "Did you see all Iranian people on television with candles?"

"Of course, Maryam." I had seen on the BBC the nightly vigils in Tehran, thousands of people gathered in memory of the fallen.

"We are all so very sad," she said.

I thanked her and then spoke with Rasool and finally with Hassan.

"I pray for you," Hassan said. Before saying goodbye, he recited the words of the poet Saadi:

"Children of Adam are all members of the same body,
Who, in creation, were made of the same essence."

Again he wanted me to look beyond.

I imagine him in Isfahan, kneeling, praying in the dark. Now I
see a bonfire blazing in my childhood alley. Dad's jazz tunes float
on the balmy breeze in our garden. My brothers' voices echo
around me as we wait for Hassan to come, swinging his lantern.

*Acknowledgments*
*Further Reading*

# Acknowledgments

I owe immense gratitude to my many Iranian friends in the United States, Europe and Iran, and in particular the Ghasemi family, who taught me profound lessons in civility and love. In this journey, I owe a special thanks to my charismatic and loving mentor, Gholam Hosain Janati-Ataie, who guided me with his wit, spirituality and wisdom through Iran's culture. Like Hassan, he has taught me to see.

I salute Gloria Loomis, my agent, for recognizing the value of this chronicle, and Eric Chinski, my editor, for his patient insight and wise counsel. I also thank Larry Cooper for his well-crafted suggestions at the eleventh hour.

I wish to thank Caroline Lockhart for her Sag Harbor cabin, which served as my writing refuge during one snowy winter, and Paola Carola for her warm hospitality in Naples, which allowed me to plunge into the library of the Istituto Universitario Orientale.

The first reader of this book was Idanna, my treasured companion. With her lyrical storytelling gift and compassionate heart, daily she unveils to me life's hermetic meanings. In this realm lies our tender and sacred bond, which will be neither broken nor bent in this life or the next.

I embrace my three brothers, Kevin, Chris, and Richard, whose esprit de corps is like a deep cool well from which I have been drinking for decades, a source that miraculously never runs dry. Finally, I toast my parents, Donna and Patrick, who are endowed with a limitless capacity for love and wisdom. It is to them that I wish to say: I am honored to be your son.

# Further Reading

If you wish to explore further the history, culture and literature of modern Iran and ancient Persia, I recommend the following books.

## HISTORICAL SOURCES

*The Histories of Herodotus* (London: Woodsworth Classics of World Literature, 1988) is by far the largest classical source of material on the lives and times of the ancient Persians and remains a joy to read. *The Persians* by Aeschylus (in *Aeschylus II*, edited by David Greene and Richmond Lattimore; New York: Pocket Books, 1973) is a surprisingly sympathetic drama set in the royal Persian court, where all await the fate of Xerxes at Salamis.

*The Heritage of Persia* by Richard Nelson Frye (London: Cambridge University Press, 1975) is a comprehensive study of pre-Islamic Persia from the birth of the Achaemenian Empire to the collapse of the Sassanian dynasty in the wake of the Arab invasion.

*The Cambridge History of Iran* (Cambridge: Cambridge University Press, 1968–91), with contributions by leading scholars, also serves as a treasure trove of information about the Achaemenians, the Sassanian dynasty, the Arab invasions, the Timurid and Safavid flowering as well as the turmoil of the twentieth century.

*Persia: From the Origins to Alexander the Great* by Roman Ghirshman (edited by André Malraux and Georges Salles, translated by Stuart Gilbert and James Emmons; London: Thames & Hudson, 1962; in The Arts of Mankind series) renders pre-Islamic Persian history enjoyable through the passionate explanations of an archaeologist who spent a lifetime in Iran.

ISLAM AND OTHER FAITHS

*The Mantle of the Prophet: Religion and Politics in Iran* by Roy Mottahedeh (New York: Simon & Schuster, 1985) remains perhaps the most accessible account of the scholarly Islamic jurists of Qom who rule Iran today. The tale follows the life of Ali Hashemi, a religious student whose journey begins with his enrollment in theological school and who later comes of age as an activist in the Islamic Revolution. Mottahedeh also provides an excellent survey of the Shia faith, the roots of Sufi and gnostic influences and the role of Ayatollah Khomeini, who galvanized the clergy and emerged as the political victor of the Revolution.

*The Koran Interpreted* by A. J. Arberry (New York: Macmillan, 1955) serves as an essential translation of this holy book.

*Zoroastrians: Their Religious Beliefs and Practices* by Mary Boyce (London: Routledge & Kegan Paul, 1979) is a great source for understanding Iran's oldest faith.

*Beyond Belief: Islamic Excursions Among the Converted Peoples* by V. S. Naipaul (New York: Random House, 1998) traces the role of Islam in non-Arabic-speaking lands. What intrigues Naipaul is the psychological complications of nations that have rich cultural identities that predate Islam.

LITERATURE

*The Conference of the Birds* by Farid ud-Din Attar (translated by Afkham Darbandi and Dick Davis; Middlesex, England: Penguin, 1984) is the inspirational twelfth-century Sufi epic poem about thirty birds in search of the mythical Simorgh and the immense revelation that lies in wait.

*The Essential Rumi* (translated by Coleman Barks; New York: HarperCollins, 1995) is, quite simply, a masterwork, an accessible and illuminating translation of an important Persian mystic poet.

The poetry of Hafez. Translations by A. J. Arberry, Gertrude Bell, Ralph Waldo Emerson, Elizabeth Gray, David Ladinsky, Haleh Pourafzal and Roger Montgomery are all fine attempts to render this master's verse into English.

*The Epic of Kings* by Ferdowsi (translated by Reuben Levy; Costa Mesa, Cal.: Mazda Publishers, 1996) offers the recently rehabilitated epic poem of pre-Islamic myth, Iranian kingship and heroic national history, all grandly told by the Persian Homer.

*The Water's Footfall: The Green Volume* by Sohrab Sepheri (translated by Abbas Zahedi; Tehran: Zabankade Publications, 1958) is a wonderful contemporary work from the much-loved poet of Kashan.

## THE CULTURAL DIVIDE

*My Dear Uncle Napoleon* by Iraj Pezeshkzad (translated by Dick Davis; Washington, D.C.: Mage Publishers, 1996). This hilarious book lampoons the ever-lurking Iranian fears of British conspiracy, collusion and interference in Iran's fragile destiny. Set in 1941 on the eve of the British occupation, the tale gallops to an operatic climax, led by the paranoid hero, Uncle Napoleon.

*In a Persian Mirror: Images of the West and Westerners in Iranian Fiction* by M. R. Ghanoonparvar (Austin: University of Texas Press, 1993). An original and intriguing survey of Iranian literature from the nineteenth century to the present.

*The Great Game: The Struggle for Empire in Central Asia* by Peter Hopkirk (New York: Kodansha America, 1990) is a riveting history of two centuries of Anglo-Russian competition in Asia, replete with secret agents, skullduggery and coups.

*Occidentosis: A Plague from the West* by Jalal Al-e Ahmad (translated by R. Campbell; Berkeley, Cal.: Mizan Press, 1984) is still a lightning rod for controversy among Iranians. Its description of *gharbzadegi*, or the "Western-intoxicated," was a touchstone of criticism of the Shah's regime.

## TRAVELERS' TALES AND ÉMIGRÉS' REFLECTIONS

*The Road to Oxiana* by Robert Byron (London: Macmillan, 1937) is a witty, insightful account of a journey across Iran and Afghanistan during the reign of Reza Shah. It is considered to be one of the great works of travel writing.

*Travels in Persia, 1673–1677* by Jean Chardin (New York: Dover Publications, 1988) is an exhaustive account by a French jeweler seeking clients in seventeenth-century Safavid Isfahan. It includes fascinating descriptions of social customs, food, natural resources, architecture and crafts of the day.

*Seven Shades of Memory: Stories of Old Iran* by Terence O'Donnell (Washington, D.C.: Mage Publishers, 1999). A collection of tales that illustrate Iran's diverse cultural mix before the Revolution.

*Saffron Sky* by Gelareh Asayesh (Boston: Beacon Press, 1999) is a poignant reflection by an Iranian-American émigré on her brave struggle to reclaim her culture. An immigrant's story, it also examines the conflicts Iranians face when they attempt to hold on to their identity in America.

*Tales of Two Cities: A Persian Memoir* by Abbas Milani (Washington, D.C.: Mage Publishers, 1996) describes a dark and troubled childhood in Tehran. After a college education in the West, where he is seduced by left-wing ideologues, Milani returns to Tehran to illuminate the masses. While he is teaching at a university, the secret police arrest him. He charts his tortuous path through Evin Prison and revolutionary Iran, and finally his escape to Berkeley.

CURRENT AFFAIRS

*Persian Mirrors: The Elusive Face of Iran* by Elaine Sciolino (New York: Free Press, 2000) and *The Last Great Revolution: Turmoil and Transformation in Iran* by Robin Wright (New York: Alfred A. Knopf, 2000) share insights on the Islamic Republic, its inner workings, its current elite, the democratic ferment and the diverse social currents rippling throughout Iran. These two American journalists, of the *New York Times* and the *Los Angeles Times* respectively, have been reporting on Iran since the Revolution of 1979. Their books explore two decades of political, religious and social developments, with special glimpses of the world of women and contemporary Iranian life.

WEB SITES TO EXPLORE

www.payvand.com
www.iranian.com
www.gooya.com
www.iranmania.com
www.Tehran24.com